LAND ENTRY BOOK
WILKES COUNTY, NORTH CAROLINA
1778-1781

SOUTHERN HISTORICAL PRESS INC

Book Publishers

Compiled by

Mrs. W.O. Absher

Please direct all correspondence and orders to:

www.southernhistoricalpress.com
or
SOUTHERN HISTORICAL PRESS, Inc.
PO BOX 1267
375 West Broad Street
Greenville, SC   29601
southernhistoricalpress@gmail.com

ISBN #0-89308-645-2

Printed in the United States of America

LAND ENTRY BOOK

Abstracting the old Land Entry Book of Wilkes County, North Carolina has been a difficult task, and in all probability, mistakes have been made; but the entries that were readable will out-weigh by far those that were almost impossible to decipher. By all rights this project should have been completed before the old Land Deed Books were abstracted, but had I not "cut my teeth" on the Deed Books, it is doubtful I would have had the nerve to tackle the Entry Book.

In the Land of Wilkes by J. J. Hayes it is stated, "The best comtemptorary documentary evidence for an accurate location of the settlers when the county was created is the original Land Entry Book. It has better details than that to be found in the subsequent land grants. It was customary for the settler to describe the location of his plantation on some stream or head waters of some stream, or on some mountain. Generally the claim would close with the statement, "and being the plantation where I (or he) now live." Each entry is dated. There were numerous transfer of entries before the issuance of a grant. Some are referred to in the entry, but generally the Entry Taker would mark through the name of the original enterer and insert the name of the one to whom it was transferred. For a fuller understanding of the Entry Book, you will observe that there will never be a grant or deed to the original enterer if he transferred his entry. The state of North Carolina did not acquire title to the land until the Confiscation Act, effective in 1778. Our county opened its Land Entry Book when the county was organized the first Monday in March 1778."

The above excerpt explains far better than I can about the Entry Book. There were many misspellings of names, places, and words. Since we had people in this locality with similar names such as Johnson and Johnston, Lowe and Laws, Morris and Norris, Calton and Carlton, and many others, I am sure some of the people listed by one name should be by the other.

Not only was the first name entered, frequently marked out, but many times erased and the next name written in its place. This explains why there will be a subsequent name entered than that which was first recorded. Many of the entries had as many as four names marked out and written in with no way of knowing whose name was the last one written.

In order to make the abstract as accurate as possible, comparisons have been made with the land entries in the above mentioned Land of Wilkes, old tax lists, two old index books that have been preserved, and other materials. There is a portion of the book that is almost faded beyond readability and many of the pages are worn and torn away completely.

If the Entry Book has been microfilmed there is no mention of it. Only a stamp stating by whom and where it was laminated is on its first page.

Fishes, Fisher, and Fishing Creek are the same stream. A question mark after a name denotes uncertainty of writing or spelling or both. The spelling of a surname in parenthesis in the index is the present day spelling of that surname in this locality.

The Genealogical Society sincerely hopes this old Entry Book Abstract will be of help to many of our members whose ancestors either passed through or remained in "The Land of Wilkes."

North Wilkesboro, N. C.   Ruby T. Absher
Summer 1971

WILKES COUNTY LAND ENTRY BOOK
1778-1781

4 March 1778. JAMES DYER e. 640 ac. being land he now lives on..both
               sides Yadkin River. Entry No. 1.

4 March 1778. GEORGE MORRIS e. 300 ac. branch N side New River below
               WM. RAY'S Mill. Entry No. 2.

4 March 1778. ABEL PENINTON e. 150 ac. being land he now lives on..N
               fork New River..W of WM. ADKINS land..transfered to ENOCH
OSBURN & from him to GIDEON LEWIS. Entry No. 3.

4 March 1778. (worn-not readable)..(?) hundred & fifty ac. he lives on
               ..N fork New River by name Big Old Fields Creek. Entry
No. 4.

4 March 1778. WILLIAM RAY e. 100 ac. fork Dog Creek. Entry No. 5.

4 March 1778. JAMES DIER e. 100 ac. Solomon's Branch. Entry No. 6.

4 March 1778. THOMAS SLONE e. 200 ac. S side Yadkin River..joining W
               side JOHN BARTONS claim..by THOMAS FARGUSON transfered
to OWEN HUMPHREY. Entry No. 7.

4 March 1778. ROBERT LEWIS e. 250 ac. both sides Stony Fork..Yadkin
               River..including Mill Seat..(ROBERT LEWIS marked out..
transfered to MOSES WATERS written in). Entry No. 8.

4 March 1778. WM. HUMPHRIES e. 200 ac. waters New River..fork Naked
               Creek..S side GEORGE MORRIS'S land..being land HUMPHRIES
now lives on. Entry No. 9.

4 March 1778. WILLIAM MITCHELL e. 300 ac. in Wilkes & part in Rowan..S
               side Hunting Creek..joining DANIEL RASH & SAMUEL NICHOL-
SON. Entry No. 10.

4 March 1778. WM. T. LEWIS e. 650 ac. N side Yadkin River..upper end
               Great Round About..including the Great Round About im-
provement. Entry No. 11.

4 March 1778. BENJAMIN CLEVELAND e. 400 ac. N side Yadkin River known
               by name of Round About..lower end of bottom..including
improvement CLEVELAND now lives on. Entry No. 11.

4 March 1778. WILLIAM T. LEWIS e. 640 ac. S side Yadkin River..upper
               end Swan Ponds..joining THOMAS PARKES' & THOMAS BICKNEL'S
claims..to BENJA HERNDON'S claim..(Caveated by SAMUEL BECKNEL): Entry
No. 12.

4 March 1778. SAMUEL BECKENELL e. 320 ac. on Yadkin River at BENJAMIN
               HERNDON'S lower corner..claim of THOMAS BECKNEL & THOMAS
PARKS (torn)..(torn) ALEXANDER GORDONS. Entry No. 12.

4 March 1778. THOMAS DUNNOHOE e. 320 ac. both sides Yadkin River..LEWIS
               DEMOSSES line..ordered by court to issue warrant of sur-
vey to ANN DONNOHE. Entry No. 13.

4 March 1778. CHARLES HICKERSON e. 320 ac. both sides Mulberry Creek..
               including his own improvement. Entry No. 14.

4 March 1778. THOMAS JOHNSTON e. 200 ac. S side Yadkin below mouth
               Lewis Fork..land whereon he now lives. Entry No. 15.

1

4 March 1778.   JACOB NICHOLDS e. 200 ac. whereon he now lives..S side
                Yadkin River below the Bent. Entry No. 16.

4 March 1778.   JOHN KEN----- e. 640 ac. on Kings Creek..S side Yadkin
                River..above JOHN KEES plantation. Entry No. 17.

4 March 1778.   JOHN BARTON e. 250 ac. S side Yadkin River joining
                AHAZAEL DYERS claim. Entry No. 18.

4 March 1778.   LARENCE ROSS e. 640 ac. whereon he now lives..Solomon's
                branch..N side Yadkin River. Entry No. 19.

4 March 1778.   CORNELIUS BOMAN e. 100 ac. S W side Buffalow Creek of
                the Yadkin..joining RUTH BARTONS improvement..including
the falls for bounds..(Caveated by JOSEPH MCCORKEL). Entry No. 20.

4 March 1778.   WILLIAM SNODDY e. 300 ac. N side Yadkin from Falls of
                Buffalow..CAPT. ISAACK'S line..(Caveated by SAMUEL
TOMPSON). Entry No. 21.

4 March 1778.   WILLIAM WILLBURN e. 400 ac. N side Yadkin River..dividing
                line between WELLBURN and EDMAN NORMAND..(Caveated by
ELIHAH ISAACS). Entry No. 22.

4 March 1778.   JOHN DOYAL e. 400 ac. S side Yadkin River..at mouth
                Moravian Creek..(Caveated by HUGH MONTGOMERY). Entry No.
23.

4 March 1778.   MEREDITH MINTON e. 50 ac. whereon he now lives on N side
                Yadkin River. Entry No. 24.

4 March 1778.   BENJAMIN GREYER (GREER) e. 200 ac. joining FRANCIS HARD-
                GRAVE..including improvement whereon GREYER lives. Entry
No. 25.

4 March 1778.   EPHRAIM COX e. 400 ac. being land he now lives on..both
                sides Kings Creek. Entry No. 26.

4 March 1778.   JAMES SHEPHERD e. 150 ac. N side Yadkin River..mouth of
                Moravian Creek. Entry No. 27.

6 March 1778.   BENJAMIN HERNDON, Esq...Entry taker for County of Wilkes
                appeared before me, CHARLES GORDON, one of the Justices
of Peace for said County and entered 500 ac. land S side Yadkin River..
ROBINS corner..upper end Swan Ponds..including improvement HERNDON now
lives on and an Island. Entry No. 28.

6 March 1778.   WILLIAM MCCLAIN e. 320 ac. lower end rich bent N fork
                New River..(name of 1st enterer erased completely..WM.
MCCLAIN written in). Entry No. 29.

6 March 1778.   WILLIAM MCCLAIN e. 150 ac. N fork at three Forks of New
                River..(1st enterer erased completely..WM. MCCLAIN
marked out..transfered to MATTHEW SPARKS written in). Entry No. 30.

6 March 1778.   JD. LEWIS e. 150 ac. N fork New River..lower end hickory
                bottom..including the two improvements of said JD. LEWIS
..(JD LEWIS marked out..JOSHUA NEAVES written in). Entry No. 31.

6 March 1778.   DANIEL WRIGHT e. 200 ac. on Big Elkin..including improve-
                ment he now lives on. Entry No. 32.

7 March 1778.   THOMAS ROBBINS e. 350 ac. N side Mulberry Creek..includ-
                ing Mill and old improvement. Entry No. 33.

7 March 1778.   SAMUEL WRIGHT e. 500 ac. land fork Grassy Creek..includ-
                ing two improvements of said SAMUEL WRIGHT..(SAM'L WRIGHT
marked out..WM. THURSTON written in). Entry No. 34.

12 March 1778. GEORGE MCKNIEL e. 120 ac. S fork Reddies River..side
                mtn...along ROLAND JUD'S line..ROBERT SHEPHERD'S line.
Entry No. 35.

13 March 1778. EBENEZER FAIRCHILD e. 150 ac. S fork Lewis Fork..includ-
                ing improvement whereon said FAIRCHILD now lives. Entry
No. 36.

13 March 1778. EBENEZER FAIRCHILD e. 150 ac. Mill Seat on Long Branch..
                waters Lewis Fork..including an old AX entry. Entry
No. 37.

14 March 1778. WILLIAM NALL e. 200 ac. Middle fork Roaring River..in-
                cluding improvement where WM. NALL now lives..(Caveated
by PETER GREENSTREET..WM. NALL marked out..AMBROSE HAMMON written in..
transfered by me, WILLIAM NALL to JAMES RAMEY also written in and marked
out). Entry No. 38.

14 March 1778. WILLIAM MCCLAINE e. 200 ac. upper falls on Bugaboe W
                side..Cross creek E including both sides creek..(Cavea-
ted by JOSEPH PORTER). Entry No. 39.

19 March 1778. ROBERT CHANDLOW e. 450 ac. Yadkin River..including two
                improvements where THOMAS TURNER and JOHN BOND claimed
on both sides river. Entry No. 40.

20 March 1778. JOSEPH HOLEMAN e. 200 ac. Yadkin River..both sides Cub
                Creek..including improvement where ISAAC NORMAN now
lives. Entry No. 41.

21 March 1778. WILLIAM LOVEING e. 250 ac. S side Yadkin River near
                Shoal where JOHN PARKES line stops running along the
line..including two improvements where RICE MODERIST and WILLIAM LOVE-
ING now live. Entry No. 42.

21 March 1778. GABRIEL LOVEING e. 300 ac. N side Yadkin River..Swan
                Shoal with JOHN PARKES, SENR'S. line..including improve-
ment where said LOVEING now lives. Entry No. 43.

21 March 1778. GABRIEL LOVEING e. 50 ac. on Little Elkin joining said
                LOVEINGS line..including the Mill. Entry No. 44.

27 March 1778. HILLIAR RUSSAU e. 200 ac. Ridge near JOHN ROBINS Mill..
                including an old cabin formerly property of MORDACI
--ULLER on Mulberry waters. Entry No. 45.

27 March 1778. HILLIAR ROUSSEAU e. 200 ac. forks path leading to
                CHARLES GORDONS, Stewarts Mill & Readys River..(Entry
cross-marked out). Entry No. 46.

27 March 1778. JAMES FLETCHER e. 400 ac. S side Yadkin River..including
                an island at Moravian Lower line..to JOHN PROPHETS
claim..including improvement said FLETCHER lives on..(Caveated by DANIEL
VANNOY). Entry No. 47.

27 March 1778. QUILLER GREYER (GREER) e. 360 ac. E side Moravian Creek
                ..joining JOSHUA GREYER on the S..ISAAC LOW on W..JOHN
LAWS, SENR. on N..on both sides main road.

27 July 1778. BENJAMIN HERNDON e. 320 ac. both sides Wrights Creek..
               including improvement made by WM. WRIGHT below main road
that leads by Lyken's ford. Entry No. 49.

1 April 1778. LEWIS ROBERTS e. 640 ac. S side Yadkin..spring branch..
               including improvement JOHN PAYN bought of HUMPHREY BESS
(BEST?)..(LEWIS ROBERTS marked out..JOHN PAYN written in). Entry No.
50.

1 April 1778. BENJAMIN CLEVELAND e. 200 ac. E side road leads up Red-
               dies River..forks of path that leads to Lewis' Fork.
Entry No. 51.

7 April 1778. CHARLES MORGAN e. 150 ac. Little River..waters of New
               River..E end Peak Mountain..(CHARLES MORGAN marked out..
JOHN OREAR written in). Entry No. 52.

7 April 1778. CHARLES MORGAN e. 150 ac. Waters Little River. Entry
               No. 53.

8 April 1778. P. SPENCER HUMPHRIES e. 200 ac. waggon ford Cub Creek..
               including improvement where SPENCER HUMPHRIES now lives..
(1st. enterer erased completely..MARY GORDON written in). Entry No. 54.

17 April 1778. TIMOTHY PURKINS e. 400 ac. both sides New River..upper
                end of what is called Old Fields..crossing Deep Gap
Creek..including three improvements: one whare said PURKINS now lives..
one whare BOYAL PORTER now lives..one that said PURKINS bought of
SAMUEL MCQUEEN..(Caveated by JOSEPH PURKINS..also Caveated by BENJAMIN
CLEVELAND). Entry No. 55.

18 April 1778. JOHN BROWN e. 200 ac. W side Yadkin River..mouth Buffa-
                low..condt. line between HUMPHREY GIBSON & SAMUEL
WILLIAMS, JUNR...including improvement CORNELIUS BOMAN now lives on..
(Caveated by RUTH BARTON). Entry No. 56.

18 April 1778. JOHN BROWN e. 300 ac. on Yadkin River..upper end JAMES
                BROWNS claim including two improvements on said land..
(Caveated by JONATHAN SNEED). Entry No. 57.

18 April 1778. JOSEPH HERNDON e. 200 ac. both sides main road up Readys
                River Settlement..about three miles from Yadkin River..
(JOSEPH HERNDON marked out..GEORGE GORDON written in). Entry No. 58.

18 April 1778. JOSEPH HERNDON e. 150 ac. Brushey Mountain..head Mill
                fork Fishers Creek..formerly called Burks Creek on
which BURK built a mill. Entry No. 59.

20 April 1778. HENRY HAND e. 320 ac. waters New River near Coxes road..
                lower end great glade called Three Forks..(HENRY HAND
marked out..CHRISTOPHER MANNARD written in). Entry No. 60.

20 April 1778. JOHN GREYOR, SR. (GREER) e. 350 ac. both sides main road
                and joining QUILLER GREYOR on S..(Caveated by JOSHUA
STEPHENS). Entry No. 61.

20 April 1778. JOHN GREYOR, SR. (GREER) e. 200 ac. both sides Cub Creek
                ..joining JACOB HAMPTONS at upper end..CAPT. FRANCIS
HARTGROVE at lower end. Entry No. 62.

22 April 1778. THOMAS BECKNALL e. 247 ac. both sides Swan Creek..join-
                ing THOMAS PARKES at lower and JOHN BOURLAND at upper
end..cornering on main road. Entry No. 63.

24 April 1778. JOHN SHEPHERD e. 405 ac. Deep Ford on Reddis River..
                including improvement where said SHEPHERD now lives.
Entry No. 64.

24 April 1778. ROBERT SHEPHERD e. 200 ac. near ford Readys River on
                JOHN SHEPHERDS line..including improvement where said
SHEPHERD now lives. Entry No. 65.

24 April 1778. JAMES BARKLEY e. 50 ac. S side Yadkin River..AHAZUR
                DIERS line..JAMES DIERS line..(Caveated by CHARLES
BOILES). Entry No. 66.

24 April 1778. JOHN WITHERSPOON e. 640 ac. Kings Creek..EPHRIAM COXES
                claim. Entry No. 67.

24 April 1778. 1st enterer erased completely..e. 100 ac. New River near
                the bent..both sides River..including improvement for-
merly made by PHILLIP DAVIS..(DANIEL JOHNSTON & ROWLAND JUDD marked
out..JOHN BROWN written in). Entry No. 68.

25 April 1778. WILLIAM GUIS (GIST?) e. 400 ac. little below mouth
                Buffalow Creek..mouth Bakers branch. Entry No. 69.

25 April 1778. JOHN THRASHER e. 100 ac. S side Yadkin..including im-
                provement whereon TIMOTHY PURKINS now lives. Entry No.
70.

25 April 1778. WILLIAM HIGGINS e. 50 ac. Yadkin River..upper Dark
                Bottom. Entry No. 71.

25 April 1778. JOSEPH MCCORKLE e. 200 ac. S side Yadkin River..MOSES
                (?) branch below line..up river to branch named ARCHI-
BALD ALLOMS (ALLEN). Entry No. 72.

25 April 1778. JAMES DIER e. 100 ac. Yadkin River..including improve-
                ment where CORNELUIS BOWMAN now lives. Entry No. 73.

25 April 1778. JAMES DIER e. 100 ac. both sides Yadkin River..commonly
                known by Lower Dark Bottom. Entry No. 74.

25 April 1778. ANDREW TATE e. 160 ac. mouth of a branch..line between
                TATE & WM. GUES (GIST or GUEST?)..joining JOHN THRASHERS
line. Entry No. 75.

25 April 1778. STEPHEN CARPENTER e. 100 ac. S side Yadkin River..on
                branch called Beaver Ponds..including improvement where
JOHN PRESTON (?) lives. Entry No. 76.

25 April 1778. HENRY HUDSON e. 100 ac. N side Yadkin River..JAMES DIERS
                line..THOMAS FORGESONS line. Entry No. 77.

25 April 1778. RUTH BARTON e. 640 ac. N side Yadkin River..Buffalow
                Creek..(Caveated by SAMUEL THOMPSON). Entry No. 78.

25 April 1778. HARDY JONES e. 640 ac. New River..lower end Big Crab
                Orchard..both sides river including improvement..(HARDY
JONES & MOSES BUTTS marked out..RUSSELL JONES written in). Entry No.
79.

25 April 1778. 1st enterer erased completely out..e. 300 ac. Flanneries
                fork New River..JAMES MARTINS line..(ROBERT AYERS marked
out..JOHN AYERS written in). Entry No. 80.

25 April 1778 . DANIEL YARNALL e. 300 ac. Bartons fork New River..join-
                 ing JAMES MARTINS line. Entry No. 81.

5

25 April 1778. JOHN DIER e. 200 ac. both sides Yadkin River at LARENCE ROSS'S line. Entry No. 82.

25 April 1778. WILLIAM VANDERPOOL e. 50 ac. Yadkin River..including improvement made by PETER KING..(Caveated by JOHN SIMPSON). Entry No. 83.

25 April 1778. WILLIAM LEWIS e. 200 ac. Fishers Creek..part of Ridge between Fishers Creek & Cub Creek..(WM. LEWIS marked out..ANDREW YEARGAIN written in). Entry No. 84.

25 April 1778. ANDREW CANADY (KENNEDY) e. 100 ac. Bugabo including improvement made by REUBEN PARKS. Entry No. 85.

1 May 1778 . FRANCIS REONALDS (REYNOLDS) e. 360 ac. N side Yadkin River near his spring branch on his deeded land..including both sides..at mouth Roch Creek..including improvement where JAMES REONALDS (REYNOLDS) now lives and the Island nearly adj. to improvement made by FRANCIS REONALDS (REYNOLDS)..(Caveated by JOHN SIMPSON). Entry No. 86.

4 May 1778. THOMAS HAMBRICK e. 150 ac. JOHN PITMANS line near the Court House..both sides of the Great Road. Entry No. 87.

8 May 1778. BENJAMIN MORGAN e. 640 ac. Middle fork Roaring River called Long Bottom Creek..near fork Brushey Creek..near LARKIN CLEVELAND'S line..whereon said MORGAN now lives. Entry No. 88.

8 May 1778. JESSE WALTON e. 100 ac. New River on both sides..(JESSE WALTON & ROBERT AYERS marked out..JOHN GREEN (?) written in). Entry No. 89.

8 May 1778. 1st enterer erased completely out..e. 100 ac. New River E side..known by name Buckeye Island..(JOHN PROFFITT marked out..JAMES TOMKINS written in). Entry No. 90.

15 May 1778. JAMES DAVIS e. 150 ac. Great Elkin Creek..DANIEL WRIGHTS line..both sides creek..including improvement whereon said DAVIS now lives. Entry No. 91.

15 May 1778. THOMAS STUBBLEFIELD e. 320 ac. N side Yadkin River..lower end THOMAS PARKES line..including an Island nearly against said STUBBLEFIELDS improvement. Entry No. 92.

15 May 1778. SIMEON CARTER e. 300 ac. Little Elkin Creek..both sides.. including improvement said CARTER now lives on. Entry No. 93.

15 May 1778. JOHN PARKES, SENR. e. 200 ac. N side Yadkin River..lower end PARKES field..along GABRIEL LOVEINGS line..including improvement said PARKES now lives on. Entry No. 94.

15 May 1778. JAMES RANEY e. 270 ac. waters Roaring River..GAMBILLS Mill Creek..both sides river..including improvement whereon said RAMEY now lives. Entry No. 95.

15 May 1778. JOHN ROBBINS, SENR. e. 400 ac. Mulberry Creek..upper Caine Brake..both sides of creek. Entry No. 96.

15 May 1778. WILLIAM LOWE e. 360 ac. both sides Moravian Creek..join-
ing old JOHN LAWS at upper end. Entry No. 97.

16 May 1778. GEORGE FOSTER e. 100 ac. Stony Fork..both sides. Entry
No. 98.

16 May 1778. JOHN ROBBINS, SENR. e. 150 ac. Mulberry Creek at Middle
Caine Brake..both sides creek. Entry No. 99.

16 May 1778. MOSES POWERS e. 200 ac. at a branch between GEORGE WHEAT-
LEY, JUNR. and his own dwelling..S to upper falls of
Moravian Creek..(MOSES POWERS marked out..transfered to ALEXANDER
MCMULLEN written in). Entry No. 100.

16 May 1778. JOHN ROBBINS, SENR. e. 100 ac. S side Mulberry Creek joining THOMAS ROBINS and lying both sides creek whereon
said ROBBINS has a mill..including the mill. Entry No. 101.

16 May 1778. BENJAMIN ELLEDGE e. 200 ac. top Brushey Mountain between
Ellets Gap & GREYERS (GREERS)..including head Grassy fork
and Garrets fork. Entry No. 102.

16 May 1778. JOSHUA GREYER (GREER) e. 200 ac. both sides S fork Moravian Creek..joining QUILLER GREYER at lower end. Entry
No. 103.

16 May 1778. NICKOLAS ANGEL e. 400 ac. both sides Beaver Creek at the
Narrows a little above..including improvement where
WILLIAM ELLISON now lives. Entry No. 104.

18 May 1778. JOHN CORNWALL e. 100 ac. S fork New River..including improvement formerly made by ROBERT BAKER..(JOHN CORNWALL
marked out..JON. JOHNSON written in). Entry No. 105.

18 May 1778. GEORGE WHITLEY, SENR. (WHEATLEY) e. 350 ac. E side Roaring
River below mouth Whitleys Creek..near the Mill ford..in-
cluding the plantation whereon he now dwells..(Caveated by EDMOND DENNY).
Entry No. 106.

19 May 1778. JOHN PARKES, JUNR. e. 600 ac. S side Yadkin River..mouth
Roaring River..including improvement whereon THOMAS PARKES
now lives. Entry No. 107.

19 May 1778. JOHN PARKS, JUNR. e. 250 ac. S side Yadkin River opposite
Fish Trap Shoal..including improvement whereon said PARKS
now lives. Entry No. 108.

20 May 1778. BENJAMIN MORGAN e. 300 ac. waters Roaring River..near
dividing line between LARKIN CLEVELAND & said MORGAN.
Entry No. 109.

20 May 1778. LARKIN CLEVELAND e. 100 ac. Middle fork Roaring River..
beginning on Spur of mountain on first fork said river.
Entry No. 110.

20 May 1778. BENJAMIN CLEVELAND e. 400 ac. N side Yadkin near the Great
Rocks opposite JOSEPH PORTER..N bank Yadkin...(Caveated
by JOHN JOHNSON). Entry No. 111.

22 May 1778. WILLIAM CARRELL e. 400 ac. N side Yadkin River..below
mouth Little Elkin..including improvement where said
CARRELL now lives. Entry No. 112.

22 May 1778. THOMAS PARKES, JR. e. 420 ac. both sides Swan Creek..
joining THOMAS BICKNEL at upper end and MAJOR WILLIAM
LEWIS at lower end. Entry No. 113.

23 May 1778. JOSEPH PORTER e. 400 ac. S side Yadkin River above..includ-
ing improvement whereon said PORTER now lives..S to HARRIS
line. Entry No. 144.

23 May 1778. ABRAHAM COOK e. 640 ac. waters Hunting Creek..Ridge above
what was called HAMLIN'S old store .including improvement
and store where ELIJAH CLAY now lives. Entry No 115.

23 May 1778. WILLIAM HARGIS e. 140 ac. head of Hollow near Roaring River
..including his improvement. Entry No. 116.

25 May 1778. MARTIN GAMBILL e. 200 ac. waters Little River..head waters
Crab Creek..N fork Little River. Entry No. 117.

25 May 1778. WILLIAM GAMBILL e. 500 ac. S fork Roaring River..including
improvement whereon he lives. Entry No. 118.

25 May 1778. WILLIAM GAMBILL e. 380 ac. waters Roaring River..beginning
on said GAMBILLS line. Entry No. 119.

25 May 1778. WILLIAM GAMBILL e. 53 ac. S fork Roaring River..including
improvement whereon said GAMBILL now lives. Entry No. 120.

26 May 1778. WILLIAM GAMBILL, JUNR. e. 192 ac. S fork Roaring River..
beginning on WILLIAM GAMBILL, JUNR'S. line. Entry No. 121.

26 May 1778. RICE MEDERIST e. 150 ac. fork Parkes Creek..beginning on
County line up main creek to school house..(RICE MEDERIST
marked out..HENRY PARKES written in). Entry No. 122.

27 May 1778. VOLENTINE NUTTERVILL e. 200 ac. waters Cub Creek..on Ashers
branch below improvement where THOMAS LOW now lives..in-
cluding said improvement. Entry No. 123.

27 May 1778. JOHN BOURLAND e. 200 ac. W fork Swan Creek on THOMAS BICK-
NELLS line..including improvement where said BOURLAND now
lives. Entry No. 124.

27 May 1778. EDMAN BOAZ e. 320 ac. N side Yadkin River..lower end Great
Meadow..including an Island & improvement where BOAZ now
lives. Entry No. 125.

28 May 1778. WILLIAM SHERRY e. 50 ac. waters New River about 3 miles
above the Old Fields..on small branch below an old cabin..
including improvement WM. SHERRY made..(WM. SHERRY marked out..SAMUEL
WILCOXON written in). Entry No. 126.

28 May 1778. WILLIAM SHERRY e. 100 ac. on New River joining his line
below. Entry No. 127.

29 May 1779. WILLIAM CARRELL e. 300 ac. on Little Elkin Creek above
LOVEING Mill near Cattail Marsh..including improvement
whereon said CARRELL now lives. Entry No. 128.

30 May 1778. JOHN HUDDLESTON e. 250 ac. Elk Creek below BENJAMIN ANGELS
Mill Seat..including BEAN'S improvement..(JOHN HUDDLESTON
marked out..SARAH KINDEL written in)..(Caveated by ELIJAH ISAACES).
Entry No. 129.

30 May 1778. JONATHAN STAMPER e. 320 ac. on Bugaboo Creek nearly against
the old Mill..to CANADYS (KENNEDY) line..including JONA-
THAN STAMPER, JR. improvement. Entry No. 130.

1 June 1778. GEORGE STUBBLEFIELD e. 100 ac. N side Yadkin River..EDON
BOAZ'S line..including improvement said STUBBLEFIELD now
lives on. Entry No. 131.

2 June 1778. HENERY DUNKIN e. 200 ac. Yadkin River..mouth Kings Creek.
Entry No. 132.

2 June 1778. WILLIAM HARBIN e. 150 ac. N side Yadkin River. Entry No.
133.

2 June 1778. JOAB WILDER e. 50 ac. N side Yadkin River..N fork LINVELS
Mill Creek..including improvement he now lives on..(JOAB
WILDER marked out..transfered to JOSEPH MCGLOCKLAND written in). Entry
No. 134.

2 June 1778. THOMAS BRYAN e. 100 ac. Kings Creek. Entry No. 135.

2 June 1778. LEWIS DEMOSS e. 200 ac. Yadkin River..mouth Suttons branch
..up Yadkin to mouth Falling Branch..both sides river..in-
cluding his improvement. Entry No. 136.

2 June 1778. 1st enterer erased completely..e. 100 ac. S side Yadkin
River..joining THOMAS JOHNSTONS & JACOB NICOLS..including
his plantation..(WILLIAM TRIBBLE written in). Entry No. 137.

2 June 1778. ROLAND HADLEY e. 200 ac. Waryer Creek at LARENCE ROSS'S
line..both sides creek..(ROLAND HADLEY marked out..JAMES
COFFEY written in..also transfared to JAMES COFFEY written in). Entry
No. 138.

2 June 1778. JOHN TRIBBLE e. 400 ac. on Moravian Creek..joining ISAAC
LOW & ZACH. WALKER..including the improvement where WM.
TRIBBLE now lives. Entry No. 139.

2 June 1778. PETER GREENSTREET e. 165 ac. both sides N fork Roaring
River. Entry No. 140.

2 June 1778. PETER GREENSTREET e. 245 ac. both sides N fork Roaring
River..joining his first entry..including his improvement.
Entry No. 141.

2 June 1778. JOHN FARGUSON e. 100 ac. S side Yadkin River at the waggon
ford. Entry No. 142.

2 June 1778. JOHN DYER e. 300 ac. Moravian Creek N side said creek.
Entry No. 143.

2 June 1778. JOHN HENRY STONESYPHER e. 640 ac. Head of Naked Creek..in-
cluding his improvement. Entry No. 144.

2 June 1778. ROWLAND JUDD e. 514 ac. S & Middle fork Readys River.
Entry No. 145.

2 June 1778. JOHN BAKER e. 200 ac. both sides New River..crossing at the
Bent above mouth of Peak Creek..including his improvement..
(JOHN BAKER marked out..WM. NALL written in). Entry No. 146.

2 June 1778. MATTHEW FRANCIS e. 300 ac. on Lewis Fork..below the improvement. Entry No. 147.

2 June 1778. JAMES WARD e. 150 ac. N fork New River..above mouth of
Fenick Creek. Entry No. 148.

2 June 1778. 1st enterer erased completely..e. 640 ac. both sides Yadkin
..joining COLO. CHARLES GORDONS lore (lower) line..includ-
ing his improvement..(Caveated by JAMES HERNDON..CHARLES GORDON written
in). Entry No. 149.

2 June 1778. EDWARD HARRIS e. 230 ac. on Fishers Creek..including his
             improvement. Entry No. 150.

2 June 1778. ABRAHAM HUNT e. 100 ac. on Fishers Creek..joining EDWARD
             HARRIS' line..including his improvement. Entry No. 151.

2 June 1778. WILLIAM TOLIVER e. 170 ac. S fork Roaring River. Entry No.
             152.

2 June 1778. FRANCIS REYNOLDS e. 200 ac. on a branch Roaring River..W
             side below the Little Mountain..including a small improve-
ment and the improvement GEORGE WHITLEY made..(FRANCIS REYNOLDS, JAMES
& JOHN WHEATLEY marked out..JOSEPH WHITLEY written)..NOTE: There are
WHITLEYS in Wilkes County in 1971. In the first recoreds it is spelled
WHEATLEY & WHITLEY..sometimes in the same transaction. Entry No. 153.

2 June 1778. JOSHUA SHURLOCK e. 300 ac. Moravian Creek..joining entry
             JON. DOYAL made at mouth said creek on both sides. Entry
No. 154.

3 June 1778. JOHN ROBERSON e. 50 ac. Head Kings Creek in the Brushey
             Mtn. known by name of the Cove. Entry No. 155.

3 June 1778. JOHN BOND e. 100 ac. Fishers Creek,.including the improve-
             ment..both sides creek..(JOHN BOND marked out..transfered
to JOHN TURNBILL and transfered to JOSEPH HORTON written in). Entry No.
156.

3 June 1778. JESSE TOLOVER e. 60 ac. both sides Mulberry Creek just
             above MOSES TOLIVER. Entry No. 157.

3 June 1778. MOSES TOLOVER e. 100 ac. both sides Mulberry Creek just
             above Stewarts Mill. Entry No. 158.

3 June 1778. JESSE TOLOVER e. 300 ac. on Mulberry waters both sides
             road..leads from JOHN ROBBINS, SENR. over to Roaring River
Settlement..being improvement JOHN TOLOVER, SENR. now lives on. Entry
No. 159.

3 June 1778. GEORGE MORRIS e. 100 ac. joining his former entry on New
             River. Entry No. 160.

3 June 1778. JOHN HOWARD e. 200 ac. on Hunting Creek..N side of Mtn..
             including his improvement..(this land first e. by ELIJAH
CLAY & forgot to be set in its right place). Entry No. 161.

3 June 1778. ELIJAH CLAY e. 320 ac. both sides Little Fork Hunting
             Creek..below SILVESTER BAKERS..including improvement
whereon JOHN HOWARD live. Entry No. 161.

3 June 1778. JOHN SIMPSON e. 150 ac. S side Yadkin River..JOSEPH PORTERS
             line..including a certain Island..(JOHN SIMPSON marked out
..JOHN CHANDLOW written in). Entry No. 162.

3 June 1778. MATTHEW SPARKES e. 400 ac. N side New River on little Naked
             Creek..including his improvement. Entry No. 163.

3 June 1778. FRANCIS HARDGRAVE e. 400 ac. on Cub Creek joining JON GREER
             Esq...including his improvement. Entry No. 164.

4 June 1778. HUGH MONTGOMERY e. 300 ac. Yadkin River joining the Bent
              line..below Castles Creek..S side Yadkin..above fish dam..
(HUGH MONTGOMERY marked out..JOHN BROWN written in). Entry No. 165.

4 June 1778. HUGH MONTGOMERY e. 399 ac. on Elk Creek..being improvement
              whereon BENJAMIN ANGEL now lives. Entry No. 166.

4 June 1778. HUGH MONTGOMERY e. 200 ac. Lewis Fork joining above entry.
              including improvement where said WATERS lives..(no other
mention of WATERS). Entry No. 167.

4 June 1778. HUGH MONTGOMERY e. 200 ac. Lewis Fork being part ROBERT
              WATERS claim he now lives on..upper end Brushey Bottom.
Entry No. 168.

4 June 1778. HUGH MONTGOMERY e. 150 ac. on Naked Creek..being improve-
              ment JOHN WEBB now lives on below said improvement.
(Caveated by JOHN WEBB). Entry No. 169.

Sept. 1778. LARENCE THOMPSON e. 640 ac. N fork Lewis..lower end of Maple
             Swamp..including improvement where THOMAS CALLAWAY now
lives..(LARENCE THOMPSON marked out..BENJAMIN CLEVELAND written in).
Entry No. 170.

4 June 1778. HUGH MONTGOMERY e. 640 ac. N fork Lewis Fork..lower end
              Maple Swamp..including improvement where THOMAS CALLOWAY
now lives..(Caveated by LARRENCE THOMPSON). Entry No. 170.

4 June 1778. JOSHUA MORGAN e. 300 ac. Cub Creek joining JOHN GREEAR and
              THOMAS WILLSON..Narrows of said creek..joining THOMAS
WILLSON..(JOSHUS MORGAN & THOMAS HAMRICK marked out..(also) JOHN CAMPBELL
to ISAAC WALKER). Entry No. 171.

4 June 1778. JOSEPH TANNER e. 200 ac. S side Yadkin River near the
              Mulberry Fields..joining Whites Bottom at lower end and
JOHN PROPHET at upper end..(JOSEPH TANNER marked out..CHARLES CRANSHAW
written in..(also) transfard to CHARLES CRANSHAW by JOSEPH TANNER (in
margin)). Entry No. 172.

4 June 1778. JOHN PITMAN e. 400 ac. S side Yadkin River..both sides Cub
              Creek..including the Court House. Entry No. 173

4 June 1778. WILLIAM SMITH e. 200 ac. joining JAMES MITCHEL..down Cub
              Creek on both sides..(WM. SMITH marked out..ALEXANDER (?)
JOHNSTON written in). Entry No. 174.

4 June 1778. JOHN BROWN e. 640 ac. on Moat camp Creek on New River..
              lower end first Big Crab Orchard below old cabbin..both
sides creek. Entry No. 175.

5 June 1778. HUGH MONTGOMERY e. 640 ac. S fork Hunting Creek..including
              the improvement JAMES BROWN now lives on..(HUGH MONTGOMERY
marked out..JAMES BROWN written in..Caveated by JAMES BROWN..given up by
HUGH MONTGOMERY). Entry No. 176.

5 June 1778. BENJAMIN HERNDON e. 500 ac. head waters Bryer Creek called
              the Cove..foot of a mtn..(BENJ. HERNDON marked out..HANCE
LAYCANS written in). (NOTE: This name is spelled several different ways
in all the first deed books as well as this entry book--HANCH, HANCE &
LYCANS, LICANS, LIKENS, LIKANS..in one of the deed book abstracts..it
was in the index as LYONS..but this is not the same name). Entry No. 177.

5 June 1778. CHARLES GORDON e. 200 ac. near head Pine Swamp of New
River..on path that leads from the Spanyards to the Old
Fields on said river..some distance below a remarkable spring on right
hand of said path..(CHARLES GORDON marked out..TELAIAH (?) CASS written
in). Entry No. 178.

6 June 1778. JAMES GRAY e. 640 ac. S side Yadkin River near bank..mouth
of SAMUEL WRIGHTS Creek..including both sides of JAMES
GRAYS Creek..improvement where SAMUEL GRAY & JAMES GRAY now lives and
WM. RIGHTS lately lived. Entry No. 179.

6 June 1778. LARKIN CLEVELAND e. 640 ac. spur of mtn...near head N fork
of Jones's Branch. Entry No. 180.

6 June 1778. JOSEPH HERNDON e. 200 ac. waters Mulberry Creek..at foot of
small mtn. that divides Mulberry & Roaring River waters..
being an improvement the said HERNDON lately bought of JESSE TOLLIVER.
(JOSEPH HERNDON marked out..EZEKIAL BARKER written in). Entry No. 181.

6 June 1778. JOHN MORGAN e. 300 ac. S side Halls Creek. Entry No. 182.

8 June 1778. THOMAS PARKES e. 300 ac. N side Yadkin River..little above
ford on Roaring River..including improvement whereon
THOMAS PARKES & REUBEN now lives. Entry No. 183

8 June 1778. JOHN PARKES e. 300 ac. S side Yadkin River..including improvement whereon said PARKES now lives..both sides mouth
Bryer Creek. Entry No. 184.

8 June 1778. WILLIAM JOHNSTON e. 127 ac. S side Yadkin River..CHANDLOWS
corner..including improvement where said JOHNSTON now
lives. Entry No. 185.

9 June 1778. WILLIAM MCCLAIN e. 300 ac. forks Buffelo Creek on New River
..including improvement GEORGE MORRIS, JUNR. claims..(WM.
MCCLAINE marked out..EZRA CAMRON (?) & TOWLAND JUDD marked out..JACOB
HUNTSINGER(?) written in). Entry No. 186.

9 June 1778. WILLIAM MCCLAINE e. 200 ac. head Crabb fork Beaver Creek..
being fork New River..did formerly go by name SAMUEL RAYS
claim. Entry No. 187.

11 June 1778. THOMAS WILMOTT (WILMOTH) e. 150 ac. head water Elkin
Creek..on ARTER SCRITCHFIELDS claim..including improvement where WILMOT now lives. Entry No. 188.

12 June 1778. RICHARD ALLEN e. 350 ac. Little Bugabo..lower end of his
bottom..both sides Bugabo..including improvement whereon
said ALLEN now lives. Entry No. 189.

12 June 1778. ABRAHAM VANDERPOOL e. 150 ac. S side Yadkin River..along
line made by THOMAS LINVILL..including improvement where
ABRAHAM VANDERPOOL, SR. and ABRAHAM VANDERPOOL, JR. now lives. Entry No.
190.

15 June 1778. JESSE LAY e. 50 ac. Linvils Mill Creek..dividing Ridge up
both sides said creek. Entry No. 191.

15 June 1778. JESSE LAY e. 100 ac. Linvils Mill Creek on LAYS lower
entry..including improvement said LAY bought of BENJ.
ANGLE. Entry No. 192.

16 June 1778.   WILLIAM SPICER e. 100 ac. waters Roreing River..little
                above improvement where said SPICER made lately. Entry No.
193.

17 June 1778.   JOHN AMBURGY e. 200 ac. E fork Roreing River..on the hill
                near the rode E of creek. Entry No. 194.

17 June 1778.   JOSEPH HERNDON e. 100 ac. head some of Mulberry waters at
                foot small Piney Mountain that divides Roreing River
waters & Mulberry waters..joining a peace of land lately purchased of
JESSE TOLOVER. Entry No. 195.

17 June 1778.   WILLIAM TAYLOR e. 100 ac. Roreing River waters..under foot
                of mountains that divides Roreing River waters from waters
of Mulberry..mouth of Salt Log Branch. Entry No. 196.

17 June 1778.   WILLIAM TAYLOR e. 200 ac. Little fork Hunting Creek..near
                Ring Fire Knob. Entry No. 197.

17 June 1778.   HENRY KERBEY e. 600 ac. near large Rock by Deep Hole in
                Fishers River known by name Millet Hole..including his
improvement. Entry No. 198.

18 June 1778.   WILLIAM STURDIE e. 50 ac. mouth of branch called Bucks
                Mire. Entry No. 199.

18 June 1778.   ISAAC GARRESON e. 100 ac. Wheatleys Creek..dividing line
                between WHEATLY & GARRESON. Entry No. 200.

18 June 1778.   BENJAMIN OAKLEY e. 230 ac. under foot Little Mountain in
                fork Roreing River..(BENJ. OAKLEY marked out..transfard to
DAVID BURN written in). Entry No. 201.

18 June 1778.   JOHN HOLDBROOK e. 175 ac. S side mountain near Camp Branch
                ..including plantation he now lives on. Entry No. 202.

18 June 1778.   JOHN FUGIT e. 120 ac. near Gap of Holdbrooks Mountain on
                Roering River. Entry No. 203.

18 June 1778.   JOHN FUGIT e. 92 ac. in hillside S side Roreing River..
                including the plantation. Entry No. 204.

22 June 1778.   JAMES WEBB e. 140 ac. waters Roreing River..called Harris
                Creek..near the rode..including improvement said WEBB now
lives on. Entry No. 205.

22 June 1778.   JAMES WEBB e. 100 ac. on Roaring River waters that is
                called Harris's Creek. Entry No. 206.

22 June 1778.   JOHN BOURLAND e. 200 ac. on BOURLAND'S fork Swan Creek..a
                small glade above the old Haystacks..down both sides of
Creek. Entry No. 207.

22 June 1778.   JAMES ROBERTS e. 300 ac. head waters S fork Lewis Fork..
                lying on left hand of path that leads from the Spainyards
to New River. Entry No. 208.

22 June 1778.   SAMUEL CASTLE e. 200 ac. S fork Lewis Fork two miles above
                TOMPKINS Mill. Entry No. 209.

24 June 1778.   EDMOND KERBY e. 640 ac. Fishes River..called thoroughfare
                run gap..including improvement where said KERBY now lives.
Entry No. 210.

24 June 1778.   JOHN UNDERWOOD e. 500 ac. Fishes River..on Roaring Gap
                Creek. Entry No. 211.

26 June 1778. WILLIAM LENOIR e. 200 ac. W side Big Bald Mountain between
heads Elk & Longhope Creek. Entry No. 212.

26 June 1778. WILLIAM SLONE e. 50 ac. both sides Roaring River..at
HENRY BRYOMS fence..including improvement whereon said
SLONE now lives. Entry No. 213.

26 June 1778. HENRY BYROM e. 100 ac. N side Roaring River..below
Stewarts Creek..including improvement where BYROM now
lives. Entry No. 214.

26 June 1778. HENRY BYROM e. 80 ac. N side Roaring River..WM. SLONES
line..including improvement where BYROM now lives, Entry
No. 215.

26 June 1778. 1st. enterer erased completely..e. 100 ac. S fork New
River..mouth of Livingstons Creek..including the improvement & claim..(BENJAMIN CUTHBEARD written in). Entry No. 216.

26 June 1778. 1st enterer erased completely..e. 100 ac. S fork New
River..including improvement whereon the said STRINGER
now lives..(BENJAMIN GREER'S name written in). Entry No. 217.

26 June 1778. REUBIN STRINGER e. 150 ac. S fork New River..(JONATHAN
HATKINGS (?) & REUBIN STRINGER marked out..THOMAS FARMER
written in). Entry No. 218.

26 June 1778. WILLIAM BREWER e. 400 ac. Big Sandy Creek near an old
mill..including the improvement said BREWER now lives on.
Entry No. 219.

26 June 1778. GILES PARMELY e. 200 ac. Little Sandy Creek..including
improvement whereon PARMELY now lives. Entry No. 220.

26 June 1778. PRITCHETT ALEXANDER e. 280 ac. W side Brier Creek..E near
line of JOHN TURNBILL. Entry No. 221.

26 June 1778. ABEL PENNINGTON e. 100 ac. N fork New River..at foard of
river below mouth Skeggs Creek..(ABEL PENNINGTON marked
out..ISAAC WEAVER written in). Entry No. 222.

29 June 1778. EMANUEL ROSE e. 100 ac. Roaring River..including improvement whereon ROSE now lives. Entry No. 223.

30 June 1778. WILLIAM CORNELIOUS e. 150 ac. land on Graves Creek..JOSEPH
GOUGES line..including improvement said CORNELIOUS lives
on. Entry No. 224.

30 June 1778. JOSEPH GOUGE e. 230 ac. Graves Creek joining WM. CORNE-
LIOUS..line made between JOSEPH GRAVES and JOHN ANGLE.
Entry No. 225.

30 June 1778. JAMES BROWN e. 160 ac. land S fork Hunting Creek..about
300 yards above mouth Caleys Creek. Entry No. 226.

2 July 1778. WILLIAM SNODDY e. 300 ac. N side New River..head Howards
Creek..(WM. SNODDY & WM. LENOIR marked out..ZEBULON BEARD
written in). Entry No. 227.

2 July 1778. WILLIAM SNODDY e. 150 ac. N fork New River called Flannerys
fork..including gap at head..(WM. SNODDY marked out..JAMES
GREENLEE written in). Entry No. 228.

14

2 July 1778.   JOSEPH MCCORKLE e. 250 ac. on Blue Ridge between head Elk
        & New River..including each path leads from head of Elk
to Three Forks..likewise including some of waters New River..(JOSEPH
MCCORKEL marked out..DANIEL EGGERS written in). Entry No. 229.

2 July 1778.   AMOS KILBURN e. 100 ac. Great Elkin..including the improve-
        ment. Entry No. 230.

4 July 1778.   JOHN WILLIAM CROSTHWAIT e. 100 ac. Beaver Creek at great
        shoals..including improvement CROSTHWAIT now lives on..
(JOHN WM. CROSTHWAIT marked out..LIVINGSTON ISBILL written in). Entry
No. 231.

4 July 1778.   FRANCIS VANNOY e. 60 ac. mouth S fork Rock Creek. Entry
        No. 232.

4 July 1778.   JOHN BROWN e. 150 ac. N fork Lewis fork..including JOHN
        ADAMS Cabin. Entry No. 233.

4 July 1778.   STEPHEN SOUTHER e. 200 ac. both sides Hunting Creek above
        WM. CRANES improvement..including improvement whereon said
SOUTHER now lives. Entry No. 234.

4 July 1778.   ISAAC PARLIER e. 320 ac. branch N fork Lewis Fork..on ridge
        between said fork and Reades River..including BELL'S Cabbin
..(ISAAC PARLIER marked out..JOHN BROWN written in). Entry No. 235.

4 July 1778.   ISAAC PARLIER e. 320 ac. branch N fork Lewis Fork..below
        the plantation where JOHN BROWN now lives..(ISAAC PARLIER
marked out..JOHN BROWN written in). Entry No. 236.

4 July 1778.   REUBEN STANDLEY e. 200 ac. Hunting Creek..foot Losey (?)
        Hill..including improvement said STANDLEY now lives on..
(REUBEN STANDLEY marked out..JAMES LOVE, JR. written in). Entry No. 237.

4 July 1778.   JOHN COOK e. 150 ac. Beaver Creek..at great falls above
        waggon road..including improvement, Entry No. 238.

4 July 1778.   JOHN CRANE e. 100 ac. both sides Hunting Creek between
        AMBROSE CRANES & ABNER BAKERS..including improvement where-
on JOHN CRANE now lives..(JOHN CRANE & DANIEL HOLMAN marked out..JOHN
LOVE written in). Entry No. 239.

4 July 1778.   WILLIAM LENOIR e. 170 ac. both sides Fishes Creek above
        EDWARD FINCHES Mill..(WM. LENOIR marked out..DEVEREAUX
BALLARD written in). Entry No. 240.

6 July 1778.   WILLIAM MCCUBBINS e. 300 ac. middle fork Bryer Creek..15
        or 20 yards above mouth Falls Branch..including improve-
ment said MCCUBBINS now lives on. Entry No. 241.

7 July 1778.   JAMES BUNYARD e. 100 ac. N side lower end of my improve-
        ment..E fork Roaring River. Entry No. 242.

8 July 1778.   RANDOLPH FUGIT e. 281 ac. on both sides Roaring River.
        Entry No. 243.

17 July 1778. HILLIAR RUSSAU (ROUSSEAU) e. 320 ac. on Mulberry Creek..
        foot of Suttons Mountain. Entry No. 244.

17 July 1778. JAMES CRANE e. 100 ac. head waters Fishes Creek..above
        improvement where RODEN TOMPSON formerly lives..(JAMES
CRANE marked out..EDWARD CARTER written in). Entry No. 245.

17 July 1778. JAMES CRANE e. 100 ac. N side Hunting Creek..AMBROSE
               CRANES line. Entry No. 246.

20 July 1778. JOSEPH COUCH e. 50 ac. New River above what is called
               the Old Fields..lower end called Adam's Bottom..including
small improvement made by ADAMS..(JOSEPH COUCH & JOSEPH ELLEDGE marked
out..SAMUEL WILCOXEN written in). Entry No. 247

20 July 1778. LARKIN CLEVELAND e. 200 ac. Beaver Creek..N branch New
               River..near NATHANIEL JUDDS Camp on said creek..(LARKIN
CLEVELAND marked out..BENJAMIN CLEVELAND written in). Entry No. 248.

20 July 1778. LARKIN CLEVELAND e. 100 ac. New River..near a horse foard
               ..including an improvement above mouth the Old Field
Creek..(LARKIN CLEVELAND marked out..JAMES HAMPTON written in). Entry
No. 249.

20 July 1778. BENJAMIN CLEVELAND e. 200 ac. Deep Gap Creek about three
               miles from mouth..(BENJ. CLEVELAND marked out..ALEXANDER
GORDON marked out..AARON MASH written in). Entry No. 250.

20 July 1778. CARLTON KEELAND e. 200 ac..(Entry withdrawn). Entry No.
               251.

23 July 1778. WILLIAM DAVIS e. 150 ac. Elk Creek..including improvement
               where said DAVIS now lives..(WM. DAVIS & MICHEL BARKER
marked out..JOHN SOUTHER (?) written in). Entry No. 252.

25 July 1778. JOHN TURNBILL e. 100 ac. Bryer Creek..mouth Mirey Branch
               a little below the falls of said Creek that lies below
the road that leads from shallow foard to the Mulberry Fields. Entry
No. 253.

25 July 1778. JOHN TURNBILL e. 200 ac. waters Bryer Creek..line said
               TURNBILL'S entry no. 253..both sides Great Road..including
improvement where BEN. JOHNSTON formerly lived..(JOHN TURNBILL marked
out..JAMES HAGOOD (HAIGWOOD) written in). Entry No. 254.

25 July 1778. JOHN TURNBILL e. 140 ac. on Bryer Creek on EDMOND CROSSES
               claim..including improvement made by WM. FRAZER (FRAZIER)
..(TRUNBILL marked out..TIMOTHY CHANDLER written in). Entry No. 255.

25 July 1778. JOHN SIMPSON e. 500 ac. Yadkin River..above LINVILLS Mill
               Creek..cross the river by WILLSON Cabbin..including the
improvement..(JOHN SIMPSON marked out..RUSSEL JONES written in). Entry
No. 256.

25 July 1778. JOHN SIMPSON e. 150 ac. both sides Yadkin River..waggon
               foard..condt. line made between JOHN FARGUSON & GEORGE
POINTERS (?)..claims joining said SIMPSONS Entry No. 256..(JOHN SIMPSON
marked out..RUSSEL JONES written in). Entry No. 257.

27 July 1778. FRANCIS VANNOY e. 320 ac. head waters Robins Creek of
               Readys River & Roan Creek on New River..near camp where
CAPT. JOSEPH HERNDON was scouting in the year 1776..(FRANCIS VANNOY and
ALEXANDER GORDON marked out..AARON MASH written in). Entry No. 258.

27 July 1778. FRANCIS VANNOY e. 100 ac. S fork Rock Creek. Entry No.
               259.

27 July 1778. FRANCIS VANNOY e. 100 ac. Robbins Creek opposite Chesnut
          Knob..(FRANCIS VANNOY, ALEXANDER GORDON & AARON MASH
marked out..GEORGE GRIMES written in). Entry No. 260.

27 July 1778. FRANCIS VANNOY e. 60 ac. Rock Creek at the falls of said
          ck..(FRANCIS VANNOY & JOHN JOHNSON marked out..JAMES
REYNOLDS written in..(also)..Caveated by TURNBILL written in). Entry
No. 261.

27 July 1778. JOHN PROPHET e. 130 ac. S side Yadkin River..JOSEPH TAN-
          NERS line..JAMES FLETCHERS line..including said PROPHET'S
improvement. Entry No. 262.

30 July 1778. CUTBURT KING e. 60 ac. Rowing River near falls..(CUTBURT
          KING marked out..GEORGE BREWER written in). Entry No.
263.

30 July 1778. CUTHBURT KING e. 100 ac. waters Roaring River between WM.
          BREWERS & GILES PARMELY..(CUTHBURT KING marked out..GEORGE
BREWER written in). Entry No. 264.

31 July 1778. MOSES DENMAN e. 100 ac. N side Yadkin River with WM.
          WILLBURNS lower line..including improvement whereon JOHN
MORE lives. Entry No. 265.

3 Aug. 1778. JOSEPH JONES e. 100 ac. both sides Elk Creek known by name
          of the Middle Cane..(JOSEPH JONES marked out..JOHN MARLEY
JONES written in). Entry No. 266.

3 Aug. 1778. JOHN HAWKINGS e. 200 ac. Mulberry Creek..foot of a mtn...
          joining BAUGAUS line..including old improvement made by
said HAWKINS. Entry No. 267.

3 Aug. 1778. JAMES WALLS e. 100 ac. both sides New River..including im-
          provement made by REUBEN STRINGER..(JAMES WALLS marked out
..THOMAS HOLMAN written in). Entry No. 268.

3 Aug. 1778. FRANCIS BROWN e. 320 ac. waters Readies River near foot of
          a small mountain..including improvement whereon said BROWN
lives. Entry No. 269.

3 Aug. 1778. EBENEZER FAIRCHILD e. 250 ac. N fork S fork Lewis Fork.
          Entry No. 270.

3 Aug. 1778. WILLIAM JACKSON e. 320 ac. both sides S fork Lewis Fork..
          including improvement by said JACKSON. Entry No. 271..

7 Aug. 1778. JOHN ROSE e. 400 ac. Grays Creek..joining GRAYS line..in-
          cluding his improvement and HENRY READ'S Mill. Entry No.
272.

8 Aug. 1778. WILLIAM MCCLANE e. 200 ac. E side Three Fork..N fork New
          River..foard at mouth of Pounding Branch..(WM. MCCLANE
marked out..a name has been erased). Entry No. 273.

8 Aug. 1778. WILLIAM MCCLANE e. 300 ac. N fork New River..to Roans
          Creek. Entry No. 274.

8 Aug. 1778. NICHOLAS ANGEL e. 100 ac. Sycamore foard N fork New River..
          (NICHOLAS ANGEL marked out..ISAAC WEAVER written in).
Entry No. 275.

8 Aug. 1778. JOHN DOYAL e. 250 ac. both sides Little fork Hunting Creek
          of Duggars Creek to ISHAM HARRELS line. Entry No. 276.

8 Aug. 1778. ISHAM HARVEL e. 550 ac. both sides little fork Hunting
          Creek..on Ridge between Duggars Creek & Ring Fire knob in
JOHN DOIALS line..including ISHAM HARVELS improvement. Entry No. 277.

8 Aug. 1778. MARK WHITAKER e. 100 ac. little fork Hunting Creek..mouth
of Maple Branch and ISHAM HARVELS line..to JOHN DOIALS..
including his improvement. Entry No. 278.

8 Aug. 1778. JOHN STANDLEY e. 200 ac. on Mill Creek of Hunting Creek..
including his improvement. Entry No. 279.

10 Aug. 1778. JOSEPH COUCH e. 150 ac. above fork Elk Creek..(JOSEPH
COUCH & WILLIAM SHERRY marked out..THOMAS FARMER written
in). Entry No. 280.

15 Aug. 1778. WILLIAM FLETCHER e. 150 ac. S fork Old Fields Creek of
New River. Entry No. 281.

19 Aug. 1778. WILLIAM RYSDON e. 100 ac. S fork Stoney Fork. Entry No.
282.

19 Aug. 1778. ELIJAH CLAY e. 100 ac. little creek of Hunting Creek..
joining JOHN DOIALS line..(Caveated by JAMES MCBRIDE Nov.
the 9th). Entry No. 283.

25 Aug. 1778. ABEDNIGO BAKER e. 100 ac. waters Hunting Creek called the
Bear Branch..(ABEDNIGO BAKER marked out..FRANCIS SANDERS
(?) & JAMES JONES written in). Entry No. 284.

25 Aug. 1778. SYLVESTER BAKER e. 100 ac. joining JOHN HOWARDS claim..up
Hunting Creek on both sides..(SYLVESTER BAKER marked out..
ISAAC REAVES written in..JON. FORBUSH written in..but marked out). Entry
No. 285.

25 Aug. 1778. JOHN ROBINS e. 100 ac. both sides middle fork Reddies
River..near Gap of mtn. between said ROBINS & OWENS..in-
cluding ROBINS improvement where he now lives. Entry No. 286.

25 Aug. 1778. BAKER AIRS e. 200 ac. Cranberry Creek of New River near
lower end Elk Hill..(BAKER AIRS marked out..BENJAMIN
HERNDON written in). Entry No. 287.

25 Aug. 1778. BAKER AIRS e. 300 ac. Bushey Creek of Little River on path
that leads from HOLDBROOKS to New River Settlement..(BAKER
AIRS & BENJ. HERNDON marked out..MOSES WOODRUFF written in). Entry No.
288.

27 Aug. 1778. BARNARD BRUMLEY e. 200 ac. Cranberry Creek at mouth dividing branch between JOSEPH MONEY and said BRUMLEY..includ-
ing his improvement..(BARNARD BRUMLEY marked out..JOHN COX written in..
(also)..Caveated by JOHN COX 20th Nov. written in). Entry No. 289.

27 Aug. 1778. WILLIAM MORGAN e. 200 ac. Hunting Creek..including his
improvement. Entry No. 290.

27 Aug. 1778. ABSALOM CLEVELAND e. 200 ac. laying partly on dividing
ridge between Bryer Creek & Grays Creek near fork of
MCCUBBINS path where it comes into ridge road..(Caveated by JOHN ROSE
18th Sept.). Entry No. 291.

28 Aug. 1778. DAVID HARVIL (or HOWARD) e. 600 ac. middle fork Hunting
Creek on BOMAN CASS'S claim..E to Bear Branch..including
his improvement..(DAVID HARVIL (or HOWARD) marked out..BENJAMIN HERNDON
written in). Entry No. 292.

28 Aug. 1778. JOSEPH PRUET e. 100 ac. S fork Roaring River near a foard
above his house..including his improvement. Entry No.
293.

29 Aug. 1778.   JOHN CALTON (CARLTON) e. 50 ac. waters Beaver Creek known
by name Hickory Knob. Entry No. 294.

1 Sept. 1778.   DANIEL WARD e. 200 ac. between the Green Mountain and
Buttals (?) Mountain..waters of Kings Creek above his
improvement..including his impt...(DANIEL WARD & MICHEL SOUTHER marked
out..JOSHUA STOREY written in). Entry No. 295.

3 Sept. 1778.   JOSEPH HERNDON e. 50 ac. both sides Mulberry Creek on
said HERNDON'S tract where he now lives..including a Griss
Mill & small impvt. Entry No. 296.

3 Sept. 1778.   WILLIAM WATTS e. 200 ac. S fork Michels (Mitchels) River..
a little above his fence..including his improvement.
Entry No. 297.

3 Sept. 1778.   WILLIAM WATTS e. 60 ac. N fork S fork Mitchels River.
Entry No. 298.

3 Sept. 1778.   WILLIAM WATTS e. 250 ac. S fork Mitchels River..including
an old improvement made by NATHANIEL SCRITCHFIELD..
(WILLIAM WATTS & BENJAMIN HERNDON marked out..ELKENER LEWIS written in).
Entry No. 299.

3 Sept. 1778.   JOHN PARKES, SENR. e. 50 ac. N side Yadkin River joining
land called Hews Bottom..to said PARKES line. Entry No.
300.

3 Sept. 1778.   ROBERT HAMMON e. 80 ac. main fork Mitchells River..taking
in an Island..including the improvement whereon JAMES
CHILDRESS lives. Entry No. 301.

3 Sept. 1778.   BENJAMIN MAY e. 80 ac. Mitchels River..including his
impvt...(THOMAS MAY marked out..JOSEPH THOMPSON written
in). Entry No. 302.

3 Sept. 1778.   THOMAS MAY e. 100 ac. Mitchells River..including his
improvement..(THOMAS MAY marked out..JOSEPH THOMPSON
written in). Entry No. 303.

3 Sept. 1778.   JAMES WALDON e. 100 ac. Mitchells River dividing line of
THOMAS MAY & himself..(JAMES WALDON marked out..JOSEPH
THOMPSON written in). Entry No. 304.

4 Sept. 1778.   WILLIAM SHERRY e. 50 ac. New River above his other entry
..near an Island. Entry No. 305.

4 Sept. 1778.   WILLIAM ADAMS e. 100 ac. S fork Lewis Fork..above GEORGE
ELMORES..both sides Lewis Fork..including his improvement.
..(WM. ADAMS & GEO. ELMORE marked out..JAMES JACKSON written in). Entry
No. 306.

4 Sept. 1778.   SAMUEL WRIGHT e. 300 ac. on the Brushey Mountain known by
name of BAILEYS place..including the improvement..(SAMUEL
WRIGHT marked out..(also)..the above entry is trandferred to THOMAS
BANDGE (BENGE) the 4th Dec. written in). Entry No. 307.

4 Sept. 1778.   ANDREW DUGLAS e. 100 ac. John's Creek of Fishes River..on
JAMES WILLIAM'S claim..including his improvement. Entry
No. 308.

4 Sept. 1778.   GIBSON MAINARD e. 250 ac. both sides Great Elkin..upper
corner his bottom..including the improvement..(GIBSON
MAINARD marked out..JACOB HEDDEN written in). Entry No. 309.

4 Sept. 1778.   JACOB MAINARD e. 100 ac. little fork Mitchels River at
the Big Cove..above his house..both sides said river..
(JACOB MAINARD marked out..JAMES FIELDER written in..(also)..JAMES FLET-
CHER transfaired to JOHN JENNINGS). Entry No. 310.

5 Sept. 1778. SAMUEL MORRISON e. 200 ac. Great Elkin..W side..including improvement whereon EDWARD HEADY lives..(SAMUEL MORRISON marked out..WM. CANNADY written in). Entry No. 311.

5 Sept. 1778. EDMOND WARD e. 400 ac. Mitchells River..including his improvement..(EDMOND WARD marked out..BARNARD FRANKLIN written in). Entry No. 312.

5 Sept. 1778. EMANUEL ROSE e. 450 ac. middle Fork Roaring River..widow ALEXANDERS line..including ROSE'S improvement. Entry No. 313.

5 Sept. 1778. WILLIAM RENOLDS (REYNOLDS) e. 200 ac. Pine Swamp about a mile above mouth on E fork..(WM. RENOLDS marked out.. JONATHAN TOMPKINS written in). Entry No. 314.

5 Sept. 1778. WILLIAM RENOLDS (REYNOLDS) e. 50 ac. New River near mouth of small branch. Entry No. 315.

5 Sept. 1778. JOHN CLEVELAND e. 640 ac. waters Buffaloe below improvement made by MOSES DARNEL and sold to SOLOMON SPARKS.. (JOHN CLEVELAND marked out..BENJAMIN CLEVELAND written in). Entry No. 316.

5 Sept. 1778. JAMES WILLIAMS e. 150 ac. John's Creek. Entry No. 317.

5 Sept. 1778. JAMES WILLIAMS e. 200 ac. on John's Creek at ANDREW DOUGLAS line..(JAMES WILLIAMS marked out..WILLIAM CUNNINGHAM written in). Entry No. 318.

5 Sept. 1778. GEORGE BROWN e. 50 ac. Big Sandy Creek above the Big Falls. Entry No. 319.

7 Sept. 1778. JEFFREY JOHNSON e. 100 ac. Dennys Mill Creek near fork. Entry No. 320.

7 Sept. 1778. (erased) JOHNSON e. 100 ac. on Rock Creek above middle fork..(JOHN JOHNSON & ELLENER (?) marked out..JOHN JOHNSON written in again). Entry No. 321.

7 Sept. 1778. ELISHA RENOLDS (REYNOLDS) e. 100 ac. lying on Roaring River waters..foot of mountain. Entry No. 322.

7 Sept. 1778. JOHN WILLIAM CROSTHWAIT e. 137 ac. Beaver Creek between his own land and THOMAS LANDS land..near waggon road. Entry No. 323.

7 Sept. 1778. THOMAS LAND e. 300 ac. Beaver Creek..including his improvement. Entry No. 324.

7 Sept. 1778. THOMAS LAND e. 50 ac. branch Beaver Creek. Entry No. 325.

7 Sept. 1778. JAMES BROWN e. 125 ac. Pipe Creek Branch..draughts of Hunting Creek. Entry No. 326.

7 Sept. 1778. JOHN HAMMON e. 100 ac. Osborns Creek..at mouth of Reedy Branch..(JOHN HAMMON marked out..SAMUEL NICLISON written in). Entry No. 327.

7 Sept. 1778. JOHN SIMPSON e. 100 ac. S side Yadkin River in a cornfield of SIMPSONS parting his land and ABRAHAM VANDERPOOLS.. dividing SIMPSONS land and JOHN KEES..including SIMPSONS improvement. Entry No. 328.

7 Sept. 1778. EDMOND TILLEY e. 400 ac. Kings Creek..fork of Kings Creek road. Entry No. 329.

7 Sept. 1778. WILLIAM SUTTON e. 150 ac. N branch Reddys River..including his improvement..(WM. SUTTON marked out..WALTER BROWN written in). Entry No. 330.

7 Sept. 1778. RICHARD SMITH e. 150 ac. N fork New River..just above Horse Creek..including plantation whereon said SMITH now lives..(RICHARD SMITH marked out..PAUL HENSON written in). Entry No. 331.

7 Sept. 1778. THOMAS TOMSON e. 100 ac. Hunting Creek above his improvement..including his improvement..(THOMAS TOMSON marked out..JOHN LOVE written in). Entry No. 332.

7 Sept. 1778. EDWARD CROSS e. 320 ac. on Bryer Creek..at FRAZERS line. Entry No. 333.

7 Sept. 1778. PHILLIP DAVIS e. 200 ac. Kings Creek..condt. line between STEPHEN TILLEY & said DAVIS..(PHILLIP DAVIS marked out.. WM. HOLT written in). Entry No. 334.

7 Sept. 1778. SAMUEL MCQUEEN e. 150 ac. on New River near mouth Mill Creek..including the old camp called BAKERS old camp.. both sides river. Entry No. 335.

7 Sept. 1778. BEVERLY WATKINS e. 400 ac. on New River..including his improvement..(BEVERLY WATKINS marked out..JOHN LONGE written in). Entry No. 336.

7 Sept. 1778. ALEXANDER GILREATH e. 100 ac. N side New River..including WALLS improvement..(ALEX. GILREATH marked out..WM. MACNIEL written in). Entry No. 337.

7 Sept. 1778. JAMES HAMPTON e. 150 ac. on Cub Creek..including his improvement on both sides creek. Entry No. 338.

7 Sept. 1778. JAMES DUGGARS e. 200 ac. on Elk Creek joining BEN DUGGARS & SAMUEL HALL..including his improvement..(JAMES DUGGARS & WM. ISAACS marked out..transferred to ELIJAH ISAACS written in). Entry No. 339.

7 Sept. 1778. SOLOMON CAMBLE e. 100 ac. N side Yadkin River..JOHN SUTTON line..including his improvement where he now lives..(this is a definite CAMBLE and not GAMBLE..possibly spelled CAMPBELL). Entry No. 340.

7 Sept. 1778. THOMAS HOPPER e. 100 ac. on Readdies River..mouth of branch that makes into the River below his house..includ- his improvement. Entry No. 341.

7 Sept. 1778. BENJAMIN BIRD e. 200 ac. S side Yadkin River below Tumb- ling Shoal..including his improvement..(BENJ. BIRD marked out..JOSEPH REED written in). Entry No. 342.

7 Sept. 1778. WILLIAM SMITH e. 200 ac. on N side Yadkin River..mouth of branch below WILLIAM KERBEYS improvement..(Ordered by court to WM. SMITH written in..WM. SMITH marked out..JEREMIAH CRICELEY (CRYSEL?) written in..Caveated by CHARLES GORDON 1st Dec. written in). Entry No. 343.

7 Sept. 1778. BENJAMIN BEYMAN e. 50 ac. in Cove of Buffalow on Jesse's fork..including his improvement..(BENJ. BEYMAN marked out..WM. LANSDOWN written in). Entry No. 344.

7 Sept. 1778. WILLIAM DAVIS e. 320 ac. both sides Hunting Creek N fork ..on road leading to shallow ford..crossing ford of Creek to Brushey Mountain..including his improvement..(Caveated by CORNELIUS SAILS 25 Nov.). Entry No. 345.

8 Sept. 1778. THOMAS CORVIN (or COWEN?) e. 400 ac. waters S fork New
River..including his improvement bought of BAKER KING..
(THOMAS CORVIN marked out..DANIEL YARNEL written in). Entry No. 346.

8 Sept. 1778. ALEXANDER HOLTON e. 100 ac. at JAMES STEPS (STAPP) line
on a branch of Kings Creek..(ALEX. HOLTON marked out..
JOHN DIROM (DURHAM) written in). Entry No. 347.

8 Sept. 1778. THOMAS HENDERSON e. 100 ac. on Beaver Creek between EDWARD
BOONS land and his own..including his improvement. Entry
No. 348.

8 Sept. 1778. WILLIAM GILREATH, JR. e. 150 ac. on Cub Creek at JAMES
WILSONS line. Entry No. 349.

8 Sept. 1778. BENJAMIN BRANHAM e. 200 ac. on Caleys Creek..including
his improvement. Entry No. 350.

8 Sept. 1778. EDWARD PINKSTON e. 120 ac. on Hunting Creek..joining JAMES
BROWNS lower line..including his improvement..(EDWARD
PINDSTON marked out..WALTER WAL--- written in). Entry No. 351.

8 Sept. 1778. SPILSBY TRIBLE e. 250 ac. waters Warryors Creek..both
sides on Maravian line below his plantation..including
his improvement. Entry No. 352.

8 Sept. 1778. JAMES STAPP e. 100 ac. branch Kings Creek..joining JAMES
TRIBLES upper line..(JAMES STAPP marked out..JOHN STAPP
written in). Entry No. 353.

8 Sept. 1778. JAMES HENDERSON e. 300 ac. branch Beaver Creek above old
WILLIAM PARKERS..taking in STEPHEN LITTLES claim..(JAMES
HENDERSON & DAVID COX marked out..PHILLIP DAVIS written in). Entry No.
354.

8 Sept. 1778. HUGH SMITH e. 150 ac. S fork New River..including improvement..(HUGH SMITH marked out..THOMAS DICKSON written in).
Entry No. 355.

8 Sept. 1778. JOHN ISAACS (??) e. 50 ác. N fork Lewis Fork at MATTHEW
FRANCIS line..(JOHN ISAAC (?) marked out..OWEN WILLIAMS
marked out..transferred to JOHN YATES written in). Entry No. 356.

8 Sept. 1778. THOMAS LAXTON e. 150 ac. both sides Fishdam Creek..at
ROBERTS path. Entry No. 357.

8 Sept. 1778. JOHN LEWIS e. 150 ac. S side Hunting Creek..below mouth
of Cayleys Creek..(JOHN LEWIS marked out..WILLIAM LEWIS
written in). Entry No. 358.

8 Sept. 1778. JOSEPH WISDOM e. 50 ac. branch Kings Creek..joining DANIEL
WARDS upper line..(JOSEPH WISDOM marked out..FANNEY MC-
KENZEY written in). Entry No. 359.

8 Sept. 1778. THOMAS WISDOM e. 150 ac. branch Kings Creek..adjoining
JOSEPH WISDOMS upper line. Entry No. 360.

8 Sept. 1778. JOHN WISDOM e. 150 ac. branch Kings Creek..adjoining said
WISDOMS upper line..(JOHN WISDOM marked out..JOHN BRADLEY
written in). Entry No. 361.

8 Sept. 1778. WILLIAM ROBERTS e. 250 ac. N fork Lewis fork..condt. line
between JOHN YATES & said ROBERTS..(WM. ROBERTS & LARKIN
CLEVELAND marked out..GEORGE MACNIEL written in). Entry No. 362.

8 Sept. 1778. THOMAS ELLIOT e. 640 ac. between EDWARD BOON and him..S
side BOONS Field Branch..including ELLIOT'S improvement.
Entry No. 363.

8 Sept. 1778. BENGAMIN HOWARD e. 350 ac. N side Yadkin River..both
sides Elk Creek..including his improvement. Entry No. 364.

9 Sept. 1778. HENRY TILLEY e. 100 ac. lying on waters Kings Creek..in-
cluding his improvement..(HENRY TILLEY marked out..ROBERT
NETHERLY written in). Entry No. 365.

9 Sept. 1778. THOMAS FORHOCK e. 300 ac. both sides New River..deep foard
on said river. Entry No. 366.

9 Sept. 1778. ENOCH OSBURN e. 640 ac. upon hills Elk Creek..New River..
on ridge between Rockey Creek & Elk. Entry No. 367.

9 Sept. 1778. ZACHARIAH WELLS e. 100 ac. on New River..mouth boundry
branch between his & MICAJAH PENNINGTONS land. Entry No.
368.

9 Sept. 1778. ANDREW BAKER e. 100 ac. S fork New River..mouth certain
branch..below MORRIS BAKERS improvement. Entry No. 369.

9 Sept. 1778. MICAJAH PENNINGTON e. 100 ac. both sides New River..mouth
branch above his improvement. Entry No. 370.

9 Sept. 1778. BENAJAH PENNINGTON e. 150 ac. on Grassy Creek..New River..
at ground hogs den below his mill. Entry No. 371.

9 Sept. 1778. BEVERLY WATKINS e. 200 ac. E fork Little Elk Creek..New
River..(BEVERLY WATKINS marked out..WM. LENOIR written in).
Entry No. 372.

9 Sept. 1778. DANIEL RICHARDSON e. 150 ac. S fork New River..both sides
river. Entry No. 373.

9 Sept. 1778. CHARLES GORDON e. 200 ac. N side Yadkin River..upper line
of his Pasturs land..including his improvement..known by
name of PETERS improvement. Entry No. 374.

9 Sept. 1778. RICHARD CHURCHILL e. 100 ac. Cove of Buffalow at foard
below his house..(RICHARD CHURCHILL marked out..THOMAS
COTRAL written in). Entry No. 375.

9 Sept. 1778. DAVID SMITH e. 100 ac. N side S fork New River..above
mouth Nathans Creek. Entry No. 376.

9 Sept. 1778. JONATHAN SMITH e. 100 ac. S side Cranberry Creek..known
by name of Roundabout..in JAMES WILLIAMS line..including
his improvement..(JONATHAN SMITH marked out..JOHN COX written in). Entry
No. 377.

9 Sept. 1778. QUILLER LOWE e. 500 ac. both sides Moravian Creek..joining
ZACHARIAH WALKERS on E..THOMAS ELLISON on S..main road on
the W. Entry No. 378.

9 Sept. 1778. JOHN PARKER e. for JOHN PARKER, JUNR. 100 ac. on a fork
of Beaver Creek just above EDWARD BOONS Mill Falls..in-
cluding an improvement bought of THOMAS ELLEDGE, SR. Entry No. 379.

9 Sept. 1778. FRANCIS HARDGRAVE e. 100 ac. on Brushey Mountain..taking
on head little fork of Cub Creek. Entry No. 380.

9 Sept. 1778.   LAZARUS SOUTHER e. 400 ac. both sides Moravian Creek..
                joining lands of AQUILLER LOWE on N..NICHELUS WALKER on
S..(LAZARUS SOUTHER & WM. DONATHAN marked out..HANKINS DONATHAN written
in). Entry No. 381.

9 Sept. 1778.   ABNER BAKER e. 50 ac. on Hunting Creek..JOHN CRANES line..
                both sides Creek..including plantation said BAKER now
lives on..(ABNER BAKER marked out..JOHN HUNT written in). Entry No. 382.

9 Sept. 1778.   CHARLES ADAMS e. 150 ac. on Reddies River above the horse
                foard..N side river..below the Plantation. Entry No. 383.

9 Sept. 1778.   1st enterer erased completely..e. 200 ac. on Bryer Creek..
                joining JOHN WILLIAM CROSTHWAITS..including improvement
whereon his father now lives..(EDWARD PARKER transfers and Deed to JOHN
WILLIAM CROSTHWAIT written in). Entry No. 384.

9 Sept. 1778.   JACOB HAMPTON e. 250 ac. waters Cub Creek..joining JOHN
                GREER..including his improvement. Entry No. 385.

9 Sept. 1778.   WILLIAM CRANE e. 100 ac. Hunting Creek in STEPHEN SOUTHERS
                line..both sides Creek..including improvement whereon
CRANE now lives..(WILLIAM CRANE marked out..OSBORNE KEELING written in).
Entry No. 386.

9 Sept. 1778.   GEORGE GORDON e. 200 ac. Saw Mill Creek at shoals below
                plantation..including saw Mill & Plantation. Entry No.
387.

9 Sept. 1778.   JOSHUA HENDRICKS e. 100 ac. S fork Stony Fork..including
                an improvement formerly belonging to JAMES OWENS above
GARRETT HENDRICS..(JOSHUA HENDRICKS marked out..BENJ. HENDRICK written
in). Entry No. 388.

9 Sept. 1778.   WILLIAM KILBY e. 300 ac. Maiden Cane Branch near the
                mouth. Entry No. 389.

9 Sept. 1778.   WILLIAM KILBY e. 200 ac. on Reddies River at the falls..
                including his improvement. Entry No. 390.

9 Sept. 1778.   WILLIAM KILBY e. 100 ac. between Maiden Cain Branch and
                Meadow branch..at a Canebrake on Meadow branch. Entry No.
391.

9 Sept. 1778.   SAMUEL CRITCHFIELD (SCRITCHFIELD) e. 200 ac. S fork
                Mitchels River..boundary line between him and RICHARD
HANKINGS. Entry No. 392.

9 Sept. 1778.   EDWARD BOON e. 200 ac. on Beaver Creek..adjoining THOMAS
                HENDERSON..including BOON'S improvement. Entry No. 393.

9 Sept. 1778.   SAMUEL CRITCHFIELD e. 200 ac. waters Big Elkin..known by
                name of Whiteoak Bottom..where the Ax entry was made by
ARTHER CRITCHFIELD..(SAMUEL CRITCHFIELD marked out..BENJ. HERNDON written
in). Entry No. 394.

10 Sept. 1778. GEORGE BAKER e. 50 ac. Buffaloe Creek between Paddy
                Knob of Three Top Mountain..near BAKERS Camp. Entry No.
395.

10 Sept. 1778. GEORGE BOON e. 640 ac. S fork Bear Creek..otherwise
                known as Warriors Creek..at the big road up THOMAS
ELLEDGES line..corner adjoining JACOB ELLEDGE'S run..condt. line to
GEORGE BROWNS..(GEORGE BOON marked out..NANCY ISBELL written in). Entry
No. 396.

10 Sept. 1778. ROWLAND JUDD e. 100 ac. N fork New River..(ROWLAND JUDD
                marked out..RANDOL SMITH written in). Entry No. 397.

10 Sept. 1778. WILLIAM GAMBILL e. 100 ac. between pine swamp..Little
                River known by name No-headed Branch. Entry No. 398.

10 Sept. 1778. HENRY GAMBILL e. 150 ac. near mouth Bledsoes Creek..
                Ridge that runs from Peach Bottom Mountain to said land.
Entry No. 399.

10 Sept. 1778. GEORGE BOON e. 260 ac. waters Bear Creek..otherwise
                called Warryors Creek..BEN ELLEDGES line..both sides
Bridge bank..(GEORGE BOON & BENJ. ELLEDGE marked out..JAMES HILL written
in). Entry No. 400.

10 Sept. 1778. THOMAS LAXTON e. 100 ac. N side New River..two miles
                above Elk Shoals..(THOMAS LAXTON marked out..JOHN BROWN
written in). Entry No. 401.

10 Sept. 1778. HUGH SMITH e. 50 ac. E side Peak Creek..down New River..
                including round meadow. Entry No. 402.

10 Sept. 1778. GEORGE GORDON e. 100 ac. top ridge head spring Lewis
                Fork.. Entry No. 403.

10 Sept. 1778. SAMUEL WRIGHT e. 250 ac...one and one-half miles above
                fork Elk Creek..on N fork. Entry No. 404.

12 Sept. 1778. BENJAMIN CUTHBERTH e. 200 ac. head waters middle fork
                Lewis Fork..top main ridge..S of his improvement..includ-
ing his improvement..(BENJ. CUTHBERTH & JOSHUA STOREY marked out..JAMES
PATTON written in). Entry No. 405.

14 Sept. 1778. WILLIAM HILL e. 100 ac. Great Elkin..condt. line between
                HILL & ARTHER CRITCHFIELD..condt. line between HILL &
THOMAS GOINS..including his improvement..(WM. HILL marked out..THOMAS
GOINS written in). Entry No. 406.

15 Sept. 1778. JAMES SHUFFIELD e. 100 ac. on Reddys River at WILSONS
                waggon road..(JAMES SHUFFIELD marked out..GERVIS SMITH
written in). Entry No. 407.

15 Sept. 1778. THOMAS EVINS e. 320 ac. on and under Duggars Mountain..
                near widow ROBERTS..including his improvement..(THOMAS
EVINS marked out..LUKE ADAMS written in). Entry No. 408.

15 Sept. 1778. BOMAN CASS e. 240 ac. middle fork Hunting Creek..joining
                DAVID HARVELS line..below his own..including his improve-
ment..(Duplicate 5 Nov. 1807..in margin). Entry No. 409.

15 Sept. 1778. JAMES MCBRIDE e. 300 ac. little fork Hunting Creek..on
                DAVID HARVELS line..JOHN DYALS (DOYAL) line..including
MCBRIDE improvement. Entry No. 410.

16 Sept. 1778. (erased) CLEVELAND e. 200 ac. S fork New River..horse
                foard below the Three Forks..including the improvement
where CHURCHILL formerly lived..(? CLEVELAND & JEN. TILLEY marked out..
JOHN FORGUSON written in). Entry No. 411. .

18 Sept. 1778. JOSHUA TURNBILL e. 300 ac. long branch of the cove.
                Entry No. 412.

18 Sept. 1778. JOSHUA TOMSON e. 300 ac. Bryer Creek..in JOHN TURNBILLS
                line. Entry No. 413.

18 Sept. 1778. WILLIAM STURDIE e. 75 ac. E side New River at mouth Bear
                Creek. Entry No. 414.

18 Sept. 1778. WILLIAM STURDIE e. 75 ac. W side New River..line of land
of MATTHEW SPARKS..including the above improvement.
Entry No. 415.

19 Sept. 1778. WILLIAM LENOIR e. 100 ac. between Cub Creek and Moravian
Creek..on THOMAS HAMBRICKS line between muddy branch
and the Yadkin River. Entry No. 416.

19 Sept. 1778. BENJAMIN CLEVELAND e. 300 ac. S side Yadkin River..THOMAS
HAMBRICKS corner..including improvement whereon JOSEPH
WILSON and his father now live..(BENJ. CLEVELAND marked out..transferred
to JOSEPH WILSON written in). Entry No. 417.

19 Sept. 1778. SPENCER HUMPHRIES e. 200 ac. both sides Cub Creek..THOMAS
HAMBRICKS line..including improvement whereon THOMAS
WILSON now lives..(SPENCER HUMPHRIES marked out..THOMAS WILSON written
in..(also)..Caveated by THOMAS WILLSON 21st Nov. written in). Entry No.
418.

21 Sept. 1778. HENRY REED e. 50 ac. in JOHN ANDERSONS line..both sides
of creek,,including improvement made by PHILIP DAVIS..
(HENRY REED marked out..JAMES STEPP, SR. written in). Entry No. 419.

21 Sept. 1778. JOHN PAYNE of Goochland County in the Colony of Virginia
e. 200 ac. S side Yadkin River..(JOHN PAYNE marked out..
THOMAS THURMAN written in). Entry No. 420.

21 Sept. 1778. JAMES TOMPKINS e. 125 ac. S fork Lewis Fork..N side
Creek..near said TOMPKINS Mill. Entry No. 421.

21 Sept. 1778. JAMES TOMPKINS e. 150 ac. top Blue Ridge..head of most
southern branch Lewis Fork between BENJAMIN CUTHBERTH
and JOHN PROPHET. Entry No. 422.

21 Sept. 1778. JAMES TOMPKINS e. 125 ac. S fork Lewis Fork..joining
said TOMPKINS entry above. Entry No. 423.

21 Sept. 1778. JOHN (?) e. 150 ac. joining JAMES TOMPKINS line..includ-
ing some waters of N fork Stony Fork..(JOHN (?) marked
out..CHARLES GORDON JUNR. written in). Entey No. 424.

23 Sept. 1778. WILLIAM COOK e. 100 ac. head Cranes Creek..waters Hunting
Creek..side of a mountain. Entry No. 425.

23 Sept. 1778. WILLIAM MCCUBBINS e. 320 ac. N side Shallow ford road..
down road joining LACKINGS (LYCANS) claim. Entry No.
426.

26 Sept. 1778. JAMES FLETCHER e. 200 ac. little Rock Creek of Hunting
Creek..known by name Cranes Creek..mouth Grassy branch.
Entry No. 427.

28 Sept. 1778. EDMOND DENNY e. 640 ac. N side Yadkin River..mouth of
Roaring River..including JEFFREY JOHNSONS..his own
plantations. Entry No. 428.

28 Sept. 1778. EDMOND DENNEY e. 300 ac. both sides Cane Creek which
runs into Roaring River..including plantation whereon
FRANCIS HILL lives. Entry No. 429.

28 Sept. 1778. EDMOND DENNEY e. 300 ac. on Roaring River..lower end of
mill floss that is called swift Shoal run..including his
Mill. Entry No. 430.

1 Oct. 1778. WILLIAM LENOIR e. 60 ac. both sides Reddies River near
foard below WILLIAM OWENS. Entry No. 431.

1 Oct. 1778.   WILLIAM LENOIR e. 60 ac. both sides Fishes Creek..mouth
                meadow branch above said LENOIRS improvement. Entry No.
432.

1 Oct. 1778.   EDWARD FINCH e. 300 ac. both sides Mulberry Creek..includ-
                ing an improvement said FINCH bought of ANDREW VANNOY.
Entry No. 433.

1 Oct. 1778.   EDWARD FINCH e. 168 ac. both sides Mulberry Creek..includ-
                ing a fork of said Creek above FINCHES other entry..(Ca-
veated by ANDREW VANNOY). Entry No. 434.

1 Oct. 1778.   EDWARD FINCH e. 50 ac. both sides Mulberry Creek..includ-
                ing fork of said creek between Rich Mountain and the Grand-
father Mountain. Entry No. 435.

1 Oct. 1778.   EDWARD FINCH e. 80 ac. head Hawkins Branch. Entry No. 436.

1 Oct. 1778.   EDWARD FINCH e. 100 ac. Top of the Blue Ridge..including
                some of waters of Obids Creek..against head of Tyrahs (?)
Fork of Reddies River. Entry No. 437.

1 Oct. 1778.   EDWARD FINCH e. 250 ac. both sides middle fork Fishes
                Creek..N side Mare Branch..including Mill and improvement
said FINCH bought of ANDREW VANNOY..(EDWARD FINCH marked out..DEVEREAUX
BALLARD written in). Entry No. 438.

2 Oct. 1778.   ISAAC WALKER e. 200 ac. waters Waryers Creek..adjoining
                THOMAS ELLEDGES & PHILIP WALKERS..including ISAAC WALKERS
improvement..(ISAAC WALKER marked out..ELISHA DYER written in). Entry
No. 439.

2 Oct. 1778.   ISAAC WALKER e. 200 ac. Cub Creek..below an old entry..
                (ISAAC WALKER marked out..WILLIAM LOW written in). Entry
No. 440.

2 Oct. 1778.   ISAAC WALKER e. 100 ac. waters Moravian Creek at JOHN
                TRIBLES claim..crossing the waggon road..(ISAAC WALKER
marked out..HANNAH HUBBARD written in). Entry No. 441.

2 Oct. 1778.   ABRAHAM DEMOSS e. 80 ac. little fork Cub Creek..adjoining
                JOHN GREYORS (GREER). Entry No. 442.

6 Oct. 1778.   WILLIAM SMITH e. 250 ac. Smitheys Creek of the Yadkin..in-
                cluding JOSHUA SCURLOCKS improvement..(WM. SMITH marked
out..HESTER ELMOR written in). Entry No. 443.

6 Oct. 1778.   WILLIAM SMITH e. 100 ac. Merediths Branch..including
                GARNET SMITHEYS improvement. Entry No. 444.

6 Oct. 1778.   WILLIAM RAGLAND e. 200 ac. middle fork Hunting Creek..N
                side under foot of mtn...below his improvement..condt. line
between BENJAMIN HERNDON & RAYLAND..including his improvement. Entry No.
445.

6 Oct. 1778.   BAKER AIRES e. 150 ac. waters Hunting Creek..above PETER
                GOODE..on a hill above PETER GOODS Tobacco house..includ-
ing the piece of land BENJ. HERNDON bought of PETER GOODE..(BAKER AIRS
and BENJAMIN HERNDON marked out..JOHN GRANT written in). Entry No. 446.

8 Oct. 1778.   BENJAMIN DUGGAR e. 100 ac. S fork Elk Creek..adjoining
                JULIAS DUGGARS line..including BENJ. DUGGARS improvement.
Entry No. 447.

8 Oct. 1778.   WILLIAM OWEN MADDLIN e. 200 ac. waters Roaring River..in-
                cluding his improvement..(Caveated by JOHN BROWN 8th Oct.).

8 Oct. 1778.   GILES PARMELY e. 100 ac. Sandy Creek of Roaring River..
               Little falls..(GILES PARMELY marked out..JOHN DEFREACE (?)
(looks like) written in). Entry No. 449.

8 Oct. 1778.   JAMES BOGGS e. 100 ac. N fork New River at Rock Foard..
               including his improvement..(JAMES BOGGS & ANDREW BAKER
marked out..RICHARD SMITH written in). Entry No. 450.

9 Oct. 1778.   ELISHA HEDDIN e. 200 ac. Great Elkin below his improvement
               and including it. Entry No. 451.

14 Oct. 1778. ALEXANDER GORDON e. 640 ac. N branch S fork Mitchells
               River..foot of mtn...including DOPETS improvement...(ALES.
GORDON marked out..SHADRICK BURK written in). Entry No. 452.

14 Oct. 1778. ALEXANDER GORDON e. 200 ac. S side Yadkin River at SAMUEL
               BECKNELLS corner..at THOMAS PARKES line..JOHN PARKES
Creek..including the Swan Sholes..MICHAEL BACONS improvement. Entry No.
453.

14 Oct. 1778. ROBERT CHANDLOW e. 100 ac. Fishes Creek above JOHN DARNELS.
               Entry No. 454.

14 Oct. 1778. ROBERT CHANDLOW e. 50 ac. waters Fishes Creek..below
               ISAAC DARNALS. Entry No. 455.

14 Oct. 1778. ROBERT CHANDLOW e. 150 ac. (Wilkes County)..no other
               description. Entry No. 456.

14 Oct. 1778. BAILY CHANDLOW e. 150 ac. N fork Fishes Creek. Entry No.
               457.

16 Oct. 1778. JOHN TIREY e. 440 ac. both forks Reddies River..including
               his improvement. Entry No. 458.

16 Oct. 1778. GEORGE TIREY e. 60 ac. joining JOHN TIREY on middle fork
               of Reddys River. Entry No. 459.

16 Oct. 1778. WILLIAM SCOTT e. 300 ac. Beaver Creek..joining WILLIAM
               COLVARTS (COLVARDS) claim..including SCOTTS improvement.
Entry No. 460.

16 Oct. 1778. ROBERT HUSBANDS e. 71 ac. Ridge near Waggon road..THOMAS
               LANDS line..including HUSBANDS improvement. Entry No.
461.

16 Oct. 1778. WILLIAM MCGILL e. 100 ac. Siside (?) waggon road..adjoin-
               ing BEN ELLEDGE'S line..including MCGILL'S cabbin and
improvement. Entry No. 462.

16 Oct. 1778. NELSON KELLY e. 200 ac. branch Warriors Creek called Fish
               Trap branch..adjoining THOMAS ELLEDGES land..including
his improvement..(NELSON KELLY marked out..HOAKINGS DONAHAN written in).
Entry No. 463.

16 Oct. 1778. JOHN HALL, SENR. e. 320 ac. on branch Mulberry Creek..in-
               cluding his improvement. Entry No. 464.

16 Oct. 1778. ISAAC ELLEDGE e. 320 ac. Warriors Creek adjoining GEORGE
               BOON'S..including his and BEN ELLEDGE'S improvement..
(ISAAC ELLEDGE marked out..WILLIAM JOHNSON written in). Entry No. 465.

16 Oct. 1778. ISAAC PARLIER e. 100 ac. branch Lewis Fork whereon he now
               lives..(ISAAC PARLIER marked out..JOHN BROWN written in).
Entry No. 466.

<u>16 Oct. 1778</u>. THOMAS LAXTON e. 320 ac. branch Reddies River known by
                name Reedy Branch..(THOMAS LAXTON & JOHN BROWN marked out
..MIKEL KILBEY written in). Entry No. 467.

<u>16 Oct. 1778</u>. THOMAS LAXTON e. 50 ac. Fishdam Creek below the falls..
                (THOMAS LAXTON marked out..JOHN BROWN written in). Entry
No. 468.

<u>16 Oct. 1778</u>. JOHN LOW, SR. e. 400 ac. land both sides Moravian Creek..
                including his improvement where he lives..(JOHN LOW, SR.
marked out..WM. TERRILL LEWIS written in). Entry No. 469.

<u>16 Oct. 1778</u>. ISAAC LOWE e. 300 ac. at AQUILLA GREARS line..mouth S fork
                Moravian Creek..including THOMAS LOWES improvement. Entry
No. 470.

<u>16 Oct. 1778</u>. THOMAS ELLEDGE e. 500 ac. on Warriors Creek..including his
                Mill and two small improvements known by the JOSEPH &
THOMAS ELLEDGE, JR. improvements..(THOMAS ELLEDGE marked out..JAMES
CUNNINGHAM & JOHN STAPP written in). Entry No. 471.

<u>19 Oct. 1778</u>. URIAH HARDIMAN e. 50 ac. adjoining ROBERT CHANDLER and
                WM. JOHNSON'S claims. Entry No. 472.

<u>19 Oct. 1778</u>. WILLIAM GILREATH e. 200 ac. Flat Top Mountain on Tumbling
                fork Hunting Creek..including head waters said fork..(WM.
GILREATH marked out..WILLIAM FLETCHER, JR. written in). Entry No. 473.

<u>20 Oct. 1778</u>. JOHN BOURLAND, JR. e. 150 ac. Swan Creek at BOURLANDS S
                corner. Entry No. 474.

<u>20 Oct. 1778</u>. JOHN JOB HANKINGS e. 200 ac. fork New River & Naked Creek
                ..Ridge between Bobs Branch and Allens Branch. Entry No.
475.

<u>20 Oct. 1778</u>. JOSHUA NICHOLS e. 300 ac. both sides Naked Creek..(JOSHUA
                NICHOLS marked out..ANDREW BAKER written in). Entry No.
476.

<u>22 Oct. 1778</u>. WILLIAM RIDGE e. 200 ac.-Great Elkin at GEORGE'S Cabin..
                including BEN SMITHS improvement..(WM. RIDGE & BENJ. SMITH
marked out..JOHN BURROW written in). Entry No. 477.

<u>22 Oct. 1778</u>. RANDOLPH MITCHEL e. 640 ac. both sides Swan Pond Creek to
                include improvement of MATTHIAS CARPETER (CARPENTER).
Entry No. 478.

<u>22 Oct. 1778</u>. JOSEPH GOOUGE e. 100 ac. little Sandy Creek in WILLIAM
                HARGUS'S line. Entry No. 479.

<u>24 Oct. 1778</u>. GEORGE PARKES e. 150 ac. on Bugaboe about a mile above
                JONATHAN STAMPERS..(GEORGE PARKES marked out..WM. TOLBEY
written in). Entry No. 480.

<u>27 Oct. 1778</u>. HENERUOS STONECYPHER e. 100 ac. waters Lewis Fork near
                Calloways Mountain or ABSALOM WIGGONS claim..(HENERUOS
STONECYPHER marked out..NICKLIS ANGEL written in). Entry No. 481.

<u>27 Oct. 1778</u>. ABSALOM (Or ABRAHAM) WIGGINS e. 100 ac. waters Lewis Fork
                ..joining HENERICO STONEYCPHERS entry. Entry No. 482.

<u>28 Oct. 1778</u>. CHESLE COCKROM e. 400 ac. both sides Yadkin River..in-
                cluding the improvement whereon the said COCKROM & GEORGE
BREWER now lives. Entry No. 483.

28 Oct. 1778. MARTIN GAMBILL e. 300 ac. Roaring River..upper end of his
bottom land. Entry No. 484.

30 Oct. 1778. FRANCIS CALLOWAY e. 300 ac. Brushey fork near Roaring
Eiver..near spring where MORGANS path turns out of New
River Road..including both sides of fork and the clearing..(FRANCIS
CALLOWAY marked out..JOHN POE written in). Entry No. 485.

30 Oct. 1778. FRANCIS CALLOWAY e. 300 ac. where New River crosses Muddy
Branch near SPICERS Path that turns out of said road..
(FRANCIS CALLOWAY & JOHN BREWER marked out..GEORGE BREWER written in).
Entry No. 486.

30 Oct. 1778. RICHARD ALLEN e. 250 ac. N fork New River..including land
known as the Ears (?) Camp. Entry No. 487.

30 Oct. 1778. ARTHUR SCRITCHFIELD e. 300 ac. The Great Elkin at WM.
HALL'S line..including his improvement. Entry No. 488.

30 Oct. 1778. ROBERT HANKINGS e. 200 ac. little fork Mitchels River..
on RICHARD HANKINS line..including his improvement..
(ROBERT HANKINS marked out..WM. WATTS written in). Entry No. 489.

30 Oct. 1778. GEORGE LEWIS e. 350 ac. Gaddis (?) Creek..an arm of Rich
Mountain opposite the Laurel Fork of said creek. Entry
No. 490.

3 Nov. 1778. JONATHAN WALL e. 600 ac. W side ridge..S side Meadow Branch.
Entry No. 491.

3 Nov. 1778. NATHANIEL VANNOY e. 200 ac. both sides Beaver Creek..adjoin-
ing WM. COLVARTS (COLVARD) claim..including his improvement. Entry No. 492.

4 Nov. 1778. BENJAMIN ANGEL e. 140 ac. N fork New River at mouth Rockey
Branch. Entry No. 493.

5 Nov. 1778. THOMAS GOINS e. 100 ac. Big Elkin..condt. line between
GOINS & ELIJAH HEDDEN..including the improvement. Entry
No. 494.

7 Nov. 1778. THOMAS PARKES e. 20 ac. on an island in the Yadkin River
opposite his entry..known by name Parkes Island. Entry No.
495.

7 Nov. 1778. SAMUEL CARTER e. 300 ac. waters Little Elkin..branch in
SIMEON CARTERS line. Entry No. 496.

10 Nov. 1778. JOSEPH VAWN (VAUGHN?) e. 100 ac. on branch that runs into
E fork Roaring River..(JOSEPH VAWN marked out..THOMAS
GOINES written in). Entry No. 497.

10 Nov. 1778. JOSEPH VAWN e. 100 ac. Little Sandy Creek. Entry No. 498.

11 Nov. 1778. RANDOLPH HOLDBROOK e. 250 ac. E side the creek..including
his improvement on waters of E fork Roaring River. Entry
No. 499.

11 Nov. 1778. EDWARD HARRIS e. 50 ac. head Bear Branch of Hunting Creek
..known by name Rich Cove. Entry No. 500.

12 Nov. 1778. BENJAMIN CLEVELAND e. 400 ac. N fork Lewis Fork..being
lower part MATTHEW FRANCIS line. Entry No. 501.

12 Nov. 1778.   REUBEN FLETCHER e. 200 ac. N fork Hunting Creek..mouth
                WILCOXES branch..including the improvement. Entry No.
502.

12 Nov. 1778.   JENKINS REYNOLDS e. 200 ac. N fork Hunting Creek near
                mouth Wilcocks Branch..including his improvement. Entry
No. 503.

13 Nov. 1778.   RICHARD WOOLBANKS e. 80 ac. Wheatleys Creek..including his
                improvement. Entry No. 504.

15 Nov. 1778.   THOMAS GORDON e. 100 ac. fork Wrights Creek. Entry No.
                505.

17 Nov. 1778.   PATRICK HAMRICK e. 200 ac. waters Cub & Moravian Creeks..
                both sides main road at JOHN GREERS line..W to WM. LOWS
line..(PATRICK HAMRICK marked out..BENJ. JOHNSON written in). Entry No.
506.

17 Nov. 1778.   SAMUEL HALL e. 100 ac. Elk Creek at JULIAS DUGGARS line..
                including HALLS improvement. Entry No. 507.

17 Nov. 1778.   JOSHUA STEPHENS e. 100 ac. waters Yadkin River and Carlays
                Creek..including the improvement..(JOSHUA STEPHENS marked
out..JOILES MARTIN written in..(also)..Caveated by SPENCER HUMPHRIES
written in). Entry No. 508.

17 Nov. 1778.   DAVID BURNS e. 150 ac. Moravian Creek..at cleft of rocks..
                including PETER BOWMAN'S improvement..(DAVID BURNS marked
out..WM. LANDSDOWN written in). Entry No. 509.

17 Nov. 1778.   BENJAMIN BEYMAN e. 50 ac. on Josephs fork of Buffaloe..
                including the cabbin..(BENJ. BEYMAN marked out..WM.
LANDSDOWN written in). Entry No. 510.

20 Nov. 1778.   DANIEL RASH e. 50 ac. S fork Hunting Creek..being line of
                Wilkes & Surry Counties..including his improvement. Entry
No. 511.

20 Nov. 1778.   SAMUEL NICHOLSON e. 320 ac. S fork Hunting Creek..S fork
                Little Hunting Creek..between WM. MITCHELS & NICHOLSON..
agreed line between NICHOLSON & WM. MORGAN. Entry No. 512.

21 Nov. 1778.   CORNELIUS SAILS (SALES) e. 400 ac. N fork Hunting Creek..
                on top of mtn...between SAILS & PETER GOODE..condt. line
of SAILS & DAVIS..condt. line between SAILS & MICAJAH WRIGHT..including
his improvement. Entry No. 513.

23 Nov. 1778.   THOMAS ROBBINS e. 200 ac. dividing ridge between Roaring
                River and Mulberry waters..including small improvement
made by JESSE TOLOVER. Entry No. 514.

23 Nov. 1778.   HAUNCH LYKINS e. 640 ac. head Grays Creek..high ridge
                above the big Glade..both sides big road to BENJ. HERNDONS
claim..including his improvement. Entry No. 515.

26 Nov. 1778.   WILLIAM GILREATH, JR. e. 100 ac. on JAMES SHEPHERDS spring
                branch..SHEPHERDS line..(WM. GILREATH, JR. marked out..
BENJ. JONES written in). Entry No. 516.

2 Dec. 1778.   GEORGE REAVES e. 600 ac. New River..mouth first branch
                above his plantation..including his improvement. Entry No.
517.

2 Dec. 1778.   JOHN COX e. 400 ac. on Crab fork Little River..including
                his improvement..(JOHN COX marked out..WM. HARDEN written
in). Entry No. 518.

3 Dec. 1778.   ANDREW CANADY e. 100 ac. both sides little branch Bugaboe..
a little below the road. Entry No. 519.

3 Dec. 1778.   NATHANIEL CRITCHFIELD e. 200 ac. little fork Mitchels
River..agreed line between CRITCHFIELD & JACOB MAINYARD..
agreed line of FILDER..joining line between NATH'S CRITCHFIELD & SAMUEL
CRITCHFIELD..including both sides of creek..(NATH'L. CRITCHFIELD marked
out..JAMES FILDER written in..(also)..transferred to JAMES JENNINGS by
J. L. FILDER written in). Entry No. 520.

5 Dec. 1778.   GEORGE PAYN e. 100 ac. N fork New River..adjoining ZACHA-
RIAH WELLS claim..(GEORGE PAYN marked out..JAMES BOGGS
written in). Entry No. 521.

5 Dec. 1778.   HUGH MONTGOMERY e. 200 ac. head Big Elkin known by name
Rich Cove..being the improvement formerly the property of
OLIVER WALACE. Entry No. 522.

7 Dec. 1778.   ROBERT WILLIS e. 250 ac. Wootings Creek..including his
improvement..(ROBERT WILLIS marked out..TRAVIS REES
written in). Entry No. 523.

7 Dec. 1778.   ARCHELAUS WALKER e. 200 ac. branch Warrior Creek..including
improvement made by MOSES WATERS adjoining RICHARD BLOOD.
Entry No. 524.

7 Dec. 1778.   BENJAMIN TRIBBLE e. 100 ac. on Warrior Creek adjoining
land of JAMES DYER..(BENJ. TRIBBLE marked out..HAMON (?)
DYER marked out..WM. COCHRAM written in). Entry No. 525.

7 Dec. 1778.   SAMUEL TUCKER e. 50 ac. Dunnahoos Creek..waters of Yadkin..
including his improvement. Entry No. 526.

7 Dec. 1778.   HENRY ISBELL e. 100 ac. branch Kings Creek..adjoining
EPHRAIM COX and JAMES WILSON..including a mill shoals..
(HENRY ISBELL marked out..JOHN WALLIS (WALLACE) written in). Entry No.
527.

7 Dec. 1778.   JAMES DYER e. 200 ac. on Warriors Creek adjoining land
SPILSBY TRIBBLE. Entry No. 528.

7 Dec. 1778.   ENEROUS GRAY e. 50 ac. waters Stony Fork on Glady Creek..
including an improvement made by CAPT. GEORGE FOSTER..
(ENEROUS GRAY marked out..DANIEL SUTHERLING written in). Entry No. 529.

7 Dec. 1778.   BENJAMIN GRAYSON e. 400 ac. Kings Creek adjoining land
EDMOND TILLER (TILLEY)..including his improvement. Entry
No. 530.

7 Dec. 1778.   WILLIAM BUNTING e. 100 ac. N side Yadkin..including his
improvement..(WM. BUNTING marked out..ABRAHAM BUSHEP
(BISHOP) written in). Entry No. 531.

8 Dec. 1778.   THOMAS CALTON e. 375 ac. fork Beaver Creek..spurs of Brus-
hie Mountain..including the improvement whereon he lives.
Entry No. 532.

8 Dec. 1778.   CALEB LOW e. 150 ac. falling fork Moravian Creek joining
GEO. WHEATLEY, JUNR...including his improvement..(CALEB
LOW marked out..THOMAS (TOMME) HAMPTON written in). Entry No. 533.

8 Dec. 1778.   WILLIAM MITCHELL e. 300 ac. W fork Lewis Fork at THOMAS
LAXTONS line..on both sides as far as Reddie Camp..up
Dawsons Branch. Entry No. 534.

8 Dec. 1778. EDWARD PARKER e. 100 ac. on Gum Branch..waters Beaver
Creek..adjoining line of JOHN WILLIAM CROSTHWAIT..(EDWARD
PARKER marked out..JAMES ISBELL written in). Entry No. 535.

8 Dec. 1778. JOHN BRADLEY e. 150 ac. at JOHN DURHAMS line..branch Kings
Creek..(JOHN BRADLEY marked out..THOMAS ALLEMS (ALLEN)
written in). Entry No. 536.

8 Dec. 1778. LAWRENCE BRADLEY e. 100 ac. on branch Kings Creek at JOHN
WISDOM'S line..(LAWRENCE BRADLEY marked out..JOHN WISDOM
written in). Entry No. 537.

8 Dec. 1778. ZACHARIAH GARSON e. 150 ac. branch Kings Creek in THOMAS
DUNCAN'S line..(ZACHARIAH GARSON & ANNIAS ALLEN marked
out..LEWIS CALTON (CARLTON) written in). Entry No. 538.

8 Dec. 1778. JAMES FORBUS e. 300 ac. N side Yadkin River adjoining
FRD. HOGS improvement..(JAMES FORBUS marked out..JESSE
COUNSIL written in). Entry No. 539.

8 Dec. 1778. JAMES STAPP e. 150 ac. on BENJ. DUNCAN'S line on branch of
Kings Creek..(JAMES STAPP marked out..GERSHAM ALLEN written
in). Entry No. 540.

8 Dec. 1778. ABNER SMALLY e. 200 ac. Howards Creek..ABNER SMALLY, BENJ.
HERNDON & JAMES BROWN marked out..EBENEZER FAIRCHILD
written in). Entry No. 541.

8 Dec. 1778. ABNER SMALLY e. 200 ac. S end Plat Mtn...(ABNER SMALLY &
WM. WHITE marked out..BENJAMIN HERNDON written in). Entry
No. 542.

8 Dec. 1778. GEORGE BARKER e. 150 ac. long branch of Mulberry Creek..
(GEO. BARKER marked out..JOSEPH HERNDON written in). Entry
No. 543.

8 Dec. 1778. THOMAS LAXTON e. 100 ac. Lewis Fork..up line made by JOHN
LAXTON & WM. MITCHELL..(THOMAS LAXTON marked out..JOHN
ADAMS written in). Entry No. 544.

8 Dec. 1778. BENJAMIN DUNCAN e. 50 ac. branch Kings Creek at JOHN BRAD-
LEYS line..(BENJ. DUNCAN marked out..GERSHAM ALLEN written
in). Entry No. 545.

8 Dec. 1778. JOHN DURHAM e. 200 ac. at JAMES STEPPS upper line. Entry
No. 546.

8 Dec. 1778. JAMES STAPP e. 100 ac. on Kings Creek at WM. BAJIOX'S
(BOLEJACK?) line..(JAMES STAPP marked out..THOMAS STAPP
written in). Entry No. 547.

9 Dec. 1778. JOHN LIPS e. 100 ac. mouth small branch SW side S fork
Lewis Fork near JAMES TOMKINS upper line..including his
improvement. Entry No. 548.

9 Dec. 1778. CHARLES CRANSHAW e. 100 ac. adjoining JOSEPH TANNERS entry
and Whites Bottom..both sides Garner branch..(CHARLES
CRANSHAW marked out..JOSEPH HERNDON written in). Entry No. 549.

9 Dec. 1778. JONATHAN TOMPKINS e. 100 ac. on Lewis Fork bounded on WM.
ROBART'S claim..(JONATHAN TOMPKINS marked out..MOSES TOM-
KINS written in). Entry No. 550.

9 Dec. 1778. JONATHAN TOMPKINS e. 50 ac. Lewis Fork..upper end his
other survey..(JONATHAN TOMPKINS marked out..MOSES TOMKINS
written in). Entry No. 551.

9 Dec. 1778. PETER FORD e. 200 ac. near Camp Spring on top of Ridge on
New River..adjoining the Yadkin waters. Entry No. 552.

9 Dec. 1778. ABNER SMALLY e. 300 ac. head Howards Creek near a gap..
near SNODDYS entry..(ABNER SMALLY marked out..BENJ. HERN-
DON written in). Entry No. 553.

9 Dec. 1778. WILLIAM MCGILL e. 100 ac. N side trading Road at BENJAMIN
ELLEDGES line. Entry No. 554.

9 Dec. 1778. WILLIAM MCGILL e. 200 ac. at LAZARUS SUMMERLIN'S line on
Moravian Creek..(WM. MCGILL marked out..JOSHUA MORGAN
written in). Entry No. 555.

9 Dec. 1778. THOMAS ELMORE e. 200 ac. S fork Lewis Fork at GEORGE
ELMORES line. Entry No. 556.

9 Dec. 1778. GEORGE ELMORE e. 100 ac. S fork Lewis Fork ½ mile from
DANIEL GULLIP'S (GULLET) plantation at mouth of a branch..
(GEORGE ELMORE & DOSSEN SEWILL marked out..WM. PROFFITT written in).
Entry No. 557.

9 Dec. 1778. THOMAS JONES e. 300 ac. on Fishes Creek above the falls..
including his improvement. Entry No. 558.

9 Dec. 1778. EDWARD CROSS e. 400 ac. on branch Bryer Creek opposite a
place agreed to by BENJ. CLEVELAND & JOHN ROSE, SENR...
including improvement whereon JOHN ROSE lives. Entry No. 559.

9 Dec. 1778. PERRIN CARDWELL e. 400 ac. near narrows of Naked Creek.
Entry No. 560.

9 Dec. 1778. ELISHA DYER e. 100 ac. waters Yadkin on Nicholas Creek..
including an improvement that was LOHN LAWS, JUNRS. Entry
No. 561.

9 Dec. 1778. THOMAS WITHERSPOON e. 200 ac. Kings Creek..including improvement where he now lives. Entry No. 562.

9 Dec. 1778. DAVID WITHERSPOON e. 50 ac. Branch Kings Creek..including
improvement made by MATTHEW LINDSEY..(DAVID WITHERSPOON
marked out..JAMES PAGGETT written in). Entry No. 563.

9 Dec. 1778. JAMES WITHERSPOON e. 150 ac. on Kings Creek..including
improvement and Mill of JOHN WITHERSPOON, deceased. Entry
No. 564.

9 Dec. 1778. ROBERT WATERS e. 200 ac. on Beaver Creek..New River..near
mouth of branch below VANINS improvement..(ROBERT WATERS
& WM. HUMPHRIES marked out..CHRISTIAN BURKHEAD written in). Entry No.
565.

9 Dec. 1778. ZACHARIAH WALKER e. 250 ac. adjoining AQUILLA LOWS & JOHN
TRIBBLE..including his improvement..(ZACHARIAH WALKER
marked out..ROBERT HAMRICK written in). Entry No. 566.

9 Dec. 1778. THOMAS LAXTON e. 100 ac. on ridge between waters Elk &
New River..(THOS. LAXTON marked out..JOHN BROWN written in).
Entry No. 567.

9 Dec. 1778. THOMAS LAXTON e. 150 ac. on branch of Lewis Fork joining
S side an entry made by ISAAC PERLIER..on place whereon
EDWARD BELL lived..down Bell's branch..(THOS. LAXTON marked out..JOHN
BROWN written in). Entry No. 568.

10 Dec. 1778. DAVID MCGEE e. 190 ac. on Beaver Creek in THOMAS HANDER-
SONS line..both sides creek..including his improvement.
Entry No. 569.

10 Dec. 1778.   JOEL DIER e. 100 ac. S side Yadkin River..branch known by
                name Reedies Branch..joining improvement that SIMION
HINDS had of NEHEMIAH FARGUSON. Entry No. 570.

10 Dec. 1778.   ROBERT SAUNDERS e. 300 ac. S side Yadkin River at mouth
                Warrior Creek..including his improvement..(ROBERT SAUNDERS
marked out..ABSOLOM CLEVELAND written in). Entry No. 571.

11 Dec. 1778.   SPENCER HUMPHREY e. 150 ac. at JOSEPH HOLDMAN'S upper
                corner. Entry No. 572.

11 Dec. 1778.   CHARLES GORDON e. 200 ac. waters Reddies River known by
                name Hoppers Branch..on both sides. Entry No. 573.

11 Dec. 1778.   HUGH MONTGOMERY e. 640 ac. S side Yadkin River near mouth
                of Moravian Creek..(Warrant 8 Feb. 1797..in margin).
Entry No. 574.

11 Dec. 1778.   WILLIAM COLVARD e. 400 ac. near mouth Sugar Tree Branch
                that empties into Beaver Creek..some distance above the
Plantation whereon he now lives..N to WM. SCOTTS line. Entry No. 575.

11 Dec. 1778.   ELISHA ISAACS e. 150 ac. on Yadkin River..a consentable
                line made by WM. SNODDY & ISAACS. Entry No. 576.

11 Dec. 1778.   ANDREW KILLPATRICK e. 100 ac. S fork New River one &
                one-half miles below HUGH SMITHS..including a small
cabbin formerly inhabited by WM. MAINERD & lately claimed by ARCHIBALD
MASION. Entry No. 577.

11 Dec. 1778.   JAMES FLETCHER e. 150 ac. MR. WITHERSPOONS line..including
                a part of a Crooked Branch. Entry No. 578.

11 Dec. 1778.   DEVERAUX BALLARD e. 150 ac. on Mare Branch joining EDWARD
                FINCHES entry..(DEVERAUX BALLARD marked out..WM. PETTY
written in). Entry No. 579.

12 Dec. 1778.   WILLIAM ELLISON e. 400 ac. S side Yadkin River..above
                mouth Beaver Creek..on both sides..(WM. ELLISON marked
out..ELIJAH ISAACS written in). Entry No. 580.

12 Dec. 1778.   WILLIAM ELLISTON e. 100 ac. joining his other entry..both
                sides Beaver Creek. Entry No. 581.

12 Dec. 1778.   BENJ. HOWARD e. 5 ac. for a small seat lying on Reedy
                Branch at falls..including the falls. Entry No. 582.

14 Dec. 1778.   WILLIAM FLETCHER e. 100 ac. Little Rocky Creek known by
                name Cranes Creek at mouth Grassy Branch..on both sides..
(WM. FLETCHER marked out..JOHN ANDERSON written in). Entry No. 583.

15 Dec. 1778.   JAMES REYNOLDS e. 100 ac. S fork Rock Creek..including
                both sides..(Entry withdrawn by the Entree (Enteree)).
Entry No. 584.

16 Dec. 1778.   JAMES RAIMY e. 100 ac. W fork Roaring River in RANDOLPH
                FUGITS line. Entry No. 585.

16 Dec. 1778.   THOMAS TURNER e. 140 ac. both sides N fork Roaring River..
                including the improvement. Entry No. 586.

17 Dec. 1778. JOHN ROBINSON e. 50 ac. on Christians Creek of Mitchel
              River..on both sides including his improvement..(JOHN
ROBINSON marked out..a name not readable written in & marked out..WM.
AUSTIN written in). Entry No. 587.

18 Dec. 1778. WILLIAM WILCOCKS e. 50 ac. S side branch between JAMES
              HARVELS & WILCOCK'S house. Entry No. 588.

18 Dec. 1778. EDWARD FINCH e. 100 ac. both sides Path between WM. LENOIR
              and his Mill..including some waters of FINCHS Mill Creek..
(EDWARD FINCH marked out..JOHN HAGINS written in). Entry No. 589.

20 Dec. 1778. WM. LENOIR e. 150 ac. on waters Fishes Creek & Hunting
              Creek..both sides Path leading from STEPHEN SOUTHER to
Wilkes Court House..(WM. LENOIR marked out..THOMAS NEWBERRY written in).
Entry No. 590.

21 Dec. 1778. PETER GOODE e. 320 ac. waters Hunting Creek above Waggon
              Road joining WM. DAVISES line..to Top of the Mtn...includ-
ing his improvement. Entry No. 591.

21 Dec. 1778. MICAJAH WRIGHT e. 200 ac. N waters Hunting Creek at the
              waggon road..E between WM. DAVISES turnip patch..and his
improvement..including his improvement. Entry No. 592.

21 Dec. 1778. RICHARD ALLEN e. 200 ac. Potatoe Creek..waters New River
              ..below the fork..including the improvement made by
CHARLES BOSTICK. Entry No. 593.

21 Dec. 1778. RICHARD ALLEN e. 80 ac. on Little Bugaboe below his Ax
              entry. Entry No. 594.

21 Dec. 1778. GEORGE FOSTER e. 50 ac. S side Elk Creek..(GEO. FOSTER
              marked out..FRANCIS SUTTLE written in). Entry No. 595.

21 Dec. 1778. JAMES TUGMAN e. 50 ac. S side Glady Branch..(JAMES TUGMAN
              marked out..ALEXANDER WEST written in). Entry No. 596.

21 Dec. 1778. RANDOLPH WALKER e. 50 ac. S side Yadkin River..including
              his improvement..(RANDOLPH WALKER marked out..SOLOMON
CROSS written in). Entry No. 597.

22 Dec. 1778. JOHN ROSE e. -----(Entry withdrawn)..(no other writting).
              Entry No. 598.

22 Dec. 1778. JOHN BROWN e. 20 ac. Reedy Branch of Stony Fork..below
              the improvement where JOHN BANKS lives..including said
improvement..(JOHN BROWN marked out..JOSHUA HAWKINS written in). Entry
No. 599.

22 Dec. 1778. JAMES JACKSON e. 100 ac. Meat Camp Creek near ledge of
              rocks..near the shuting in of the Hills. Entry No. 600.

22 Dec. 1778. JAMES JACKSON e. 100 ac. Meat Camp Creek near JOHN BROWNS
              line..down both sides of Creek. Entry No. 601.

22 Dec. 1778. AMBROUS CRANE e. 100 ac. S fork Hunting Creek..joining
              JOHN CRANES at lower end up creek on both sides to WM.
CRANES line..including his improvement. Entry No. 602.

22 Dec. 1778. JAMES JONES e. 200 ac. W fork Fishes Creek at THOMAS
              JONES line..on both sides Creek..including his improve-
ment. Entry No. 603.

23 Dec. 1778. WILLIAM HARVEY e. 50 ac. N side Yadkin River at mouth
              small branch at upper end RLANERYS Bottom..including the
improvement where he now lives..(WM. HARVEY marked out..JOSEPH YOUNGER
written in). Entry No. 604.

36

23 Dec. 1778. WILLIAM CARROL e. 100 ac. both sides Elk Branch at WM.
CARROL'S own line. Entry No. 605.

23 Dec. 1778. JACOB WALL e. 100 ac. on Adams Creek of Reedy River..
upper end of the bottom..(JACOB WALL & WALTER BROWN
marked out..JAMES HAIS (HAYES) written in). Entry No. 606.

23 Dec. 1778. ROBERT HANKINS e. 150 ac. little fork Mitchels River at a
condt. line between HANKINS & SAMUEL CRITCHFIELD..includ-
ing RICHARD HANKINS plantation..(ROBERT HANKINS & RICHARD HANKINS marked
out..EZEKIAL WILMONTH written in). Entry No. 607.

23 Dec. 1778. MICHAEL ISRAEL e. 300 ac. formerly belonging to BEASOM on
N fork Warrior Creek..above ROWLAND HONSLEYS entry. Entry
No. 608.

24 Dec. 1778. WILLIAM HULEN e. 500 ac. Hunting Creek at Muddy Branch..
being dividing line between him & WM. MORGAN..including
his improvement. Entry No. 609.

25 Dec. 1778. THOMAS STUBBLEFIELD e. 120 ac. on Stubblefield Creek..in
THOMAS PARKS line. Entry No. 610.

25 Dec. 1778. NATHAN BARNETT e. 50 ac. middle fork Hunting Creek..on
both sides..including his improvement..(NATHAN BARNETT
marked out..HENRY REED written in). Entry No. 611.

26 Dec. 1778. WILLIAM OWENS, SENR. e. 250 ac. both sides N fork Reddies
River..E LUKE FIELDS plantation..including said OWENS
improvement. Entry No. 612.

26 Dec. 1778. GEORGE REAVES e. 200 ac. on Rockey Creek..lower end of
Turkey Mountain..including his improvement. Entry No.
613.

26 Dec. 1778. BARNARD (BARNET) OWENS e. 200 ac. both sides Reddies
River..in ROBERT SHEPHERDS line..including improvement
whereon said OWENS now lives. Entry No. 614.

26 Dec. 1778. LUKE FIELDS e. 150 ac. on S side..N fork Reddies River..
including said FIELDS improvement..(LUKE FIELDS erased
completely..FRANCIS VANNOY written in). Entry No. 615.

26 Dec. 1778. MORRIS BAKER e. 100 ac. both sides S fork New River..at
an Island in said River..including improvement whereon
said BAKER now lives. Entry No. 616.

26 Dec. 1778. WILLIAM OWENS, SENR. e. 300 ac. both sides Riddes River..
above his Mill..including said OWENS improvement. Entry
No. 617.

NOTE: Here in the book on a small piece of paper bound within the pages
is the following: "To: JAS. FLETCHER, sir, please to transfair
that 75 acres lying above STEPHEN SOUTHERS on Hunting Creek to JOHN
STANDLEY JUNR. and oblige, Yours, SAM FENDALL".

26 Dec. 1778. WILLIAM LENOIR e. 250 ac. N side Yadkin River near MORAY
(MEREDITH?) MINTONS field..including plantation whereon
JEPHS MOSS now lives. Entry No. 618.

26 Dec. 1778. WM. LENOIR e. 200 ac. N side Yadkin between JAMES SHEP-
HERDS and the Bent..including Plantation whereon JOHN
SUTTON now lives..near JAMES SHEPHERDS line. Entry No. 619.

26 Dec. 1778. WILLIAM LENOIR e. 100 ac. both sides Fishes Creek at an
old Cane Brake on said creek..including small field.
Entry No. 620.

26 Dec. 1778. WILLIAM LENOIR e. 250 ac. both sides Fishes Creek at
LENOIRS other line..including improvement whereon LENOIR
now lives. Entry No. 621.

26 Dec. 1778. WILLIAM LENOIR e. 150 ac. both sides N fork Reddies River
..forks River above THOMAS OWENS and up both forks..in-
cluding Bottom called the Battle Ground. Entry No. 622.

26 Dec. 1778. WILLIAM LENOIR e. 80 ac. both sides Reddies River above
his other entry..(Entry withdrawn by enterer). Entry No.
623.

28 Dec. 1778. JOHN WHITAKER e. 100 ac. at Moravian line above JAMES
WILSONS..up the big branch. Entry No. 624.

28 Dec. 1778. JOHN WHITAKER e. 100 ac. at a steep hollow on big branch
Cub Creek. Entry No. 625.

28 Dec. 1778. WILLIAM FLETCHER e. 100 ac. on Southern Mountain..includ-
ing head spring branch..(WM. FLETCHER marked out..JACOB
STANDLEY written in). Entry No. 626.

28 Dec. 1778. MICHAEL CHILDRES e. 100 ac. N side Stoney Fork. Entry
No. 627.

28 Dec. 1778. BENJAMIN GREAR e. 350 ac. waters Little Cub Creek..joining
VOLENTINE NUTTERVILLS..to said GREERS former entry..in-
cluding the improvement..(BENJ. GREAR marked out..JOHN GRIER written in).
Entry No. 629.

28 Dec. 1778. ISAAC WALKER e. 300 ac. Stoney fork above improvement
where MOSES WATERS now lives..upper end ROBERT LENOIR (?)
entry..including the Mill Seat. Entry No. 630.

28 Dec. 1778. ISAAC WALKER e. 300 ac. little Cub Creek at JAMES FREE-
MANS claim. Entry No. 631.

28 Dec. 1778. THOMAS LOWE e. 100 ac. Little Cub Creek at VOLENTINE
NUTTERVILLS line..(THOMAS LOWE marked out..JOSEPH SOUTH
written in). Entry No. 632.

29 Dec. 1778. THOMAS HOLEMAN e. 320 ac. N side Yadkin River..both sides
Lewis Fork..including improvement. Entry No. 633.

29 Dec. 1778. Name completely erased e. 100 ac. S fork New River..mouth
Do (?) Creek known by name Bryer Bottom..below his Mill..
(GEORGE MORRIS written in). Entry No. 634.

29 Dec. 1778. MORDACAI FULLER e. 200 ac. on fork Creek he lives on..
(MORDACAI FULLER marked out..JERVIS SMITH written in).
Entry No. 635.

29 Dec. 1778. BENJAMIN SCOTT e. 200 ac. both sides Mitchels River on
the County line..including BENJAMIN & JOHN SCOTTS improvements. Entry No. 636.

29 Dec. 1778. JAMES SHOREFIELD e. 200 ac. waters Reddies River..head
MILLS Cabbin branch..(JAMES SHOREFIELD marked out..GERVIS
SMITH written in). Entry No. 637.

29 Dec. 1778. JOHN GREAR, JUNR. e. 200 ac. little Cub Creek at the
Moravian line..(JOHN GREAR, JR. marked out..GEORGE REAVES
written in). Entry No. 638.

29 Dec. 1778.   JACOB ELLEDGE e. 350 ac. joining THOMAS ELLEDGE, GEORGE
                BOONS, THOMAS ELLET & FRANCIS ELLEDGES on waters Warrior
Creek..including his improvement..(JACOB ELLEDGE marked out..AARON PARKES
written in).   Entry No. 639.

29 Dec. 1778.   BENJAMIN BROWN e. 640 ac. adjoining THOMAS ELLOTT & FRAN-
                CIS ELLEDGE on waters Warrior Creek..including his im-
provement.   Entry No. 640.

29 Dec. 1778.   JOHN COOK e. 50 ac. head N fork Beaver Creek.   Entry No.
                641.

29 Dec. 1778.   MOSES DICKERSON e. 100 ac. on waters Warrior Creek on
                Sweet Lauril Hill..including his improvement.   Entry No.
642.

29 Dec. 1778.   THOMAS ELLEDGE e. 100 ac. waters Warrior Creek..on branch
                called Wolf Pen Branch..near the wagon road at GEORGE
BOONS corner..including said ELLEDGES school house and dwelling house.
Entry No. 643.

29 Dec. 1778.   THOMAS e. 150 ac. waters Warrior Creek at THOMAS ELLIOT
                corner..including small field known by name EDWARD BOONS
field..(THOMAS ELLEDGE marked out..HUGH MONTGOMERY written in).   Entry
No. 644.

29 Dec. 1778.   THOMAS LEWIS e. 150 ac. middle fork Beaver Creek..joining
                JOHN WILLIAM CROSTHWAIT & JOHN COOK..including said
LEWIS improvement..(THOMAS LEWIS & ROBERT NATHAREY marked out..JOHN
LIVINGSTON written in).   Entry No. 645.

29 Dec. 1778.   ABRAHAM VANDERPOOL e. 50 ac. Elk Creek..(ABRAHAM VANDER-
                POOL, ISAAC PARLIER & JOHN SELLERS marked out..DANIEL
EGGERS written in).   Entry No. 646.

29 Dec. 1778.   ABRAHAM VANDERPOOL e. 50 ac. Elk Creek..(ABRAHAM VANDER-
                POOL & WM. FERGUSON marked out..WILLIAM MILLER written
in).   Entry No. 647.

29 Dec. 1778.   ABRAHAM VANDERPOOL e. 100 ac...including his improvement..
                (ABRAHAM VANDERPOOL marked out..RICHARD BROWN written in).
Entry No. 648.

30 Dec. 1778.   NATHANIEL HART e. 400 ac. both sides N fork Yadkin River..
                one and one-half miles below mouth Elk Creek..upper end
JAMES BROWNS claim..so as to include the improvement DANIEL BOON sold
to JOSEPH WARREN and by WARREN to said HART..(Caveated by JOHN BROWN
2 Mar. 1779).   Entry No. 649.

30 Dec. 1778.   JOHN ROBBINS, SR. e. 300 ac. N side Mulberry Creek at
                JESSE TOLEVORS line.   Entry No. 650.

30 Dec. 1778.   PETER PEARSON e. 200 ac. little fork Mitchels River..
                joining claim BENJ. HERNDON bought of WM. WATTS..includ-
ing PEARSONS improvement.   Entry No. 651.

30 Dec. 1778.   JOHN MILLER e. 100 ac. Bakers Branch..Yadkin River..in-
                cluding his improvement.   Entry No. 652.

30 Dec. 1778.   WILLIAM OWENS, JUNR. e. 50 ac. N fork Reddies River..in-
                cluding a bottom above WM. LENOIRS entry.   Entry No. 653.

30 Dec. 1778.   JOHN OWEN e. 100 ac. N fork Reddies River..mouth of a
                branch.   Entry No. 654.

30 Dec. 1778.   JOHN OWEN e. 100 ac. Falling Rock Branch of New River..
                fork Reddies River.   Entry No. 655.

30 Dec. 1778.   THOMAS OWEN e. 150 ac. N fork Reddies River at the Mill
                Pond..including his improvement. Entry No. 656.

30 Dec. 1778.   THOMAS OWEN e. 75 ac. N fork Reddies River..joining his
                other entry. Entry No. 657.

30 Dec. 1778.   GEORGE BAKER e. 100 ac. waters New River in GEORGE MORRIS
                line..WM. RAYS line..including said BAKERS cabbin..
(GEORGE BAKER, ALEXANDER GORDON & JOHN MASH marked out..JONATHAN COURT-
NEY written in). Entry No. 658.

30 Dec. 1778.   JAMES HARVILLE e. 100 ac. waters Hunting Creek..little
                gap in Brushey Mountain in MICHELS line..including his
improvement..(JAMES HARVILL & THOMAS BURROWS marked out..JAMES DENNEY (?)
written in). Entry No. 659.

30 Dec. 1778.   JOHN GAMBILL e. 100 ac. middle fork Roaring River..above
                his improvement and including it. Entry No. 660.

30 Dec. 1778.   WILLIAM ADAMS, SENR. e. 100 ac. on Lewis Fork..including
                the improvement. Entry No. 661.

30 Dec. 1778.   WILLIAM ADAMS, SENR. e. 100 ac. on Lewis Fork..joining
                WM. MITCHELS entry..including ADAMS improvement. Entry
No. 662.

30 Dec. 1778.   JONAS MARSHAL e. 100 ac. Mitchels River joining EDMOND
                WOOD. Entry No. 663.

30 Dec. 1778.   WILLIAM HIGGINS e. 100 ac. S side Yadkin River at foard
                of said river..including his improvement. Entry No. 664.

30 Dec. 1778.   WILLIAM HIGGINS e. 25 ac. S fork Yadkin River at Gibsons
                branch. Entry No. 665.

30 Dec. 1778.   WILLIAM TRIPLETT e. 150 ac. lower end of bottom on N side
                Yadkin River..including improvement ALEXANDER WEST lives
on. Entry No. 666.

30 Dec. 1778.   JOHN DARNALL e. 500 ac. near small branch below ISAAC
                DARNALLS..E side Fishes Creek..condt. line between ISAAC
DARNALL & JOHN DARNALL..condt. line between EDWARD FINCH & JOHN DARNALL
..including the straight fork. Entry No. 667.

31 Dec. 1778.   WILLIAM FRAZER e. 80 ac. on Mountainside head straight
                fork Fishes Creek. Entry No. 668.

31 Dec. 1778.   JOHN ANDERSON e. 50 ac. old dividing line between HENRY
                REED & JOHN ANDERSON down Kings Creek..(JOHN ANDERSON
marked out..JAMES STAPP, SENR. written in). Entry No. 669.

31 Dec. 1778.   WILLIAM STUBBLEFIELD e. 50 ac. at COLO. BENJAMIN CLEVE-
                LANDS corner..W to EDMON BOAZS line. Entry No. 670.

31 Dec. 1778.   JOHN ROBERTS e. 200 ac. on dividing ridge between Hunting
                Creek and Cranes Creek..including part of Glady Branch..
(JOHN ROBERTS marked out..WILLIAM LENOIR written in). Entry No. 671.

31 Dec. 1778.   JAMES WILLSON e. 100 ac. S fork Cub Creek..E corner
                WILLIAM GILREATH line..including said WILLSONS improvement.
Entry No. 672.

31 Dec. 1778.   ISAAC DARNALL e. 240 ac. S side Fishes Creek.   Entry No. 673.

31 Dec. 1778.   WILLIAM WILCOX e. 300 ac. N fork Hunting Creek at REUBEN
                FLETCHERS line..including WILCOX improvement.   Entry No.
674.

31 Dec. 1778.   ANDREW VANNOY e. 600 ac. S side Mulberry Creek..E along
                dividing line made by JOHN DARNALL & GEORGE WHEATLEY.
Entry No. 675.

31 Dec. 1778.   JOHN MASON e. 50 ac. head Swan Pond..down both sides.
                Entry No. 676.

31 Dec. 1778.   JOHN JONES e. 200 ac. N fork Lewis Fork.   Entry No. 677.

31 Dec. 1778.   DAVID AUSTIN e. 70 ac. Mitchels River on JONAS MARSHALS
                line.   Entry No. 678.

31 Dec. 1778.   PHILIP MASON e. 50 ac. waters Swan Creek..condt. line
                between SPENCER WALKER & MASON.   Entry No. 679.

31 Dec. 1778.   ABRAHAM COOK e. 400 ac. Hunting Creek waters..said COOKS
                other entry..including BARNETTS improvement.   Entry No.
680.

Entry No. 681 skipped.

31 Dec. 1778.   JOHN LINTCH e. 300 ac. N side New River..mouth branch
                runs in above horse foard..(JOHN LINTCH marked out..trans-
ferered by Sherriff to AARON ENGLISH written in).   Entry No. 682.

31 Dec. 1778.   JOHN LINTCH e. 340 ac. under S side Holstons Knob at
                spring..divides land claimed by THOMAS HODGES & JOHN
LINTCH..(JOHN LINTCH marked out..JAMES WEATHERSPOON written in).   Entry
No. 683.

31 Dec. 1778.   JAMES BROWN e. 150 ac. S side Yadkin River..joining
                WILLIAM ELLISONS entry at mouth Beaver Creek.   Entry No.
684.

1 Jan. 1779.   WILLIAM OWEN, JUNR. e. 180 ac. both sides N fork Reddies
                River..near THOMAS OWENS line.   Entry No. 685.

1 Jan. 1779.   LITTLEBERRY TONEY e. 200 ac. N side New River..including
                JOSEPH & BENJAMIN TAYLORS improvements..(LITTLEBERRY TONEY
& THOMAS CALLOWAY marked out..BENJAMIN RIGHT written in).   Entry No. 686.

1 Jan. 1779.   WILLIAM TIREY e. 100 ac. S fork Reddies River joining JOHN
                TIREYS entry..including his improvement.   Entry No. 687.

1 Jan. 1779.   JAMES MITCHEL e. 200 ac. on Cub Creek..joining FRANCIS
                HARDGRAVES entry..on both sides creek..including his im-
provement..(JAMES MITCHEL marked out..CHARLES WALKER written in).   Entry
No. 688.

1 Jan. 1779.   BENJAMIN SEBASTIAN e. 50 ac. Sebastians Branch..above
                FRANCIS VANNOYS..below the improvement..including his
improvement.   Entry No. 689.

1 Jan. 1779.   BENJAMIN SEBASTIAN e. 100 ac. Mulberry Creek on ANDREW
                VANNOYS line.   Entry No. 690.

1 Jan. 1779.   WILLIAM GRAY e. 50 ac. main River at JOHN PAYNES line..E
                to JAMES GRAYS line.   Entry No. 691.

1 Jan. 1779. JOHN TIREY e. 100 ac. S fork Reddies River at WM. TIREYS
upper line. Entry No. 692.

2 Jan. 1779. CHARLES GORDON e. 300 ac. Naked Creek in ANDREW BAKERS
line..including improvement whereon JAMES VANINCLE (VAN
WINCKLE?) now lives. Entry No. 693.

2 Jan. 1779. WILLIAM LENOIR e. 200 ac. both sides S fork New River..
below Posixon Bottom..including said bottom. Entry No. 694.

2 Jan. 1779. WILLIAM LENOIR e. 200 ac. both sides N fork New River..
near foard below improvement whereon JAMES WARD now lives
..including said improvement..(WM. LENOIR marked out..transfard to WM.
ADKINS written in). Entry No. 695.

2 Jan. 1779. WILLIAM LENOIR e. 400 ac. both sides N fork New River on
GIDEON LEWIS line..including improvements whereon EDWARD
KING & CHARLES LITTLE lives..(WM. LENOIR marked out..STEPHEN REED written
in). Entry No. 696.

2 Jan. 1779. WILLIAM LENOIR e. 400 ac. both sides Little Elk Creek..S
side New River..in OSBORNS line..near head big meadow..
including improvement whereon WM. HARVEL now lives..the improvement
HARVEL bought of MASH. Entry No. 697.

2 Jan. 1779. WILLIAM LENOIR e. 400 ac. both sides Grassy Creek N side..
N fork New River on BENAJAH PENINGTONS line..including
improvement JOSHUA YATES & BENAJAH PENINGTON, JUNR. now lives. Entry
No. 698.

2 Jan. 1779. WILLIAM LENOIR e. 320 ac. on waters New River near LEWIS
old cabbin..including improvement whereon BAKER KING formerly lived..(WM. LENOIR marked out..JESSE COUNCILL written in). Entry
No. 699.

2 Jan. 1779. WILLIAM LENOIR e. 400 ac. both sides Rockey Creek below
CHARLES COLLENS old waste cabbin. Entry No. 700.

2 Jan. 1779. BENJAMIN CLEVELAND e. 640 ac. both sides S fork New River
and Cranberry Creek..near bottom below mouth creek..includ-
ing improvements whereon MICAJAH BUNCH & JONATHAN SMITH now lives. Entry
No. 701.

2 Jan. 1779. BENJAMIN CLEVELAND e. 200 ac. S side S fork New River at
foot hill below improvement whereon VINCENT JONES now
lives..including the improvement..(BENJ. CLEVELAND & WM. NALL marked out
..MARTIN GAMBILL written in). Entry No. 702.

2 Jan. 1779. BENJAMIN CLEVELAND e. 200 ac. S side S fork New River at
foard...upper end bottom above improvement that REUBIN
STRINGER & SAMUEL COLLENS now live..including said improvement..(BENJ.
CLEVELAND & JOHN COUCH marked out..HENRY HARDIN written in). Entry No.
703.

2 Jan. 1779. BENJAMIN CLEVELAND e. 200 ac. both sides N fork New River..
below little Old Fields..including improvement FRANCIS
GILLY & PETER GILLY now lives..(BENJ. CLEVELAND marked out..JONATHAN
SMITH written in). Entry No. 704.

2 Jan. 1779. BENJAMIN CLEVELAND e. 200 ac. both sides N fork New River..
below improvement whereon JOHN FLANNERY now lives..includ-
ing said improvement..(BENJ. CLEVELAND marked out..JAMES BUNYARD
written in). Entry No. 705.

2 Jan. 1779. BENJAMIN CLEVELAND e. 200 ac. both sides S fork New River
              on DANIEL RICHARDSONS line, including improvement whereon
JAMES MULKEY now lives..(BENJ. CLEVELAND marked out; JAMES MULKEY written
in).. Entry No. 706.

2 Jan. 1779. BENJAMIN CLEVELAND e. 200 ac. both sides Heltons Creek on
              N side N fork New River below improvement, whereon BENJAMIN
PENNINGTON formerly lived, including said improvement..(BENJ. CLEVELAND
marked out; WILLIAM HUFF written in).. Entry No. 707.

2 Jan. 1779. BEVERLY WATKINS e. 200 ac. both sides New River branch
              above old plantation..up said River joining the Virginia
line, including the mountain and Elk Creek.. Entry No. 708.

2 Jan. 1779. BEVERLY WATKINS e. 50 ac. N side New River at Foard against
              mouth Fighting Creek, including GEORGE GIPSONS improvement
on the Va. line..(BEVERLY WATKINS marked out; WM. LENOIR written in)..
Entry No. 709.

2 Jan. 1779. THOMAS PAYN e. 100 ac. Mitchels River near lower and bottom,
              including improvement whereon SAMUEL CANADY lives..(THOMAS
PAYN marked out; JACOB CANADY written in).. Entry No. 710.

2 Jan. 1779. THOMAS PAYN e. 320 ac. on Obeds Creek of New River near
              lower end bottom.. Entry No. 711.

2 Jan. 1779. THOMAS PAYN e. 320 ac. both sides Hunting Creek above
              WILLIAM LEWIS, JUNR. including improvement whereon WILLIAM
LEWIS & WILLIAM LEWIS, JUNR. now lives..(THOMAS PAYN & JOHN CLEVELAND
marked out; WILLIAM LEWIS, SENR. written in..(also) transfared per
WILLIAM STURDIE written in).. Entry No. 712.

2 Jan. 1779. THOMAS PAYN e. 200 ac. on Obeds Creek of New River below
              pine marsh.. Entry No. 713.

2 Jan. 1779. THOMAS PAYNE E. 200 ac. both sides Heltons Creek N side
              N fork New River below improvement whereon MARK FOSTER
now lives including said improvement.. Entry No. 714.

SKIPPED   Entry No. 715

2 Jan. 1779. JOHN CLEVELAND e. 100 ac. on Mitchels River lower end bottom,
              including improvement whereon JACOB CANADY now lives..
Entry No. 716.

2 Jan. 1779. JOHN CLEVELAND e. 150 ac. on Bushey fork Little River, in-
              cluding improvement that ROBERT HAMON claims..(JOHN
CLEVELAND marked out; JONATHON HUGHES written in)..   Entry No. 717.

2 Jan. 1779. JOHN CLEVELAND e. 320 ac. waters Hunting Creek, lower end
              BENNET ROBERTS' claim, including improvement where BENNET
ROBERTS now lives. Entry No. 718.

2 Jan. 1779. JOHN CLEVELAND e. 320 ac. on Big Elkin at county line, in-
              cluding improvement where MICHAEL VANINCLE (Van Winckle?)
lives..(this entry is cross-marked out).. Entry No. 719.

2 Jan. 1779. ANDREW BAKER e. 200 ac. on New River near fork Naked Creek..
              mouth Little Naked Creek, along MATTHEW SPARKS line,
including great Crab Orchard and EZRA CAMRONS improvement..(ANDREW BAKER
marked out; JOHN JOHNSTON written in).. Entry No. 720.

2 Jan. 1779.   JAMES FOX e. 640 ac. middle fork Swan Creek near Three
               forks..including his improvement. Entry No. 721.

2 Jan. 1779.   MICHAEL VANINCLE (VAN WINCKLE) e. 200 ac. between his
               house & THOMAS KILBURNS..crossing Big Elkin. Entry No.
722.

2 Jan. 1779.   ABSOLAM CLEVELAND e. 150 ac. on Mitchels River on both
               sides..including improvement whereon ROBERT HAMMON lives.
Entry No. 723.

2 Jan. 1779.   ABSOLAM CLEVELAND e. 200 ac. head waters Big Elkin..in-
               cluding improvement whereon BENJAMIN SMITH lives..(ABSOLAM
CLEVELAND marked out..WILLIAM REYNOLDS written in). Entry No. 724.

2 Jan. 1779.   ABSOLAM CLEVELAND e. 200 ac. on Mitchels River near upper
               end of bottom..including improvement BENJAMIN SUMMON lives
on..(ABSOLAM CLEVELAND marked out..RICHARD HORN (?) written in). Entry
No. 725.

2 Jan. 1779.   ABSOLAM CLEVELAND e. 100 ac. on Fishes River..including
               improvement whereon WILLIAM UNDERWOOD now lives..(ABSALOM
CLEVELAND marked out..JOHN WRIGHT written in). Entry No. 726.

2 Jan. 1779.   CHARLES GORDON e. 140 ac. Dividing Ridge between head
               waters Buffalow and Naked Creek..including improvement of
PAUL PATRICK. Entry No. 727.

2 Jan. 1779.   CHARLES GORDON e. 640 ac. on Buffaloe Creek..S side N fork
               New River..including PATRICKS improvement..(CHARLES GORDON
& JAMES BUNYARD marked out..AARON MASH written in). Entry No. 728.

2 Jan. 1779.   BEVERLY WATKINS e. 320 ac. both sides Bakers road..waters
               of Cranberry Creek..including improvement whereon THOMAS
LITTLE & JOSEPH MASSEY formerly lived..(BEVERLY WATKINS marked out..
BENJAMIN CLEVELAND written in). Entry No. 729.

2 Jan. 1779.   WILLIAM LENOIR e. 200 ac. on N side New River..including
               improvement ZACHARIAH WELLS sold to LENOIR (?). Entry No.
730.

2 Jan. 1779.   BENJAMIN CLEVELAND e. 100 ac. waters New River..Little fork
               Pine Swamp..including the plantation whereon CHURCH now
lives..(BENJ. CLEVELAND marked out..JOHN CHURCH written in). Entry No.
731.

2 Jan. 1779.   LITTLEBERRY TONEY e. 150 ac. S fork Lewis Fork..above
               DANIEL GULLETS improvement and including it..(LITTLEBERRY
TONEY & DAWSON SEWAL marked out..DANIEL GULLOT written in). Entry No.
732.

2 Jan. 1779.   WILLIAM WATTS e. 200 ac. on Bushey Fork..Mitchels River.
               Entry No. 733.

2 Jan. 1779.   LITTLEBERRY TONEY e. 200 ac. Lewis Fork..including improve-
               ment JOHN BIARS & JOHN HARMON lives on..(LITTLEBERRY TONEY
marked out..JESSE GULLET written in). Entry No. 734.

2 Jan. 1779.   JOHN ROSE, JUNR. e. 200 ac. Waters Mill Creek at MR. LYKENS
               line. Entry No. 735.

2 Jan. 1779.   BENJAMIN HERNDON e. 200 ac. head waters SAMUEL WRIGHTS
               Creek..both sides main road leads thru Gap of Brushey
Mountain on HANCH LIKENS line..including part of a mountain..(BENJ. HERN-
DON marked out..THOMAS SAILS written in). Entry No. 736.

2 Jan. 1779. BENJAMIN HERNDON e. 600 ac. on Dogg Creek of New River
near the Rattlesnakes Den on Dugouth..including two old
cabbins formerly belonging to GEORGE COLLINS..an old cabbin that WILLIAM
HARVEL lives in..on waters Fighting Creek. Entry No. 737.

2 Jan. 1779. BENJAMIN HERNDON e. 300 ac. on New River below Three Forks
..lower end CLEVELANDS entry at the Horse foard..(BENJ.
HERNDON marked out..HENRY CHAMBERS written in). Entry No. 738.

4 Jan. 1779. BENJAMIN HERNDON e. 320 ac. on top Brushey Mountain..in-
cluding the improvement bought of CORNELUIS SALE where
WM. RYSDEN lives. Entry No. 739.

4 Jan. 1779. BENJAMIN HERNDON e. 300 ac. on Brushey Mountain on BENJA-
MIN HERNDONS other entry..including some of waters of
Hunting Creek. Entry No. 740.

4 Jan. 1779. JOEL DIER e. 50 ac. S side Yadkin River known by name
Reedy Branch..including the cabbin where THOMAS FERGUSON
formerly lived. Entry No. 741.

4 Jan. 1779. JOEL DIER e. 150 ac. S side Yadkin River at dividing line
of AHAZUL DIER..a branch known by name Reedy Branch..in-
cluding all the improvements thereon..(JOEL DIER marked out..THOMAS
FERGUSON written in). Entry No. 742.

4 Jan. 1779. JOEL DIER e. 25 ac. N side Yadkin River at JOHN DIERS
entry..(JOEL DIER marked out..THOMAS COFFEY written in).
Entry No. 743.

4 Jan. 1779. JOHN CUSON (?) e. 300 ac. joining JOHN KEYS line..little
fork Kings Creek..(JOHN CUSON (?) marked out..JOHN ROBERT-
SON written in). Entry No. 744.

4 Jan. 1779. GEORGE WHEATLEY, JUNR. e. 100 ac. N side Mountain near
Rich Mountain or Cove Gap on top of mtn...extending both
sides road leads thru Cove Gap..(GEORGE WHEATLEY, JUNR. marked out..
THOMAS LOW written in). Entry No. 745.

4 Jan. 1779. GEORGE WHEATLEY, JUNR. e. 150 ac. on Falling fork Moravian
Creek at CALEB LOWS line..including said WHEATLEYS im-
provement..(GEORGE WHEATLEY, JUNR. & ARCHILUS WALKER marked out..ISAAC
LOW written in). Entry No. 746.

4 Jan. 1779. JOHN FLANNERY e. 100 ac. N fork New River above mouth
Buffalow..both sides creek..including improvement where
JOHN HINSON lives..(JOHN FLANNERY marked out..JOHN HENSON written in).
Entry No. 747.

4 Jan. 1779. ARCHILUS COFFEE e. 60 ac. N fork Kings Creek..joining lower end JOHN ANDERSONS entry..including improvement whereon
LAURENCE DUNKIN lives. Entry No. 748.

4 Jan. 1779. THOMAS BICKNELL e. 50 ac. at BENJ. HERNDONS line..along
THOS. BICKNELLS line..S to BOLENS. Entry No. 749.

5 Jan. 1779. JOHN PAYN e. 200 ac. on Reddies River..upper end CHARLES
ADAMS Claim..up both sides said river..including improve-
ment JOHN DARNALL bought of REUBEN ROBBINS..(JOHN PAYN marked out..WM.
SUTTON written in). Entry No. 750.

5 Jan. 1779. THOMAS FERGUSON e. 50 ac. both sides Yadkin River above
Stoney fork. Entry No. 751.

5 Jan. 1779. JOHN FERGUSON e. 320 ac. Stoney fork Creek..including
improvement whereon JOHN FERGUSON now lives. Entry No.
752.

5 Jan. 1779.   BENJAMIN HOWARD e. 50 ac. N side Yadkin..including the
               improvement. Entry No. 753.

5 Jan. 1779.   JAMES MARTIN LEWIS e. 200 ac. above CAPT. ALLENS Muster
               Ground on Little Elkin. Entry No. 754.

6 Jan. 1779.   JAMES MARTIN LEWIS e. 200 ac. Little Elkin..joining his
               other entry. Entry No. 755.

6 Jan. 1779.   JOHN SMITHERS e. 150 ac. on N side Yadkin River below said
               SMITHERS plantation..including improvement whereon SMITHERS
now lives. Entry No. 756.

6 Jan. 1779.   JOSEPH HERNDON e. 640 ac. long branch of Mulberry Creek..
               near MOSES TOLOVORS lower corner. Entry No. 757.

6 Jan. 1779.   JOSEPH HERNDON e. 150 ac. on MOSES TOLOVORS branch..above
               said TOLOVORS line. Entry No. 758.

6 Jan. 1779.   JOHN BROWN e. 300 ac. waters New River on Obids Creek..in-
               cluding CALLOWAYS Camp..(JOHN BROWN marked out..SPILSBY
TRIBBLE written in). Entry No. 759.

6 Jan. 1779.   JAMES BROWN e. 50 ac. N side New River..mouth Howards
               Creek..(JAMES BROWN marked out..JOSEPH AYERS written in).
Entry No. 760.

6 Jan. 1779.   JOEL DIER e. 150 ac. on Buffaloe Creek in the Cove..lower
               end plantation whereon TIRY (?) ROBINS now lives..includ-
ing said plantation. Entry No. 761.

6 Jan. 1779.   JOEL DYER e. 100 ac. N side Yadkin River at JOHN SIMPSONS
               lower line..including improvement whereon JOHN VANDERPOOL
now lives..(JOEL DIER marked out..Entry withdrawn by order of JOEL DIER
written in..(also)..JOSHUA CURTIS written in). Entry No. 762.

6 Jan. 1779.   JOHN BROWN e. 100 ac. on New River..mouth Beaver Creek..
               (JOHN BROWN marked out..LITTLEBERRY TONEY written in..
entire Entry cross-marked out). Entry No. 763.

6 Jan. 1779.   JOHN ROSE, JUNR. e. 120 ac. waters Mill Creek..corner his
               other entry..then running four points of compass, etc.
Entry No. 764.

6 Jan. 1779.   JOHN ROSE, JUNR. e. 200 ac. lower fork Bryer Creek at
               JOHN PARKES line. Entry No. 765.

7 Jan. 1779.   THOMAS PAYNE e. 200 ac. Bryshey fork Little River..includ-
               ing improvement whereon WM. DAVIS lives..(THOMAS PAYNES
Entry withdrawn). Entry No. 766.

7 Jan. 1779.   THOMAS PAYNE Entry withdrawn..(no other wording). Entry
               No. 767.

7 Jan. 1779.   THOMAS PAYNE, SR. e. 320 ac. Brushey fork Little River..
               (THOS. PAYNE marked out..CLISBY COBB written in). Entry
No. 768.

7 Jan. 1779.   (?) REYNOLDS e. 200 ac. waters Lewis Fork near WM. MITCHELS
               line..including improvement that formerly belonged to
ABRAHAM LAND (?)..(? REYNOLDS marked out..JOHN WHITAKER written in).
Entry No. 769.

2 Feb. 1779.   CHARLES REYNOLDS e. 50 ac. S side Cub Creek at Waggon road
               ..including improvement said REYNOLDS now lives on. Entry
No. 770.

2 Feb. 1779. LITTLEBERRY TONEY e. 200 ac. on Yadkin River..including
             improvement whereon JOHN HAMBEA (?) now lives..(LITTLE-
BERRY TONEY & ABRAHAM BISHOP marked out..JOHN ELLEDGE written in).
Entry No. 771.

2 Feb. 1779. THOMAS PAYNE, SR. e. 320 ac. on Peak Creek. Entry No. 772.

2 Feb. 1779. GEORGE ELMORE e. 150 ac. S fork Lewis Fork near Cliff..
             including improvement whereon GEORGE ELMORE now lives..
(GEORGE ELMORE marked out..MOSES TOMPKINS written in). Entry No. 773.

4 Feb. 1779. HUMPHREY PRICE e. 80 ac. long branch of Big Elkin..includ-
             ing his improvement. Entry No. 774.

4 Feb. 1779. ANDREW CANADY e. 60 ac. joining his entry on big Bugaboo.
             Entry No. 775.

4 Feb. 1779. NICHOLAS MITCHELL e. 200 ac. middle fork Moravian Creek..
             including his improvement..(NICHOLAS MITCHELL marked out..
ISAAC LOW written in). Entry No. 776.

4 Feb. 1779. URIAH HARDEMAN e. 50 ac. at ROBERT CHANDLOWS line. Entry
             No. 777.

4 Feb. 1779. EPHRAIM PARMELY e. 50 ac. E fork Roaring River at agreed
             line between JAMES BUNYARD & RICHARD DODSON. Entry No.
778.

4 Feb. 1779. WILLIAM SPICER e. 100 ac. E side Elk Spur..waters E fork
             Roaring River at head of branch. Entry No. 779.

4 Feb. 1779. SAMUEL HYNDS e. 100 ac. between Brushey fork and Grays
             fork..Little River waters..on E end Bald Head mountain..
including his improvement..(SAMUEL HYNDS marked out..JOHN ALLEN WOODRUFF
written in). Entry No. 780.

4 Feb. 1779. THOMAS BENGE e. 200 ac. waters Swan Creek..near the moun-
             tain at JOHN BOLONS line. Entry No. 781.

5 Feb. 1779. WILLIAM CORNELIUS e. 100 ac. head spring of Bugaboe.
             Entry No. 782.

5 Feb. 1779. SAMUEL MCQUEEN e. 100 ac. S fork New River below said
             MCQUEENS improvement..(SAMUEL MCQUEEN marked out..JOHN
CHURCH written in). Entry No. 783.

5 Feb. 1779. SAMUEL MCQUEEN e. 50 ac. on New River. Entry No. 784.

5 Feb. 1779. JEFFREY JOHNSON e. 100 ac. N side Yadkin River at upper
             end EDMOND DENNYS line. Entry No. 785.

5 Feb. 1779. WILLIAM LENOIR e. 150 ac. N end Flat Mountain..including
             some of waters of Three Forks. Entry No. 786.

5 Feb. 1779. WILLIAM LENOIR e. 200 ac. both sides Howards Creek..below
             Esqr. SMALLYS entry..including a small improvement made
by JAMES MILIGIN. Entry No. 787.

5 Feb. 1779. WILLIAM SNODDY e. 100 ac. N side Yadkin River in MOSES
             DENMANS line..a small distance below the improvement that
ELIAS WOOD now lives on..(WM. SNODDY marked out..ELIAS WOOD written in).
Entry No. 788.

5 Feb. 1779. WILLIAM SNODDY e. 100 ac. N side Yadkin River on Branch
             joining LEWIS DEMOSS above ANN DUNAWHO..including the
improvement that FRANCIS TOLBY now lives on..(WILLIAM SNODDY marked out
..ISAAC PRESTON written in). Entry No. 789.

47

5 Feb. 1779.   WILLIAM SNODDY e. 300 ac. Blue Ridge between head Buffaloe
and head Elk Creek. Entry No. 790.

5 Feb. 1779.   WILLIAM LENOIR e. 400 ac. W side New River..near head 1st
branch below mouth Howards Creek..near WALTONS entry.
Entry No. 791.

5 Feb. 1779.   WILLIAM SNODDY e. 200 ac. both sides Meat Camp Creek..
above BROWNS entry..including an old Cabbin. Entry No.
792.

5 Feb. 1779.   WILLIAM LENOIR e. 200 ac. on Long Branch that runs into
Elk Creek..including an old cabbin..(WM. LENOIR marked out
..Transferred to ISAAC PRESTON written in). Entry No. 793.

5 Feb. 1779.   WILLIAM LENOIR e. 200 ac. E side New River..against EAST-
RIDGES field near CAPT. HERNDONS entry..(WM. LENOIR marked
out..transferred to ANDREW BAIRD written in). Entry No. 794.

6 Feb. 1779.   JAMES FREEMAN e. 100 ac. at CHARLES WALKERS line..both
sides little Cub Creek. Entry No. 795.

6 Feb. 1779.   JESSE COFFEE e. 100 ac. on Kings Creek..joining JOHN
ANDERSONS & KELLIS (ARCHILUS) COFFEES..including improvement PATRICK DUNCAN lives on..(JESSE COFFEE marked out..LARENCE DUNCAN
written in). Entry No. 796.

6 Feb. 1779.   DEVEREUX BALLARD e. 150 ac. both sides Mill fork Fishes
Creek..at CAPT. LENOIRS line. Entry No. 797.

6 Feb. 1779.   JONATHAN STAMPER, JUNR. e. 250 ac. Little Bugaboe..above
RICHARD ALLENS. Entry No. 798.

6 Feb. 1779.   JONATHAN STAMPER, SENR. e. 100 ac. waters Bugaboe Creek..
at his other entry. Entry No. 799.

8 Feb. 1779.   JOSEPH PRUET e. 100 ac. on Camp Branch at mouth of Johna-
cake Branch..including improvement he now lives on. Entry
No. 800.

8 Feb. 1779.   JOHN HOLDBROOK e. 150 ac. head Camp Branch. Entry No. 801.

8 Feb. 1779.   NATHAN BARNETT e. 150 ac. head Middle fork Hunting Creek..
on mountain..(NATHAN BARNETT & DEVEREUX BALLARD marked
out..JOHN VICKAS written in). Entry No. 802.

8 Feb. 1779.   1st enterer unreadable..e. 100 ac. below Glady fork &
Brushey fork Little River..including GEORGE MAYNERDS old
Camp..(WM. HARDEN written in). Entry No. 803.

9 Feb. 1779.   GEORGE BREWER e. 50 ac. foot of mtn. called Holdbrooks
Mtn...including small improvement..(GEORGE BREWER marked
out..entry withdrawn). Entry No. 804.

9 Feb. 1779.. DANIEL EASLEY e. 300 ac. waters Cranes creek joining the
County line against an entry he made in Rowan..dividing
ridge above HAMMONS cabbin. Entry No. 805.

9 Feb. 1779.   RICHARD DODDSON e. 100 ac. E fork Roaring River..above his
improvement..including the improvement. Entry No. 806.

9 Feb. 1779.   TIMOTHY SISK e. 100 ac. fork Swan Creek near THOMAS PARKES
               S corner. Entry No. 807.

9 Feb. 1779.   ABRAHAM COOK e. 500 ac. waters Hunting Creek..S side his
               own entry near County line..including JACKSONS improvement.
Entry No. 808.

9 Feb. 1779.   ROBERT SAUNDERS e. 100 ac. waters Little Warriors Creek..
               including small improvement..(ROBERT SAUNDERS marked out..
JOHN HAMBY written in). Entry No. 809.

9 Feb. 1779.   BENJAMIN ELLEDGE e. 100 ac. branch Warrior Creek..joining
               THOMAS ELLIOTT..including improvement made by JOHN LINCH
where MIMEY (?) SOSB---Y (?) now lives..(BENJ. ELLEDGE marked out..
SEBEAT SHOAT written in). Entry No. 810.

9 Feb. 1779.   BENJAMIN ELLEDGE e. 150 ac. fork Warrior Creek..(alias
               Bear Creek)..joining FRANCIS ELLEDGE and joining or near
to BENJAMIN BROWN. Entry No. 811.

9 Feb. 1779.   FRANCIS ELLEDGE e. 300 ac. on Warrior Creek..otherwise Bear
               Creek..including improvement where JOSEPH ELLEDGE, SR. &
himself live. Entry No. 812.

9 Feb. 1779.   ROBERT SAUNDERS e. 200 ac. Warrior Creek at SPILSBY TRIB-
               BLES line. Entry No. 813.

9 Feb. 1779.   ROBERT SAUNDERS e. 150 ac. Little Warrior Creek..below WM.
               JONES improvement..(ROBERT SAUNDERS & MANOAH DYER marked
out..JESSE HALL written in). Entry No. 814.

9 Feb. 1779.   EDWARD FINCH e. 100 ac. both sides path that leads from
               NATHAN BARNETTS to old MR. CRANES opposite WM. HOLLANDS
cabin. Entry No. 815.

9 Feb. 1779.   JOSEPH HERNDON e. 200 ac. N side Yadkin River..upper end
               said HERNDONS Old Pattent land..including improvement
whereon GEORGE BARKER now lives. Entry No. 816.

9 Feb. 1779.   WILLIAM TOLOVER e. 50 ac. Harris's Creek at said TOLOVERS
               entry. Entry No. 817.

9 Feb. 1779.   JOHN ROBBINS, JR. e. 200 ac. on Reddies River below mouth
               Tumbling Shoal Branch..including a Mill Seat. Entry No.
818.

9 Feb. 1779.   SAMUEL SIMPSON e. 250 ac. on top Blue Ridge..down waters
               Peak Creek. Entry No. 819.

9 Feb. 1779.   WILLIAM LENOIR e. 180 ac. both sides Naked Creek. Entry
               No. 820.

9 Feb. 1779.   WILLIAM LENOIR e. 320 ac. both sides N fork New River..
               below improvement made by EDWARD SWEETEN..(said FIELD now
claimed by DUTTON SWEETEN)..including deer foard at rich hill..(WM.
LENOIR marked out..VINSON HOLLONSWORTH written in). Entry No. 821.

9 Feb. 1779.   WILLIAM LENOIR e. 100 ac. both sides Long Branch..N fork
               New River..including Creek Bottom. Entry No. 822.

9 Feb. 1779.   DEVERAUX BALLARD e. 250 ac. head Sams Branch..S side Fishes
               Creek..including cabin where DAVID GIBSON now lives..
(DEVERAUX BALLARD marked out..JAMES REYNOLDS written in). Entry No. 823.

9 Feb. 1779.   JOHN SUTTON e. 150 ac. N side Mulberry Creek near Chestnut
               Mountain..(JOHN SUTTON marked out..JOHN HALL written in).
Entry No. 824.

9 Feb. 1779.   JOSEPH WHARTON e. 100 ac. joining entry that JOHN BOND
               made..E waters Fishers Creek..including forks of road &
Meeting house.   Entry No. 825.

9 Feb. 1779.   JOEL DYER e. 640 ac. on Flannerys fork New River above
               ABNER SMALLY..including THOMAS WILLIAMS improvement..(En-
try withdrawn by order JOEL DIER).   Entry No. 826.

11 Feb. 1779.   ISHAM WESTMORELAND e. 100 ac. on little River..including
                SIZEMORES claim..(ISHAM WESTMORELAND marked out..CLESBEY
COBB & JOHNATHAN HAINES written in).   Entry No. 827.

11 Feb. 1779.   STEPHEN HARRIS e. 100 ac. S fork Hunting Creek..condt.
                line JOHN STANDLEY..including HARIS STANDLEYS plantation.
Entry No. 828.

11 Feb. 1779.   JOHN COMBS e. 100 ac. on condt. line STEPHEN HARRIS..viz
                both sides Bryer Branch between STEPHEN HARRIS and Finches
Mill..(JOHN COMBS marked out..STEPHEN HARRIS written in).   Entry No. 829.

11 Feb. 1779.   THOMAS SISK e. 100 ac. N side Yadkin River at WILLIAM
                CARRELS corner..to WM. CARRELS line..to GABRIEL LOVEINGS
line.   Entry No. 830.

12 Feb. 1779.   SAMUEL WALKER e. 200 ac. joining AQUILLA LOWS line..in-
                cluding WALKERS shop.   Entry No. 831.

12 Feb. 1779.   JOHN FIELDER e. 150 ac. little fork Mitchels River..near
                SAMUEL CRITCHFIELDS upper line..including improvement
whare JOHN LAWRENCE lives.   Entry No. 832.

13 Feb. 1779.   DUTTON SWEETING e. 50 ac. N fork New River..mouth Laurel
                fork..including his improvement..(DUTTON SWEETING & WM.
COLVARD marked out..transfard to STEPHEN READ written in).   Entry No. 833.

13 Feb. 1779.   1st enterer erased completely..e. 50 ac. S side Elk Creek
                ..in JULIUS DUGERS line..including small improvement..
(JOHN BEVERLY written in).   Entry No. 834.

15 Feb. 1779.   ISHAM WESTMORELAND e. 100 ac. head S branch Little River..
                (ISHAM WESTMORELAND marked out..JONATHAN HAINS written in)
Entry No. 835.

15 Feb. 1779.   ISHAM WESTMORELAND e. 100 ac. waters Alexanders fork of
                Roaring River..including Meat Camp.   Entry No. 836.

15 Feb. 1779.   ISHAM WESTMORELAND e. 150 ac. head Glady fork..including
                MARTIN GAMBILLS Camp..(ISHAM WESTMORELAND, CLISBEY COBB &
JONATHAN HAINS marked out..WILLIAM LENOIR written in).   Entry No. 837.

15 Feb. 1779.   THOMAS GOODIN transfared the following entry to..Viz:
                JOHN CARTER, SR. e. 200 ac. on Little River..(THOMAS GOOD-
IN, JOHN CARTER, SENR. & CLISBEY COBB marked out..WILLIAM LENOIR written
in).   Entry No. 838.

15 Feb. 1779.   THOMAS GOODING transfared following entry to, viz: JOHN
                CARTER, JUNR. e. 200 ac. Bledsoes Creek of Little River..
(THOMAS GOODIN, JOHN CARTER, JR., JOHN CARTER, SENR. marked out..CLISBEY
COBB written in).   Entry No. 839.

15 Feb. 1779.   THOMAS GOODIN transfared the following entry to viz..JOHN
                CARTER, JUNR. e. 300 ac. on Bledsoes Creek of Little
River..(THOMAS GOODIN, JOHN CARTER, JUNR. & JOHN CARTER, SENR. marked
out..CLISBEY COBB written in). Entry No. 840.

15 Feb. 1779.   THOMAS GOODIN transferred following entry to viz..JOHN
                CARTER, JUNR. e. 200 ac. on Hands Creek..Little River
above HANDS entry..(THOMAS GOODIN, JOHN CARTER, JR. & JOHN CARTER, SENR.
marked out..CLISBEY COBB written in). Entry No. 841.

15 Feb. 1779.   DAVID ALLEN, JR. e. 640 ac. on County line joining WILLIAM
                CARRELS line. Entry No. 842.

15 Feb. 1779.   DAVID ALLEN e. 640 ac. on County line joining his other
                entry. Entry No. 843.

16 Feb. 1779.   GEORGE WHEATLEY, SR. e. 100 ac. N side Roaring River..near
                mouth second branch..below WM. SLONES. Entry No. 844.

16 Feb. 1779.   WILLIAM SLONE e. 50 ac. in ISAAC GARRISONS line..including
                waste land between GARRISONS & WOOLBANKS lines together
with SLONES improvement. Entry No. 845.

16 Feb. 1779.   ISAAC GARRISON e. 200 ac. between Wheatleys Creek and
                Bugaboe near large spring on Wheatleys Creek. Entry No.
846.

16 Feb. 1779.   JAMES MARTIN e. 100 ac. on New River on mtn. between JAMES
                DUGLAS (DOUGLAS) improvement..JOHN ROBINSONS cabbins..
including ROBINSONS cabbins. Entry No. 847.

16 Feb. 1779.   JAMES MARTIN e. 100 ac. waters Kings Creek between PHILIP
                DAVIS & JOHN GUSSON (?). Entry No. 848.

16 Feb. 1779.   JACOB MAINARD e. 100 ac. on Glady Creek of Little River
                at HEADSPETHS Camp. Entry No. 849.

16 Feb. 1779.   JAMES FRANKLIN e. 100 ac. Big Glady Creek..(JAMES FRANKLIN
                marked out..YOUNG EDWARDS written in). Entry No. 850.

16 Feb. 1779.   ABRAHAM ----(?) e. 150 ac. Falls of the crooked branch of
                Hunting Creek..including improvement whare ZACHARIAH
PINKSTON lives..(ABRAHAM ----(?) & JOB COAL marked out..SAMUEL CRABTREE
written in). Entry No. 851.

16 Feb. 1779.   JACOB MAINARD e. 640 ac. Brushey fork Little River..fork
                of Creek where AMBROUS HAMMON had a claim..(JACOB MAINARD
marked out..BENJ. HERNDON written in). Entry No. 852.

16 Feb. 1779.   GEORGE LEWIS e. 100 ac. Top Rich Mountain between head
                Gladys Creek & (?). Entry No. 853.

19 Feb. 1779.   JACOB PATE e. 100 ac. both sides Hunting Creek..below
                ABNER BAKERS improvement. Entry No. 854.

19 Feb. 1779.   JOHN HAMMON e. 100 ac. middle fork Roaring River..on
                GREENSTREETS line near road towards BREWERW line. Entry
No. 855.

19 Feb. 1779. JOHN HAMMON e. 50 ac. waters Little River..including
            HAMMONS improvement..(JOHN HAMMON & STEPHEN HOLLOWAY
marked out..WM. CONNELY written in). Entry No. 856.

19 Feb. 1779. GEORGE BREWER e. 100 ac. Big Sandy Creek near Little
            falls..including a small improvement. Entry No. 857.

19 Feb. 1779. AMBROUS HAMMON e. 6 ac. middle fork Roaring River..join-
            ing said HAMMONS line..(AMBROUS HAMMON marked out..NATHAN
COX written in). Entry No. 858.

19 Feb. 1779. AMBROUS HAMMON e. 100 ac. on a ridge near Mades Knob..
            including improvement whare said AMBROUS HAMMON now lives.
Entry No. 859.

19 Feb. 1779. ROBERT HAMMON e. 100 ac. branch of Little River near Mades
            Knob..including his improvement..(ROBERT HAMMON marked
out..THOMAS ENDICOTT written in). Entry No. 860.

19 Feb. 1779. WILLIAM HARGUS e. 100 ac. on top Holdbrooks mountain..E
            fork Roaring River..at the rich cove. Entry No. 861.

19 Feb. 1779. JOHN CARTER, JR. e. 100 ac. S side Little River at the
            hunting path..(JOHN CARTER, JR. & CLISBY COBB marked out..
WM. LENOIR written in). Entry No. 862.

20 Feb. 1779. JAMES BUNYARD e. 100 ac. one of forks..E fork Roaring
            River at JOHN AMBURGY, JUNRS. line. Entry No. 863.

20 Feb. 1779. WILLIAM NALL e. 150 ac. top Peach Bottom Mountain..:
            (WILLIAM NALL marked out..JONATHAN HAINES written in).
Entry No. 864.

20 Feb. 1779. WILLIAM NALL e. 150 ac. top Peach Bottom Mountain joining
            his other entry. Entry No. 865.

20 Feb. 1779. MARTIN GAMBILL e. 150 ac. waters Little River..near said
            GAMBILLS old camp. Entry No. 866.

20 Feb. 1779. MARTIN GAMBILL e. 100 ac. at GILES PARMELYS line. Entry
            No. 867.

20 Feb. 1779. NICHOLUS ANGEL e. 150 ac. on S side Roans Creek at ROBERT
            BAKERS line..up said creek of New River..(NICHOLUS ANGEL
marked out..COONRAD DICK written in). Entry No. 868.

20 Feb. 1779. WILLIAM SHARPE e. 100 ac. waters Moravian Creek..both
            sides path leading thru Rich Cove Gap..joining his entry
in Roan County. Entry No. 869.

23 Feb. 1779. DANIEL EASLEY e. 200 ac. waters Crane Creek joining Roan
            County line and ANDREW KINGS entry about a mile above
EASTLEYS (ENSLEYS) entry. Entry No. 870.

23 Feb. 1779. DANIEL EASLEY e. 80 ac. on Roan County line. Entry No.
            871.

23 Feb. 1779. WILLIAM LENOIR e. 320 ac. E side Cranberry Creek..includ-
            ing Elk Ridge. Entry No. 872.

24 Feb. 1779. ROGER TURNER e. 100 ac. on Muddy fork Roaring River.
            Entry No. 873.

25 Feb. 1779. WILLIAM FLOYD e. 100 ac. Lewis Fork..under foot of moun-
              tain..a mile N CALLOWAYS path over Ridge..(WILLIAM FLOYD
marked out..JOHN CHURCH written in). Entry No. 874.

25 Feb. 1779. WILLIAM FLOYD e. 50 ac. branch Reddies River called Cane
              Brake branch..being on JOHN SHEPHERDS line..(WM. FLOYD
marked out..JOHN SHEPHERD, JUNR. written in). Entry No. 875.

25 Feb. 1779. WILLIAM FLOYD e. 30 ac. on Reddies River below the deep
              ford to JOHN SHEPHERDS line. Entry No. 876.

25 Feb. 1779. STEPHEN UNDERWOOD e. 200 ac. Meadow branch below the Cane
              Brake. Entry No. 877.

25 Feb. 1779. STEPHEN UNDERWOOD e. 100 ac. joining the S end Sharpers
              Mountain..near NED BELLS Branch. Entry No. 878.

25 Feb. 1779. JOHN DYAL (DOYAL) e. 200 ac. Pipe Camp Branch. Entry No.
              879.

25 Feb. 1779. JOHN DIAL (DOYAL) e. 200 ac. on said DIALS S line whereon
              he lives..on Fosters Branch. Entry No. 880.

25 Feb. 1779. HENRY HAYS e. 100 ac. at JOHN HOWARDS line..W side Osbor-
              nes Creek..(HENRY HAYS marked out..SAMUEL NICKLESON writ-
ten in). Entry No. 881.

25 Feb. 1779. THOMAS MUNUY e. 100 ac. between S fork Hunting Creek and
              Osbornes Creek..joining ISHAM HARVILS entry next to JOHN
HOWARDS entry..on Osbornes Creek..(THOMAS MUNUY marked out..ISHAM HARVILL
written in). Entry No. 882.

25 Feb. 1779. ABNER BAKER e. 100 ac. Rock House..E side Osborne Creek.
              Entry No. 883.

26 Feb. 1779. JACOB STAMPER e. 100 ac. fork branch Little Elkin near
              the little mountain. Entry No. 884.

26 Feb. 1779. THOMAS HEMBRICK e. 100 ac. waters Moravian Creek on part
              of SCURLOCKS entry..joining DAVID BURNS claim..(Warrant
issued Sept. 20, 1808..in margin..(also)..Caveated by ROBERT HAYS. Entry
No. 885.

26 Feb. 1779. NICHOLAS ANGEL e. 200 ac. S fork New River..mouth of Roans
              Creek..to BAKERS line..including improvement that SUSANNA
BAKER now lives on..(NICHOLAS ANGEL marked out..JOHN BAKER written in).
Entry No. 886.

27 Feb. 1779. PHILIP DAVIS e. 50 ac. Kings Creek below the mill on a
              branch that runs from Buttays (?) Mountain. Entry No.
887.

2 March 1779. JONATHAN TOMPKINS e. 20 ac. S fork Lewis Fork..bounding
              on HUGH MONTGOMERYS entry. Entry No. 888.

2 March 1779. THOMAS ELLEDGE e. 100 ac. Little Warrior Creek near fork
              of paths..one leading to WILLIAM TRIPLETTS..the other to
CHESLEY COCKERHAMS. Entry No. 889.

2 March 1779. ROBERT OBAIR e. 100 ac. on Elk Creek at HUGH MONTGOMERYS
              line..(ROBERT OBAIR marked out..THOMAS STEED written in).
Entry No. 890.

2 March 1779. WILLIAM CRANE e. 200 ac. waters Lewis Fork on condt. line
              between him & WM. JACKSON..(WM. CRANE marked out..WM.
JACKSON written in). Entry No. 891.

2 March 1779.   JOEL DIER e. 200 ac. on New River at JAMES MARTINS line..
including CHARLES GERMANS improvement. Entry No. 892.

2 March 1779.   THOMAS LAY e. 50 ac. joining JESSE LAYS line up LINVILS
Mill. Entry No. 893.

2 March 1779.   JOEL DIER e. 100 ac. both sides Yadkin River at HUDSONS
line. Entry No. 894.

2 March 1779.   ROBERT KIRKPATRICK e. 50 ac. small branch..N side Yadkin
River at JOHN BROWNS line. Entry No. 895.

2 March 1779.   WILLIAM BAYS e. 100 ac. middle branch Kings Creek at
JAMES STEPPS lower line..(WM. BAYS marked out..JOHN STAPP
written in). Entry No. 896.

2 March 1779.   WILLIAM DICKERSON e. 100 ac. on Reedy Branch of Kings
Creek in Brushey Mountain at the Rock House..(WM. DICKER-
SON marked out..THOS. DICKERSON written in). Entry No. 897.

2 March 1779.   ISAAC PARLIER e. 100 ac. waters Lewis Fork on Bells
branch. Entry No. 898.

2 March 1779.   MICAJAH PENINGTON e. 100 ac. on Elk Creek of New River..
below OSBURNS Mill place. Entry No. 899.

2 March 1779.   DANIEL RICHARDSON e. 200 ac. Hilton Creek of New River..a
branch below WALINGS Camp..(DANIEL RICHARDSON marked out..
WM. MCCLAINE written in). Entry No. 900.

2 March 1779.   BENJAMIN HAMBRICK e. 100 ac. branch Fishdam Creek..adjoin-
ing THOMAS LAXTON..(BENJ. HAMBRICK & JACOB MADKIFF marked
out..JOHN R. JOHNSON written in). Entry No. 901.

2 March 1779.   MANOAH DIER e. 100 ac. on the Bent joining lands of HUGH
MONTGOMERY below..BENJAMIN LAWS above. Entry No. 902.

2 March 1779.   ENOCH OSBURN e. 200 ac. on Elk Creek below his other entry.
Entry No. 903.

3 March 1779.   THOMAS LEWIS e. 100 ac. head Middle fork Lower Creek.
Entry No. 904.

3 March 1779.   THOMAS LEWIS e. 50 ac. middle fork Lower(?) Creek..head
Turkey Pen Branch..(THOS. LEWIS, THOS. NATHERLY marked
out..JOHNON LIVINGSTON written in). Entry No. 905.

3 March 1779.   DAVID LAWS e. 150 ac. both sides Middle fork Moravian
Creek. Entry No. 906.

3 March 1779.   THOMAS PAYNE, SR. e. 400 ac. head waters Peak Creek..
including land GEORGE MORRIS entered in ARMSTRONGS office.
Entry No. 907.

3 March 1779.   BENJAMIN ANGEL e. 50 ac. N side Elk Creek..mouth Millstone
Branch..joining HUGH MONTGOMERYS entry..including an Entry.
Entry No. 908.

3 March 1779.   STEPHEN TRIBBLE e. 100 ac. S side Naked Creek..joining
PERRIN CARDWELLS below..both sides new waggon road..
(STEPHEN TRIBBLE marked out..ISAAC ELLEDGE written in). Entry No. 909.

3 March 1779. HENRY MULLEN e. 100 ac. waters Reddies River..head Tumb-
              ling Shoal..including both sides Chesnut Mountain. Entry
No. 910.

4 March 1779. (erased) BAKER e. 50 ac. joining entry JAMES BOGGS made
              on N fork New River..(? BAKER & ANDREW BAKER marked out..
RICHARD SMITH written in). Entry No. 911.

4 March 1779. ROBERT JONES e. 50 ac. on Coltons branch below Plantation.
              Entry No. 912.

4 March 1779. LEONARD EATON e. 50 ac. on Beaver Creek at WILLIAM HUMPH-
              RIES line..(LEONARD EATON marked out..CLOSS TOMSON written
in). Entry No. 913.

4 March 1779. WILLIAM JACKSON e. 20 ac. branch below said JACKSONS
              improvement on Lewis Fork..(WM. JACKSON marked out..JO-
NATHAN TOMKENS written in). Entry No. 914.

4 March 1779. JOHN HAWKINS e. 120 ac. waters Mulberry Creek near FRANCIS
              BROWNS line..including HAWKINS improvement. Entry No.
915.

4 March 1779. JOHN HAWKINGS e. 100 ac. on Mulberry Creek..joining THOMAS
              ROBBINS line. Entry No. 916.

4 March 1779. AQUILER LOW e. 200 ac. waters Warriors Creek..including
              improvement where RICHARD BLOOD now lives..(AQUILER LOW
marked out..WM. GILL (MCGILL) written in). Entry No. 917.

4 March 1779. STEPHEN HARRIS e. 50 ac. S fork Hunting Creek at JOHN
              STANDLEYS line..down both sides creek..(STEPHEN HARRIS
marked out..JOBE COLE written in). Entry No. 918.

4 March 1779. ANDREW VANNOY e. 100 ac. waters Mulberry..S side joining
              EDWARD FINCH..(ANDREW VANNOY marked out..JOHN HALL written
in). Entry No. 919.

4 March 1779. JOHN DIER e. 250 ac. waters Warriors Creek at SAUNDERS
              path..including old burnt cabbins of BERRY LAWS. Entry
No. 920.

5 March 1779. BENJAMIN HERNDON e. 320 ac. both sides N fork Little
              Elk Creek..Big Crab Orchard..including BUNCHES Camps..
(BENJ. HERNDON marked out..BARNABAS EVENS written in). Entry No. 921.

5 March 1779. BENJAMIN HERNDON e. 300 ac. S side Little River..toward
              Rich Mountain. Entry No. 922.

5 March 1779. BENJAMIN HERNDON e. 200 ac. Great Elkin Creek..including
              an old cabbin..small improvement where THOMAS PARKS,
JUNR. formerly lived..(BENJ. HERNDON marked out..JOHN POE written in).
Entry No. 923.

5 March 1779. BENJAMIN HERNDON e. 400 ac. on Little River of New River..
              mouth Glady Creek..including the Great Bend. Entry No.
924.

5 March 1779. BENJAMIN HERNDON e. 200 ac. fork Pine Swamp..(BENJAMIN
              HERNDON marked out..WINDAL CROWIS written in). Entry No.
925.

5 March 1779. BENJAMIN HERNDON e. 300 ac. Little River..mouth Fletchers
              Creek..(BENJ. HERNDON marked out..CLEZBY COBB written in).
Entry No. 926.

8 March 1779.　GIBSON MAINARD e. 200 ac. E side Piney Branch..including
　　　　　　　　his improvement where he now lives..(GIBSON MAINARD
marked out..JOHN GATE written in).　Entry No. 927.

11 March 1779.　1st enterer erased completely to..e. 100 ac. at MATTHEW
　　　　　　　　FRANCIS line..little fork Lewis Fork..(BENJAMIN CLEVE-
LAND written in).　Entry No. 928.

11 March 1779.　1st enterer erased completely..e. 100 ac. at MATTHEW
　　　　　　　　FRANCIS line..little fork Lewis Fork..(BENJAMIN CLEVE-
LAND written in).　Entry No. 929.

11 March 1779.　CHARLES B--SEY e. 250 ac. waters Hunting Creek on Fall-
　　　　　　　　ing branch..including said B--SEYS improvement..(CHARLES
B--SEY marked out..BENJAMIN HERNDON & JOBE COAL marked out..SAMUEL
CRABTREE written in).　Entry No. 930.

11 March 1779.　OWIN WILLIAMS e. 50 ac. N fork Lewis Fork at MATTHEW
　　　　　　　　FRANCIS line..(OWIN WILLIAMS marked out..JOHN YATES
written in).　Entry No. 931.

11 March 1779.　WILLIAM ROBERTS e. 50 ac. little fork Lewis Fork..
　　　　　　　　(WILLIAM ROBERTS marked out..WILLIAM FLOID written in).
Entry No. 932.

11 March 1779.　JAMES CRANE e. 150 ac. on Yadkin waters..creek called
　　　　　　　　Fish-Dam.　Entry No. 933.

11 March 1779.　ISAAC ELLEDGE e. 320 ac. on Naked Creek & Lewis Fork..
　　　　　　　　joining PERIN CARDWELL..including spring called sinking
spring.　Entry No. 934.

11 March 1779.　PAUL PATRICK e. 320 ac. on Buffalow Creek of New River..
　　　　　　　　including his improvement..(PAUL PATRICK marked out..
GILES PARMELY written in).　Entry No. 935.

11 March 1779.　PAUL PATRICK e. 320 ac. head waters Naked Creek & Buffa-
　　　　　　　　low..including his improvement..(PAUL PATRICK marked out
..JAMES BAKER written in).　Entry No. 936.

11 March 1779.　GEORGE MORRIS e. 200 ac. near ridge path between head
　　　　　　　　Peak Creek & Cranberry Creek..(GEORGE MORRIS & GEORGE
BAKER marked out..transfaird by GEORGE BAKER to MORRIS BAKER written in).
Entry No. 937.

12 March 1779.　GEORGE MORRIS e. 150 ac. S side Praters Creek of New
　　　　　　　　River.　Entry No. 938.

12 March 1779.　GEORGE MORRIS e. 200 ac. E fork Praters Creek of New
　　　　　　　　River.　Entry No. 939.

12 March 1779.　JOSEPH MAKUY (MULKEY?) e. 100 ac. N side S fork New
　　　　　　　　River..near mouth Cranberry Creek.　Entry No. 940.

12 March 1779.　CHARLES GORDON e. 300 ac. at Great Falls of Cranberry
　　　　　　　　Creek.　Entry No. 941.

12 March 1779.　WILLIAM HUMPHRIES e. 100 ac. at line dividing WILLIAM
　　　　　　　　SCOTT and WILLIAM COLVARD on waters Beaver Creek towards
the Rich Mountain..(WM. HUMPHRIES & GEORGE MORRIS marked out..JOHN DICK
written in).　Entry No. 942.

12 March 1779.　JAMES MULKEY e. 100 ac. above mouth Praters Creek..in-
　　　　　　　　cluding the big Meadow.　Entry No. 943.

12 March 1779.　JOHN BROWN e. 100 ac. Bakers Branch below SHARPER BAKERS
　　　　　　　　improvement.　Entry No. 944.

12 March 1779. JOSEPH WRIGHT e. 100 ac. on Woottons Creek..including his improvement. Entry No. 945.

12 March 1779. 1st enterer erased completely..e. 100 ac. on Hunting Creek waters..including his improvement..(WILLIAM WIL-COCKS written in). Entry No. 946.

13 March 1779. JAMES HARVEL e. 50 ac. head waters N fork Hunting Creek on Brushey Mountain..including a small improvement made by LIAH MASON. Entry No. 947.

13 March 1779. WILLIAM LENOIR e. 100 ac. both sides Buffaloe Creek..a little above JOSEPH MCCORKLES line. Entry No. 948.

15 March 1779. TIMOTHY CHANDLOW e. 60 ac. on Brier Creek..joining PRICHET ALEXANDERS entry. Entry No. 949.

15 March 1779. JAMES HAGOOD e. 40 ac. waters Bryer Creek..joining W end PRITCHETT ALEXANDERS entry..(JAMES HAGOOD marked out.. PARTEN HAGOOD written in). Entry No. 950.

15 March 1779. JOHN COOK e. 150 ac. on Warriors creek..joining BEN BROWN ..under spur Brushey Mountain..extending towards the mtn. Entry No. 951.

17 March 1779. JOHN WILLIAM CROSTHWAIT e. 150 ac. on Cox's Knob of Brushey Mountain..on the County line. Entry No. 952.

18 March 1779. JOHN BARLOW e. 150 ac. in THOMAS CARLTONS line. Entry No. 953.

25 March 1779. WILLIAM TERREL LEWIS e. 400 ac. waters Middle..W forks of Swan Creek..small creek above THOMAS BECKNELS. Entry No. 954.

26 March 1779. JOHN SLONE e. 100 ac. S side Yadkin River..joining JOHN THRASHERS..including the improvement whereon he now lives..(JOHN SLONE marked out..RUBEN ROWLAND written in). Entry No. 955.

26 March 1779. BENJ. ELLEDGE e. 50 ac. under foot Ripskin Mountain.. large branch of Buffaloe on both sides..(BENJ. ELLEDGE marked out..WILLIAM LENOIR written in). Entry No. 956.

26 March 1779. BENJAMIN ELLEDGE e. 50 ac. on Buffaloe Creek..including upper Cane Brake..(BENJ. ELLEDGE marked out..WM. LENOIR written in). Entry No. 957.

26 March 1779. LAURENCE ROSS e. 40 ac. Warrier Creek..fork of Yadkin.. joining ROWLAND HONLEYS entry..(LAURENCE ROSS marked out..ABRAHAM A. STRINGE (STRANGE) written in). Entry No. 958.

29 March 1779. REUBEN EASTERS e. 640 ac. on ridge N side Elk..path leads Three Forks New River..including his improvement..(REUBEN EASTER & JOHN SELLERS marked out..WILLIAM MILLER written in). Entry No. 959.

29 March 1779. (?) RICE (?) e. 400 ac. on Ridge near DETENS cabin..both sides S fork New River..including plantation where (?) RICE (?) now lives..(? RICE ? marked out..DANIEL JOHNSON (JOHNSTON?) written in). Entry No. 960.

31 March 1779. ABRAHAM VANDERPOOL 4. 40 ac. on Elk above Cross Mountain. Entry No. 961.

31 March 1779.   ABRAHAM VANDERPOOL e. 40 ac. on Elk..(ABRAHAM VANDERPOOL
                 marked out..JOSEPH MOSS written in). Entry No. 963.

31 March 1779.   HENRY DUNCAN e. 40 ac. mouth Turkey branch near mouth
                 Kings Creek. Entry No. 964.

31 March 1779.   THOMAS SISK e. 200 ac. waters E fork Swan Creek called
                 Sims Creek..on the County line. Entry No. 965.

31 March 1779.   GEORGE REAVES e. 300 ac. S side New River..mouth Fiting
                 (Fighting) Creek..(GEORGE REAVES marked out..MOSES
TOLEVOR written in). Entry No. 966.

2 April 1779.   GEORGE GIBSON e. 60 ac. on New River..on the Virginia line
                 near mouth Dogg Creek..including his improvement. Entry
No. 967.

5 April 1779.   THOMAS JOHNSTON e. 120 ac. S side Yadkin River..on his
                 upper line of his other entry. Entry No. 968.

5 April 1779.   DANIEL WRIGHT e. 50 ac. below little falls Big Elkin.
                 Entry No. 969.

6 April 1779.   SAMUEL CARTER e. 100 ac. joining MICHAEL VANINCLES (VAN
                 WINCKLE) land on long branch. Entry No. 970.

6 April 1779.   SAMUEL CARTER e. 100 ac. on Wheatfield branch. Entry No.
                 971.

7 April 1779.   THOMAS EVINS e. 100 ac. Osburns branch..joining the
                 County line..(THOMAS EVINS marked out..JOHN WATSON written
in). Entry No. 972.

9 April 1779.   JESSE LAY e. 100 ac. between his entrys on Linvils Mill
                 Creek..(JESSE LAY marked out..EDWARD GRAYHAM written in).
Entry No. 973.

9 April 1779.   JESSE LAY e. 50 ac. on Elk Creek..joining JOHN HUDDLE-
                 STONES entry. Entry No. 974.

16 April 1779.   ISAAC GARRISON e. 50 ac. E fork Wheatleys Creek to
                 WOOLBANKS line. Entry No. 975.

19 April 1779.   JOHN YATES e. 100 ac. N fork Lewis Fork..mouth branch
                 near head..(JOHN YATES marked out..WILLIAM FLOID written
in). Entry No. 976.

19 April 1779.   JOHN YATES e. 50 ac. waters Lewis Fork above BENJAMIN
                 CLEVELANDS entry..(Entry withdrawn by the enterer..(also)
..entry cross-marked out. Entry No. 977.

21 April 1779.   LEONARD MILLER e. 50 ac. on Mulberry Creek..joining
                 CHARLES HICKERSONS lower corner..(LEONARD MILLER marked
out..DAVID HICKERSON written in). Entry No. 978.

22 April 1779.   THOMAS WILSON e. 400 ac. on Cub Creek above the improve-
                 ment..including his improvement. Entry No. 979.

22 April 1779.   WILLIAM WRIGHT e. 100 ac. on branch Cub Creek on THOMAS
                 WILSONS line. Entry No. 980.

23 April 1779.   SAMUEL TATE e. 200 ac. on Cow Camp..fork New River..
                 (SAM'L TATE marked out..JOHN BROWN written in). Entry
No. 981.

23 April 1779. SAMUEL TATE e. 100 ac. some head waters N fork New River
                ..top high mtn...S side road leads from New River to
Roans Creek..including RUSSELS Camp..(SAMUEL TATE marked out..JOHN BROWN
written in). Entry No. 982.

23 April 1779. SAMUEL TATE e. 100 ac. head waters N fork New River at
                the Washington County line..including DENTONS Camp..
(SAMUEL TATE marked out..JOHN BROWN written in). Entry No. 983.

23 April 1779. ELIJAH ISAACS e. 100 ac. large Branch enptyeth into
                Buffalow..W side Ripskin. Entry No. 984.

27 April 1779. THOMAS BUNTING e. 100 ac. branch emptyeth into New River
                ..including his improvement..(THOMAS BUNTING marked out..
EDWARD GRAHAM written in). Entry No. 985.

1 May 1779. JOHN HUDDLESTON e. 50 ac. on Elk Creek..upper end his other
             entry. Entry No. 986.

1 May 1779. JOHN VANDERPOOL e. 50 ac. Jones's Branch..Elk Creek below
             improvement that DURHAM lives on..(JOHN VANDERPOOL marked
out..JOAL VANDERPOOL written in). Entry No. 987.

1 May 1779. JOHN VANDERPOOL e. 50 ac. N fork Long Branch..Elk Creek near
             foard where path crosses. Entry No. 988.

10 May 1779. JOHN BROWN e. 100 ac. Fish Dam Creek..joining entry made
              by THOMAS LAXTON. Entry No. 989.

10 May 1779. HUGH MONTGOMERY e. 150 ac. on Fish Dam Creek..upper end
              CRANES entry. Entry No. 990.

10 May 1779. HARRIS STANDLEY e. 100 ac. Meadow Branch..first fork of
              JAMES BROWNS Mill Creek..waters Hunting Creek..(HARRIS
STANDLEY marked out..JOB COLE written in). Entry No. 991.

29 May 1779. WILLIAM LENOIR e. 100 ac. N side Yadkin River..joining
              ELIJAH ISAACS land..WILLIAM SNODDEYS land on Buffaloe
Creek. Entry No. 992.

29 May 1779. JOHN BARTON e. 100 ac. waters Yadkin..S side at his former
              entry. Entry No. 993.

29 May 1779. ELIJAH ISAACS e. 300 ac. S side Yadkin River between
              WILLIAM GUEST..the mountain at his and TATES corner..in-
cluding both sides fort branch. Entry No. 994.

29 May 1779. ELIJAH ISAACS e. 100 ac. waters Yadkin at MCCORKLES &
              GUESTS corner..to BARTONS line. Entry No. 995.

29 May 1779. SPENCER HUMPHRIES e. 100 ac. S side Deep Gap..(SPENCER &
              JOSEPH HUMPHRIES marked out..ELIJAM WILLIAMS written in).
Entry No. 996.

29 May 1779. SPENCER HUMPHRIES e. 150 ac. on Beaver Creek under Buck
              Mtn...above COLVERDS..(SPENCER & JOSEPH HUMPHRIES & ROLAND
JUDD marked out..GEORGE BAROGON (BARDGON ?) written in). Entry No. 997.

1 June 1779. SAMUEL BIRDINE e. 100 ac. on Meadow Branch..waters Readys River..joining JONATHAN WALLS entry. Entry No. 998.

1 June 1779. CHARLES CREANSHAW e. 300 ac. Brushey Mountain..on waters Hunting Creek..joining JOSEPH HERNDONS entry. Entry No. 999.

1 June 1779. WILLIAM CORNELOUS e. 100 ac. waters Little River near Spring..including part Glady fork waters..(WM. CORNELOUS marked out..CHARLES CATE written in). Entry No. 1000.

1 June 1779. WILLIAM CORNELIUS e. 100 ac. on Graves Creek..lower end his other survey..(WM. CORNELIUS marked out..ROBERT KING written in). Entry No. 1001.

1 June 1779. RANDOLPH MABERY e. 500 ac. waters Hunting Creek..N side ABRAHAM COOKS former entry..near County line..including vacant land betwixt the entries of said ABRAHAM COOK, WILLIAM WILLCOX, JENKINS REYNOLDS & PETER GOODE. Entry No. 1002.

3 June 1779. WILLIAM TERREL LEWIS e. 640 ac. top of Ridge at QUEENS path..including CALLOWAYS Camp..(WM. T. LEWIS marked out.. THOMAS TERREY written in). Entry No. 1003.

3 June 1779. WILLIAM TERRELL LEWIS e. 400 ac. head branch Obeds Creek to head Bear Creek..(WM. T. LEWIS marked out..BETTEY SANDRIDGE written in). Entry No. 1004.

3 June 1779. WILLIAM TERRELL LEWIS e. 200 ac. Top of Ridge at the Hunters Path one half mile from OWENS camp..including the springs..(WM. T. LEWIS marked out..THOMAS CARR written in). Entry No. 1005.

5 June 1779. MATTHEW FRANCIS e. 100 ac. near head small branch of Lewis Fork. Entry No. 1006.

5 June 1779. JOHN HARMON e. 100 ac. Ridge divides LITTLEBERRY TONEYS entry and JOHN HARMONS. Entry No. 1007.

9 June 1779. BENJAMIN HERNDON e. 500 ac. both sides OSBURNS path on the Virginia line..including some waters of Potato Creek and Elk Creek. Entry No. 1008.

9 June 1779. BENJAMIN HERNDON e. 160 ac. Long Branch Elk below old WASTE Cabbin..formerly property of PETER GUIN..(BENJ. HERNDON withdraws entry). Entry No. 1009.

9 June 1779. BENJAMIN HERNDON e. 200 ac. on Ready Branch..waters of Yadkin. Entry No. 1010.

9 June 1779. 1st enterer erased completely..e. 100 ac. both sides Kings Creek..joining above his former entry that joined EPH. COXES and JAMES EHIYDON..(HENRY ISBELL marked out..JOHN BARLOW, JUNR. written in). Entry No. 1011.

9 June 1779. JOHN LIVINGSTON e. 140 ac. head waters Bever Creek..joining THOMAS LAND & THOMAS COLLENS line..including his improvement. Entry No. 1012.

9 June 1779. 1st enterer erased completely..e. 100 ac. on Kings Creek.. joining EPHRAIM COX & BENJAMIN ELLEDGE..including his improvement..(ROBERT NETHERLY marked out..JAMES WALLIS written in). Entry No. 1013.

9 June 1779. ANDREW TATE e. 50 ac. S side Yadkin River joining JOHN THRASHERS. Entry No. 1014.

9 June 1779.   ANDREW TATE e. 50 ac. branch divides WILLIAM GUEST & TATE.
               Entry No. 1015.

9 June 1779.   LIVINGSTON ISBELL e. 100 ac. branch Beaver Creek..joining
               JOHN WILLIAM WHITE & ISBELLS line. Entry No. 1016.

9 June 1779.   THOMAS CALTON e. 100 ac. near Top Brushey Mountain..under
               Cox's Nob..including heads of some branches Kings Creek &
Little River. Entry No. 1017.

9 June 1779.   JOHN HUDDLESTON e. 50 ac. branch of Elk Creek against
               BEANS Cabbin..between mouth said branch and Cabbin called
PETERS cabbin. Entry No. 1018.

9 June 1779.   FRANCIS VANNOY e. 100 ac. Bear Creek..N side New River..
               mouth Sugar Tree Branch above WILLIAM COLVARDS..joining
his upper line. Entry No. 1019.

9 June 1779.   FRANCIS VANNOY e. 100 ac. S Beaver Creek..near path goes
               from WILLIAM COLVARDS to Old Fields. Entry No. 1020.

9 June 1779.   BENJAMIN PENINGTON e. 50 ac. Elk Creek at ROBERTS OBARRS
               line. Entry No. 1021.

9 June 1779.   BENJAMIN HERNDON e. 300 ac. N side Yadkin River..joining
               entry where he lives. Entry No. 1022.

9 June 1779.   ELISHA REYNOLDS e. 100 ac. head Camp branch..S side Roaring
               River..near FRANCIS REYNOLDS upper line..including head of
branch..(ELISHA REYNOLDS marked out..JOHN BURK written in). Entry No.
1023.

9 June 1779.   GIBSON STAPP e. 50 ac. one forks Kings Creek at LAWRENCE
               BRADLEYS upper line..(GIBSON STAPP marked out..DAVID
CONSTABLE written in). Entry No. 1024.

9 June 1779.   JOILES PARMELY e. 100 ac. Brushey fork Little River..in-
               cluding his improvement..(JOILES PARMELY marked out..
THOMAS ENDICOTT written in). Entry No. 1025.

10 June 1779. GEORGE BREWER e. 100 ac. S side Yadkin River..joining
               CHESLEY COCKRAMS..including improvement whereon he now
lives. Entry No. 1026.

10 June 1779. JOSEPH HUMPHRIES e. 200 ac. N fork Meat Camp..(JOSEPH
               and SPENCER HUMPHRIES & WILLIAM MILLER marked out..JOSEPH
HAGAMAN written in). Entry No. 1027.

10 June 1779. SOLOMON CROSS e. 100 ac. top Brushey Mountain on Cedar
               Knob..including the good land between said Knob and
ELLIOT Gap..(SOLOMON CROSS marked out..ROGER BISHIP written in). Entry
No. 1028.

10 June 1779. JOHN BANKS e. 80 ac. waters Yadkin near fork Husors (?)
               Branch..including the good land on both sides said branch
..(JOHN BANKS marked out..JOSHUA HAWKINS written in). Entry No. 1029.

11 June 1779. WILLIAM SAWYER e. 50 ac. including his improvement. Entry
               No. 1030.

11 June 1779. 1st enterer erased completely..e. 50 ac. Big Branch N
               side Elk Creek below JOHN HUDDLESTONS..including the
improvement..(JOHN HUDDLESTON written in). Entry No. 1031.

11 June 1779. LEVI JACKSON e. 50 ac. Ready Branch..including what they
               call TOM ELLISONS Cabbin..(LEVI JACKSON marked out..THOMAS
ELLISON written in). Entry No. 1032.

12 June 1779.   JOSEPH HERNDON e. 200 ac. Mulberry Creek just below said
                HERNDONS entry he bought of JESSE TOLOVER. Entry No.
1033.

12 June 1779.   JOSEPH HERNDON e. 200 ac. branch Mulberry Creek known by
                name of Haymeadow..including a cabin. Entry No. 1034.

12 June 1779.   MOSES TOLOVER e. 100 ac. branch Mulberry Creek below
                JESSE TOLOVERS lower corner..to ridge road. Entry No.
1035.

15 June 1779.   WILLIAM SMITH e. 150 ac. N side Yadkin River..near road
                leads to Reddies River..including heads of branches..(WM.
SMITH marked out..JERIMIAH CRISEL written in). Entry No. 1036.

16 June 1779.   JOHN BOWMAN e. 400 ac. at LAWRENCE ROSS'S line..up both
                forks Warrior Creek..(JOHN BOWMAN marked out..JAMES BLARE
written in). Entry No. 1037.

19 June 1779.   EDMOND TILLY e. 150 ac. at a condt. line between BENJAMIN
                GRAYSON and said EDMOND TILLY. Entry No. 1038.

19 June 1779.   EDMOND TILLEY e. 100 ac. top of Bruahey Mountain..includ-
                ing head waters N fork Kings Creek. Entry No. 1038.

19 June 1779.   THOMAS ELLEDGE e. 50 ac. Reedy Branch..waters Stoney Fork
                ..near Rockey sholes..including the good land up said
branch..(THOMAS ELLEDGE & JOHN GRAY marked out..WILLIAM ADAMS written
in). Entry No. 1039.

19 June 1779.   WILLIAM BANKS e. 50 ac. waters Naked Creek..including the
                improvement. Entry No. 1040.

19 June 1779.   DAVID WITHERSPOON e. 100 ac. said WITHERSPOONS line..
                including branches Kings Creek..(DAVID WITHERSPOON marked
out..JAMES PAGGETT written in). Entry No. 1041.

21 June 1779.   GIBSON STEPP e. 200 ac. between head Howards Creek and
                Meat Camp Creek..including the improvement..(GIBSON STEPP
& AARON MASH marked out..JAMES BROWN written in). Entry No. 1042.

21 June 1779.   LEVI JACKSON e. 50 ac. Glady Creek that runs into Stoney
                fork. Entry No. 1043.

21 June 1779.   LEVI JACKSON e. 50 ac. branch runs into New River..includ-
                ing SAM DECONS (?) improvement. Entry No. 1044.

21 June 1779.   GIBSON STEPP e. 200 ac. New River..ridge between Howards
                Creek and his improvement..(GIBSON STEPP marked out..
ROBERT AYEARS written in). Entry No. 1045.

21 June 1779.   THOMAS ELLISON e. 50 ac. on Reedy Branch..N side Yadkin
                River. Entry No. 1046.

21 June 1779.   THOMAS ELLISON e. 50 ac. on N fork Beaver Creek called
                Longfork said creek..(THOMAS ELLISON marked out..JOHN
NORRIS written in). Entry No. 1047.

21 June 1779.   ALEXANDER POOR e. 200 ac. N fork Lewis Fork. Entry No.
                1048.

21 June 1779.   THOMAS WITHERSPOON e. 50 ac. on Kings Creek. Entry No.
                1049.

22 June 1779.   THOMAS WITHERSPOON e. 100 ac. on a branch said WITHER-
                SPOONS line. Entry No. 1050.

22 June 1779. THOMAS WITHERSPOON e. 100 ac. Kings Creek above said
WITHERSPOONS line. Entry No. 1051.

22 June 1779. BENJAMIN HERNDON e. 100 ac. on Salt Log Branch..waters
Roaring River..upper line of Entry WILLIAM TOLOVER made.
Entry No. 1052.

22 June 1779. THOMAS JONES e. 100 ac. on Chestnut mountain..old Mill
Creek. Entry No. 1053.

23 June 1779. THOMAS JONES e. 100 ac. N side N fork Reddies River above
LUKE FIELDS. Entry No. 1054.

23 June 1779. CHARLES BURNS (?) e. 100 ac. land on Elk Creek at DAVID
ALLENS lower line..(CHARLES BURNS marked out..NATHAN
STANBURY written in). Entry No. 1055.

26 June 1779. WILLIAM LENOIR e. 150 ac. both sides Buffalo Creek of
New River..on path that leads to BAKERS Settlement. Entry
No. 1056.

26 June 1779. JOSEPH HOPKINS e. 200 ac. on Roaring River..(JOSEPH HOP-
KINS marked out..JAMES ISBELL, SR. written in). Entry No.
1057.

29 June 1779. HENRY TILLEY e. 100 ac. fork road runs S to EPHRAM COXS
line..including improvement whereon HENRY TILLEY now
lives..(HENRY TILLEY marked out..JAMES ISBELL, SR. written in). Entry
No. 1058.

30 June 1779. BURWELL BREWER e. 100 ac. on Naked Creek..between PAUL
PATRICKS line..including Rich Cove at N end Negro Moun-
tain..(BURWELL BREWER marked out..CHRISTEFOR SHAN (?) written in). Entry
No. 1059.

30 June 1779. NICHOLAS CHAPMAN e. 100 ac. waters Hunting Creek near WM.
MITCHELS line..including an improvement made by THOMAS
DAVIS. Entry No. 1060.

6 July 1779. OWEN WILLIAMS e. 100 ac. fork Beaver Creek joining NATHAN-
IEL VANNOYS line. Entry No. 1061.

30 June 1779. BURWELL BREWER e. 100 ac. fork Naked Creek..(Entry withdrawn). Entry No. 1062.

6 July 1779. BENJ. ELLEDGE e. 200 ac. joining GEORGE BOON, LAZARUS
SUMMERLIN, WM. MCGILL & ISAAC ELLEDGES. Entry No. 1063.

8 July 1779. ISAAC ELLEDGE e. 150 ac. both sides N fork Lewis Fork..at
lower end maple swamp somewhere in line..tract entered by
HUGH MONTGOMERY..where THOMAS CALLAWAY formerly lived..now transferred
by LAWRENCE TOMPSON to BENJAMIN CLEVELAND..down said fork to BERRY
TONEYS line..(ISAAC ELLEDGE marked out..JOHN CLEVELAND written in).
Entry No. 1064.

8 July 1779. BENJAMIN CLEVELAND e. 200 ac. both sides small branch..S
side Little Elkin. Entry No. 1065.

8 July 1779. BENJAMIN CLEVELAND e. 200 ac. N side Lewis Fork..lower
corner his other entry..(BENJ. CLEVELAND marked out..JOHN
CLEVELAND written in). Entry No. 1066.

8 July 1779. BENJAMIN CLEVELAND e. 300 ac. on Lewis Fork..lower end his
other entry. Entry No. 1067.

8 July 1779. BENJAMIN CLEVELAND e. 100 ac. waters Buffaloe Creek of
New River..joining his other entry..(BENJ. CLEVELAND marked
out..HANDREW BAKER written in). Entry No. 1068.

8 July 1779. BENJAMIN CLEVELAND e. 320 ac. fork Buggaboe Creek..includ-
ing both sides both forks. Entry No. 1069.

8 July 1779. BENJAMIN CLEVELAND e. 300 ac. N side Yadkin River..lower
corner of the round about tract. Entry No. 1070.

8 July 1779. ISAAC ELLEDGE e. 100 ac. branch Warrior Creek..joining
THOMAS ELLOTS & BENJAMIN ELLEDGES entry..(ISAAC ELLEDGE
marked out..MATHEW WALKER written in). Entry No. 1071.

8 July 1779. WILLIAM FLETCHER e. 150 ac. waters Bryer Creek at TIMOTHY
CHANDLOWS line near long branch..(WM. FLETCHER marked out
..WM. COLVARD, SR. written in). Entry No. 1072.

14 July 1779. LAZARUS TILLEY e. 100 ac. Chesnut Knob..including head
waters creek at bent of New River..(TILLEY marked out..
JESSE CONNELL written in). Entry No. 1073.

21 July 1779. GEORGE WHEATLEY e. 100 ac. on Dogg Creek of New River..
adjoining WILLIAM RAYS entry. Entry No. 1074.

21 July 1779. GEORGE WHEATLEY e. 100 ac. on Camp Branch..fork Roaring
River..above lower falls. Entry No. 1075.

26 July 1779. WILLIAM NALL e. 300 ac. N fork New River..including
Plantation GIDION LEWIS and EDWARD KING now lives on..
(Entry withdrawn by consent). Entry No. 1076.

26 July 1779. WILLIAM NALL e. 300 ac. on Elk Creek..near head creek..
including plantation whereon MICAJAH BUNCH now lives..
(Entry withdrawn by consent). Entry No. 1077.

26 July 1779. WILLIAM NALL e. 300 ac. Mitchels River..lower end bottom
whereon JAMES WALING now lives..including plantation
WALING lives..(Entry withdrawn by consent). Entry No. 1078.

26 July 1779. WILLIAM NALL e. 200 ac. S fork New River..near mouth Peak
Creek..including plantation whereon HUGH SMITH now lives..
(entry withdrawn). Entry No. 1079.

26 July 1779. MARTIN GAMBILL e. 300 ac. on New River..lower end bottom
..including plantation whereon MICAJAH PENINGTON now
lives..(Entry withdrawn). Entry No. 1080.

26 July 1779. MARTIN GAMBILL e. 200 ac. S fork New River..including
plantation whereon VINCENT JONES now lives. Entry No.
1081.

26 July 1779. CARLTON KEELING e. 75 ac. on Hunting Creek above STEPHEN
SOUTHER..(CARLTON KEELING & MIAHAEL SOUTHER marked out..
HENRY SOUTHER written in). Entry No. 1082.

26 July 1779. REZON BAKER e. 100 ac. on draughts of Hunting Creek at
ABRAHAM SAUNDERS line..N to County line..(REZON BAKER
marked out..JOHN LUNSFORD written in). Entry No. 1083.

26 July 1779. SOLOMON CROSS e. 25 ac. N side Yadkin River..first branch
below falls..(SOLOMON CROSS marked out..ROGER BUSHIP
(BISHOP) written in). Entry No. 1084.

26 July 1779.   JOHN VICKERS e. 100 ac. N side S fork New River..first
                Bluff point of Peaks..above mouth Beaver Creek. Entry No.
1085.

27 July 1779.   JAMES FLETCHER e. 300 ac. N side New River above ZACK
                WELLS..(MICAJAH PENINGTON marked out..entire entry marked
out). Entry No. 1086.

NOTE: On a separate paper bound within the pages of this book is this
       entry. No date..BENNAJAH PENNINGTON e. 100 ac. on Martins Branch
..some waters New River..including improvement whereon WILLIAM SPENCER
lives. Entry No. 1086.

27 July 1779.   ELIJAH PENINGTON e. 100 ac. on Grassy Creek of New River
                ..below Old WILLIAM PENNINGTONS lower line..including
Mill Seate..(ELIJAH PENINGTON marked out..JAMES FLETCHER written in).
Entry No. 1087.

No Date.   JOHN HENSON e. 150 ac. between old MR. HENSON and his son..
           including all the good land between said line. Entry No. 1088.

27 July 1779.   JAMES FLETCHER e. 100 ac. N fork New River above MR.
                WEAVERS..including a Rich bottom..(JAMES FLETCHER marked
out..BENNAJAH PENNINGTON written in). Entry No. 1088.

27 July 1779.   JOHN CARGILE e. 150 ac. on waters Bryer Creek near his
                former entry. Entry No. 1089.

28 July 1779.   EBENEZER FAIRCHILD e. 30 ac. lone Branch S fork Lewis
                Fork..at FAIRCHILDS former entry. Entry No. 1090.

28 July 1779.   JOHN SMITH e. 150 ac. at JOHN MILLERS old path where it
                crosses Reddies River..road above GEORGE GORDONS..toward
THOMAS HOPPER..(JOHN SMITH marked out..GEORGE GORDON written in). Entry
No. 1091.

29 July 1779.   OWIN WILLIAMS e. 50 ac. at ROBERT WATERS line down Beaver
                Creek. Entry No. 1092.

29 July 1779.   JOSEPH HUMPHRIES e. 200 ac. on Meat Camp Creek..at upper
                line JOHN BROWN..(JOSEPH & SPENCER HUMPHRIES marked out..
WILLIAM MILLER written in). Entry No. 1093.

29 July 1779.   BAILY CHANDLOW e. 50 ac. on EDMONS CROSS'S line. Entry
                No. 1094.

30 July 1779.   JOHN JOHNSTON e. 200 ac. joining WILLIAM HUMPHRIES former
                entry on waters Naked Creek. Entry No. 1095.

2 Aug. 1779.   JOHN JOHNSTON e. 100 ac. S side S fork New River..mouth
                Roans Creek..ROBERT BAKERS entry. Entry No. 1096.

2 Aug. 1779.   JOSEPH PERKINS e. 150 ac. Wilkes County..(PERKINS marked
                out..JAMES FLETCHER written in). Entry No. 1097.

2 Aug. 1779.   JOSEPH HOLT e. 100 ac. waters Kings Creek near County
                line..along JOEL COFFEES line. Entry No. 1098.

3 Aug. 1779.   BAILEY CHANDLOW e. 125 ac. at URIAH HARDIMANS corner..one
                WILLIAM JOHNSTONS line. Entry No. 1099.

3 Aug. 1779.   WILLIAM CANADY (KENNEDY) e. 150 ac. on Big Elkin..upper
               end of entry CANADY had of SAMUEL MONEY. Entry No. 1100.

3 Aug. 1779.   RANDOLPH ALEXANDER e. 100 ac. mouth Stewarts Creek on
               Roaring River. Entry No. 1101.

4 Aug. 1779.   ROBERT KIRKPATRICK e. 100 ac. both sides Yadkin between
               upper and lower Dark Bottom..including dry ford at fork
of River. Entry No. 1102.

4 Aug. 1779.   JOHN PARKER e. 100 ac. head first branch above RODDIN
               THOMPSON old improvement as you go from AMBROUS CRAINS to
BURKS old Mill. Entry No. 1103.

4 Aug. 1779.   JOHN M. C. QUARY e. 100 ac. below THOMAS OWENS spring..
               said OWENS Mill Creek. Entry No. 1104.

4 Aug. 1779.   BENJAMIN HOWARD e. 50 ac. N side Yadkin River..joining his
               former entry..including mouth Reedy Branch. Entry No.
1105.

4 Aug. 1779.   WILLIAM NALL e. 250 ac. on New River..below JAMES LEWIS..
               including said LEWIS plantation..(Entry withdrawn by the
enterer). Entry No. 1106.

4 Aug. 1779.   RICHARD WOOLBANKS e. 50 ac. on Stewarts Creek..HENRY BYRAMS
               (BRYOM) corner. Entry No. 1107.

5 Aug. 1779.   FRANCIS REYNOLDS e. 150 ac. waters little River..including
               a small improvement made by WILLIAM HILL. Entry No. 1108.

5 Aug. 1779.   FRANCIS REYNOLDS e. 150 ac. waters little River..including
               TAYLORS camp. Entry No. 1109.

7 Aug. 1779.   JOHN PARKER e. 50 ac. Fishes Creek at RICHARD CHANDLOWS
               corner..STEPHEN HARRIS'S corner. Entry No. 1110.

7 Aug. 1779.   WILLIAM ROBINSON e. 200 ac. upper side Meat Camp Creek.
               Entry No. 1111.

7 Aug. 1779.   FRANCIS VANNOY e. 100 ac. about 100 yards below mouth first
               branch on W fork Roaring River. Entry No. 1112.

7 Aug. 1779.   JOHN TURNBILL e. 150 ac. adjoining his late survey called
               the MCCUBBINS place. Entry No. 1113.

7 Aug. 1779.   JOHN TURNBILL e. 150 ac. N corner his land to the main
               road. Entry No. 1114.

7 Aug. 1779.   JOHN TURNBILL e. 100 ac. waters Bryer Creek to main road.
               Entry No. 1115.

7 Aug. 1779.   JOSEPH HORTON e. 100 ac. JAMES HAGOODS line..both sides
               road. Entry No. 1116.

9 Aug. 1779.   CARLTON KEELING e. 100 ac. on Fishes Creek at JAMES CRAINES
               line..(CARLTON KEELING & WM. MORRISON marked out..ALEXANDER
MORRISON written in). Entry No. 1117.

9 Aug. 1779.   WILLIAM FLETCHER e. 50 ac. waters Bryer Creek at PRITCHETT
               ALEXANDERS line. Entry No. 1118.

10 Aug. 1779. WILLIAM NALL e. 200 ac. S fork New River above field
               where on MR. MASON (?) lives..including improvement..
(Caveated by JOSHUA NICHOLS or NICHOLAS..Entry withdrawn by the enterer).
Entry No. 1119.

10 Aug. 1779. VOLUNTINE NUTTERVILLE e. 70 ac. big branch Cub Creek at
said NUTTERVILLES old line..SAMUEL WILCOXSONS line..along
JOHN GREERS line..(Entry withdrawn by enterer). Entry No. 1120.

14 Aug. 1779. BENJAMIN GLOVER e. 200 ac. LUKE LEES Creek..near path
crosses said creek that goes from CRANES to SUTTONS.
Entry No. 1121.

14 Aug. 1779. THOMAS ELLEDGE & JOHN BROWN, partnership. e. 400 ac.
waters New River and Elk Creek at the Yadkin..near
REUBIN EASTERGES upper line..including Allen's Knob. Entry No. 1122.

14 Aug. 1779. ABRAHAM ELLEDGE e. 50 ac. New River near Fire Springs..
including the good land on each side path leads from TIM
PERKINS to CUTHBERTHS Cabin on top mtn...head Lewis Fork..(ABRAHAM
ELLEDGE marked out..ROWLAND JUDD written in). Entry No. 1123.

14 Aug. 1779. GEORGE MORRIS e. 50 ac. S side New River on NICHOLAS
ANGLES lower line..including improvement whereon ROBERT
BAKER now lives..(GEO. MORRIS, WM. HUMPHRIES & LENARD EATON marked out..
JAMES BUNYARD written in). Entry No. 1124.

14 Aug. 1779. REUBIN STRINGER e. 100 ac. S fork New River..E side New
River..(REUBIN STRINGSER marked out..DANIEL JOHNSTON
written in). Entry No. 1125.

14 Aug. 1779. JAMES BROWN e. 125 ac. Pipe Camp branch..joining his own
entry. Entry No. 1126.

16 Aug. 1779. MATTHEW SPARKS e. 250 ac. S of N fork (no stream mentioned)..(MATTHEW SPARKS & WM. MCCLAINE marked out..JAMES
KING written in). Entry No. 1127.

16 Aug. 1779. LAZARUS TILLEY e. 50 ac. S fork New River..(LAZAURS TILLEY
marked out..JAMES TOMKINS written in). Entry No. 1128.

16 Aug. 1779. 1st enterer unreadable..e. 100 ac. both sides Hunting
Creek between REDDIN TOMPSONS & ISAAC PATES (?)..including
past improvement ABNER BAKER lately lived..(JOHN HUNT written in). Entry
No. 1129.

16 Aug. 1779. JOHN SCURLEY (?) e. 100 ac. on New River..(JOHN SCURLEY
(?) marked out..SAMUEL MCQUEEN written in). Entry No.
1130.

18 Aug. 1779. JOHN PROPHET e. 100 ac. waters Yadkin River..to join
JAMES FLETCHERS line. Entry No. 1131.

21 Aug. 1779. JAMES GARRISON e. 150 ac. Pipe Camp Creek at JAMES BROWNS
line. Entry No. 1132.

21 Aug. 1779. ISAAC ELLEDGE e. 200 ac: on Warrior Creek at Mill Sholes
..including GEORGE BROWNS improvement..joining GEORGE
BROWNS line..(ISAAC ELLEDGE marked out..HANKINS JOHNATHAN written in).
Entry No. 1133.

23 Aug. 1779. ELIJAH DIER e. 100 ac. waters Warrior Creek..adjoining
entry he bought of ISAAC WALKER W side. Entry No. 1134.

23 Aug. 1779. CHARLES ROWLAND e. 400 ac. on MARTIN MAINS & JOSHAUA
TATES improvements N side N fork New River..into Grassy
Creek. Entry No. 1135.

23 Aug. 1779. JOSEPH HORTON e. 100 ac. adjoining his other entry.
Entry No. 1136.

23 Aug. 1779. BETHUEL RIGGS e. 50 ac. branch Lewis Fork..said branch puts out of S side Chesnut Spur of Blue Ridge..(BOTHUEL RIGGS marked out..JAMES FLETCHER written in..(also)..transfered to JAMES FLETCHER). Entry No. 1137.

24 Aug. 1779. EDWARD FINCH e. 150 ac. including some waters of Phenix Mtn..(EDWARD FINCH marked out..JAMES FLETCHER written in). Entry No. 1138.

25 Aug. 1779. JOHN ELLEDGE e. 100 ac. waters New River near CUTHBRAITHS plantation..including good land on both sides path leads to the Old Fields on New River. Entry No. 1139.

25 Aug. 1779. JAMES FLETCHER e. 300 ac. fork Little River at mouth of Brushey Creek. Entry No. 1140.

25 Aug. 1779. THOMAS (?) e. 100 ac. on waters Hunting Creek..N side Mill Creek near road leads from JACOB PARKS to THOMAS ROBERTS..(THOMAS (?) marked out..ROBERT WHITAKER written in). Entry No. 1141.

27 Aug. 1779. THOMAS ROBINS e. 100 ac. on said ROBBINS Mill Creek. Entry No. 1142.

27 Aug. 1779. THOMAS ROBBINS e. 200 ac. on said ROBBINS Mill Creek. Entry No. 1143.

27 Aug. 1779. THOMAS ROBBINS e. 50 ac. branch Mulberry below an improvement that is called ROBINS, ROBINS, & so (?). Entry No. 1144.

28 Aug. 1779. ROBERT KING e. 600 ac. on Big Bushey fork Creek of New River..(ROBERT KING & CLISBY COBB marked out..WM. LENOIR written in). Entry No. 1145.

28 Aug. 1779. WILLIAM LEWIS e. 50 ac. Hunting Creek. Entry No. 1146.

30 Aug. 1779. BAZIL BAKER e. 100 ac. on draughts of Hunting Creek..on JAMES BROWNS line..including his improvement..(BAZIL BAKER marked out..MARYANN BEARD written in). Entry No. 1147.

1 Sept. 1779. SAMUEL SIMPSON e. 50 ac. on SLONES line. Entry No. 1148.

1 Sept. 1779. JOHN ROBERTS e. 50 ac. on Little Fork Lewis Fork..upper end line that COLO. CLEVELAND bought of JOHN TIREY (?). Entry No. 1149.

3 Sept. 1779. WILLIAM MCCLAINE e. 200 ac. N fork New River..including improvement where DUTTEN SWEETEN & MOSES SMITH now lives. Entry No. 1150.

4 Sept. 1779. JAMES FLETCHER e. 150 ac. below mouth Pine Creek..N fork N side New River..(JAMES FLETCHER & JOHN FLANNERY marked out..EDWARD PENINGTON written in). Entry No. 1151.

4 Sept. 1779. JAMES FLETCHER e. 300 ac. New River above ZACK WELLS.. (JAMES FLETCHER marked out..MICAJAH PENINGTON, JUNR. written in). Entry No. 1152.

4 Sept. 1779. JAMES FLETCHER e. 200 ac. N fork New River at JAMES WARDS upper line..including all the good land both sides river.. (JAMES FLETCHER marked out..WILLIAM YADKINS (ADKINS?) written in). Entry No. 1153.

4 Sept. 1779. THOMAS COLIAR e. 100 ac. on Haw branch..waters Roaring River. Entry No. 1154.

4 Sept. 1779. THOMAS HAMMON e. 100 ac. waters Roaring River..joining
WILLIAM HARGUS line..(THOMAS HAMMON marked out..MOSES
WOODRUFF written in). Entry No. 1154.

4 Sept. 1779. 1st enterer not readable..e. 100 ac. N side S fork New
River..(1st enterer, WM. RIGHT, LITTLEBERRY TONEY & SAMUEL
CARTER marked out..THOMAS CALLOWAY marked out..but written in again).
Entry No. 1155.

4 Sept. 1779. JAMES S------ (?) e. 300 ac. Little fork Beaver Creek..
(JAMES S------ & DAVID MITCHEL marked out..WILLIAM BRAD-
BERRY written in). Entry No. 1156.

4 Sept. 1779. 1st enterer not readable..e. 50 ac. on New River..(1st
enterer, SAMUEL CARTER, THOMAS CALLOWAY & BENJAMIN WRIGHT
marked out..LENVIL WASHBUN written in). Entry No. 1157.

No date. MACAJAH PININGTON, SENR. e. 150 ac. N fork New River..mouth
Sileses Creek. Entry No. 1157.

6 Sept. 1779. WILLIAM HUMPHRIES, JUNR. e. 100 ac. N side fork New River
..(WM. HUMPHRIES, JUNR. marked out..GEORGE MORRIS written
in). Entry No. 1158.

6 Sept. 1779. ISAAC PRESTON e. 50 ac. Dunawhoes line up Dunawhoes Creek.
Entry No. 1159.

6 Sept. 1779. GEORGE MAINARD e. 150 ac. on Kings Creek..(GERORGE MAIN-
ARD marked out..DABNEY HARRIS written in). Entry No.
1160.

6 Sept. 1779. LUKE ADAMS e. 320 ac. near JOSHUA MIZES line..lying between said MIZE & DUGGARS Cove. Entry No. 1161.

7 Sept. 1779. FRANCIS REYNOLDS e. 70 ac. E & W survey line he now lives
on..(Entry withdrawn). Entry No. 1162.

7 Sept. 1779. GEORGE MORRIS e. 25 ac. S side New River..upper corner of
said MORRIS line..(GER. MORRIS marked out..ANDREW BAKER
written in). Entry No. 1163.

7 Sept. 1779. 1st enterer not readable..e. 150 ac. New River waters..
small branch below Beaver Dam..(1st enterer marked out..
THOMAS HIGHSMITH marked out..MOSES WOODRUFF written in). Entry No. 1164.

7 Sept. 1779. ALEXANDER HOLTON e. 100 ac. S fork New River..including
an Island called Bills (or Bells) Island..(ALEX. HOLTON
marked out..JAMES JACKSON written in). Entry No. 1165.

8 Sept. 1779. CORNELUE SAILS e. 100 ac. on his own line..(CORNELIUS SAIL
marked out..WILLIAM SALE written in). Entry No. 1166.

8 Sept. 1779. ALEXANDER WEST e. 100 ac. N side branch runs through JOHN
FARGUSONS plantation..(ALEX. WEST, WM. BROWN & DANIEL
JOHNSON marked out..JOHN FARGUSON written in). Entry No. 1167.

8 Sept. 1779. CHARLES HENDERSON e. 50 ac. on top Kings Mountain..head
flat branch. Entry No. 1168.

8 Sept. 1779. JAMES HENDERSON e. 100 ac. waters Beaver Creek..joining
EDWARD BOONS entry. Entry No. 1169.

8 Sept. 1779.   THOMAS HENDERSON e. 100 ac. waters Beaver Creek..joining
                EDWARD BOONS Entry..on BOONS line. Entry No. 1170.

8 Sept. 1779.   BENADICK -----SON (?) e. 290 ac. near Bald Knob. Entry
                No. 1171.

8 Sept. 1779.   JOHN STUART e. 50 ac. on Tolovers Creek..above old Cabbin.
                Entry No. 1172.

8 Sept. 1779.   JOHN MURPHY e. 25 ac. on Kings Creek at JOHN KEYS line.
                Entry No. 1173.

8 Sept. 1779.   CALTON KEELING e. 150 ac. Fishes Creek on his line..
                (CALTON KEELING marked out..METHEAS BATES & ALEXANDER
MORRISON written in). Entry No. 1174.

8 Sept. 1779.   DANIEL GULLETT e. 100 ac. Rockey branch Lewis Fork..join-
                ing where he now lives..(DANIEL GULLETT, ABRAHAM SEWEL &
THOMAS WHITAKER marked out..ROBERT HAIS (HAYS) written in). Entry No.
1175.

8 Sept. 1779.   DAWSON SEWEL e. 50 ac. big branch Lewis Fork at WIGGINS
                line. Entry No. 1176.

8 Sept. 1779.   DANIEL GULLETT e. 100 ac. waters Lewis Fork..both sides
                meadow Branch..joining or near line land where he now
lives. Entry No. 1177.

8 Sept. 1779.   JOSEPH SEWEL e. 100 ac. waters Lewis Fork at path that
                leads from DANIEL GULLETS. Entry No. 1178.

8 Sept. 1779.   GARRET HENDRICK e. 150 ac. on Stoney fork at ROBERT
                LENOIRS line..(GARRET HENDRICK & WM. WHITAKER marked out..
transfered to THOMAS FARMER written in). Entry No. 1179.

8 Sept. 1779.   JESSE GREER e. 100 ac. on Cub Creek on JAMES HAMPTONS line
                ..(JESSE GREER marked out..PETER JONES written in). Entry
No. 1180.

8 Sept. 1779.   ALEXANDER MARTIN e. 400 ac. N fork New River..head of
                Yadkin..including the spring near road leads from Mul-
berry Creek to Three Forks of New River. Entry No. 1181.

9 Sept. 1779.   WILLIAM GUESS e. 50 ac. on fork branch. Entry No. 1182.

9 Sept. 1779.   WILLIAM WILLBURN e. 100 ac. N side his former entry he
                now lives on. Entry No. 1183.

9 Sept. 1779.   ABEL PENNINGTON e. 150 ac. N fork New River..including
                improvement where RANDOLPH SMITH & PAUL HENSON lives..
(Entry withdrawn). Entry No. 1184.

9 Sept. 1779.   ABEL PENNINGTON e. 150 ac. N fork New River..including
                improvement where THOMAS SMITH now lives..(Entry with-
drawn). Entry No. 1185.

9 Sept. 1779.   ABEL PENNINGTON e. 50 ac. N fork New River..below VINCENT
                HOLLANDS improvement..including improvement VINCENT
HOLLAND lives on..(Entry withdrawn). Entry No. 1186.

9 Sept. 1779.   ELIJAH ISAACS e. 150 ac. Kings Creek at JESSE COFFEES
                upper line..(ELIJAH ISAACS marked out..JESSE COFFEE
written in). Entry No. 1187.

9 Sept. 1779.   GEORGE ELLISON e. 100 ac. Stoney Fork..(GEORGE ELLISON &
                SPILSBY TRIBBLE marked out..THOMAS HAMPTON written in).
Entry No. 1188.

9 Sept. 1779. JACOB GOODWIN LYCANS e. 150 ac. on roundabout on lower
end of HAUNCH LYCANS line..to condt. line between HAUNCH
LYCANS & JOHN ROSE, JR. Entry No. 1189.

9 Sept. 1779. ALEXANDER GILREATH e. 200 ac. Pine Swamp Creek on New
River near Beaver Dam..both sides Little fork..including
CHURCHES improvement..(ALEX. GILREATH marked out..BETHUEL RIGGS written
in). Entry No. 1190.

11 Sept. 1779. GODFRAY ISAACS e. 100 ac. on Millseat River..including
said ISAACS improvement. Entry No. 1191.

11 Sept. 1779. REAZON BAKER e. 50 ac. on draughts Hunting Creek..down
spring branch where he now shall settle..where it runs
into Calleys branch..(REAZON BAKER marked out..JOHN RICHARDSON written
in). Entry No. 1192.

15 Sept. 1779. WILLIAM BROWN e. 100 ac. on Stoney Fork at BURDINES
Cabbin. Entry No. 1193.

16 Sept. 1779. WILLIAM RAY e. 100 ac. W sawmill Branch..(Creek). Entry
No. 1194.

16 Sept. 1779. GEORGE GORDON e. 300 ac. N fork Sawmill Creek. Entry No.
1195.

17 Sept. 1779. JONATHAN TOMPKINS e. 125 ac. Pine Swamp Creek above
Beaver Dam..(JONATHAN TOMPKINS marked out..WILLIAM JACK-
SON written in). Entry No. 1196.

17 Sept. 1779. BETHEUL RIGGS e. 100 ac. New River & Pine Swamp Creek..
near mouth small branch..near Beaver Dam. Entry No. 1197.

17 Sept. 1779. WILLIAM DAVIS e. 25 ac. on his open line..S to Little
fork Hunting Creek. Entry No. 1198.

17 Sept. 1779. PETER GOOD e. 100 ac. at WILLIAM DAVIS N corner to
RANDOLPH MITCHELS line. Entry No. 1199.

17 Sept. 1779. JOSEPH SCRITCHWORTH e. 150 ac. N fork Hunting Creek on
WILLIAM WILCOCKES line..(JOSEPH SCRITCHWORTH marked out
..LUKE BROWNEN (BROWNING) written in). Entry No. 1200.

20 Sept. 1779. VANAM (?) OLIVER e. 100 ac. Lewis Fork..including his
improvement..(VANAM OLIVER marked out..RICHARD BENNETT
written in). Entry No. 1201.

20 Sept. 1779. JAMES CADLING e. 100 ac. at Laurel Branch on Roaring
River..(JAMES CADLING marked out..RICHARD BENNETT written
in). Entry No. 1202.

20 Sept. 1779. HENRICUS STONECYPHER e. 100 ac. waters N fork Lewis Fork
..N side Calloways Mountain..joining near JOSEPH LEEDS
claim. Entry No. 1203.

20 Sept. 1779. RANDOLPH MITCHELL e. 100 ac. at his N corner to BOLINS
line. Entry No. 1204.

21 Sept. 1779. REUBIN FLETCHER e. 100 ac. waters Hunting Creek near
his own corner. Entry No. 1205.

21 Sept. 1779. WILLIAM RAGLAND e. 100 ac. to include all vacant land
between RAGLANDS line and BENJAMIN HERNDON. Entry No.
1206.

24 Sept. 1779. ALEXANDER GORDON e. 200 ac. N side New River..S fork..
opposite mouth Praters Creek..(Entry withdrawn). Entry
No. 1207.

27 Sept. 1779. WILLIAM MCGILL e. 100 ac. at his other line..both sides
main road. Entry No. 1208.

27 Sept. 1779. ANDREW VANNOY e. 50 ac. S side Mulberry Creek..at forks
big branch..W side VANNOYS entry. Entry No. 1209.

27 Sept. 1779. WILLIAM TERREL LEWIS e. 2 ac. at the Swan pond Creek..S
side Yadkin River..including that small island and LEWIS
fishtrap. Entry No. 1210.

27 Sept. 1779. JOHN BOURLAND e. 150 ac. head Boons branch. Entry No.
1211.

27 Sept. 1779. JOHN BOURLAND e. 150 ac. N fork Elk above VANDERPOOLS..
(JOHN BOURLAND marked out..DANIEL EGGERS written in).
Entry No. 1212.

27 Sept. 1779. BAZIL BAKER e. 50 ac. draughts Hunting Creek at CHARLES
BUSYS (?) line..N of falling branch. Entry No. 1213.

27 Sept. 1779. JOHN ROBERTS e. 50 ac. N fork Lewis Fork N branch..in-
cluding improvement. Entry No. 1214.

28 Sept. 1779. JOSHUA TOMSON e. 100 ac. Cove of Bryer Creek on BENAJMIN
HERNDONS line..joining JOHN TURNBILLS line. Entry No.
1215.

28 Sept. 1779. WILLIAM MCCUBBINS e. 50 ac. waters Bryer Creek..N to
EDWARD CROSS'S line. Entry No. 1216.

28 Sept. 1779. WILLIAM HOLDER e. 100 ac. on Fishes Creek..fork above
his spring. Entry No. 1217.

28 Sept. 1779. ELIJAH VICKERS e. 200 ac. near Pond (?) Mountain..includ-
ing waters Piney Creek and Potato Creek. Entry No. 1218.

30 Sept. 1779. THOMAS GOINS e. 50 ac. main branch runs by RANDOLPH
HOLDBROOKS..towards HOLDBROOKS line. Entry No. 1219.

30 Sept. 1779. THOMAS GOINS e. 50 ac. NE prong branch that runs by
RANDOLPH HOLDBROOKS. Entry No. 1220.

1 Oct. 1779. THOMAS GOINS e. 100 ac. branch between JOHN BURGEY (AMBUR-
GEY) & PARMELY. Entry No. 1221.

1 Oct. 1779. ROBERT CLEVELAND e. 150 ac. N side Lewis Fork adjoining
COLO. BENJAMIN CLEVELANDS survey. Entry No. 1222.

1 Oct. 1779. ROBERT CLEVELAND e. 50 ac. branch Lewis Fork adjoining
BENJAMIN CLEVELAND survey..(ROBERT CLEVELAND marked out..
ELIAS DEHART written in). Entry No. 1223.

1 Oct. 1779. ABRAHAM SAUNDERS e. 100 ac. Hunting Creek waters..at his
own line..then towards CHARLES BUSEYS..(ABRAHAM SAUNDERS
marked out..EDWARD PINKSTON written in). Entry No. 1224.

1 Oct. 1779. LAWRENCE ROSS e. 40 ac. W side Yadkin River..lower end his
other survey..(LAWRENCE ROSS. marked out..ELIJAM ISAACKS
written in). Entry No. 1225.

1 Oct. 1779. ROBERT HUSBANDS e. 100 ac. waters Beaver Creek..joining his
              former entry..towards THOMAS CARSONS..(ROBERT HUSBANDS
marked out..ISBELL written in). Entry No. 1226.

1 Oct. 1779. CLOSS TOMPSON e. 50 ac. branch called Harvels Branch at
              CLEVELANDS line. Entry No. 1227.

4 Oct. 1779. JOHN OREAR e. 320 ac. Little River..near fork Peak
              Mountain. Entry No. 1228.

4 Oct. 1779. ROBERT OBARR e. 25 ac. at HUGH MONTGOMERYS lower line..
              (ROBT. OBARR marked out..THOMAS LAY, JUNR. written in).
Entry No. 1229.

4 Oct. 1779. EDWARD KETCHAM e. 150 ac. Bank Creek on CUTHBEARDS line.
              Entry No. 1230.

4 Oct. 1779. EDWARD KETCHAM e. 50 ac. the Blue Ridge..near the spring..
              including improvement he bought of JESSE BARKER. Entry No.
1231.

4 Oct. 1779. EDWARD KETCHAM e. 100 ac. ridge called Gosons Ridge.
              Entry No. 1232.

4 Oct. 1779. EDWARD KETCHAM e. 50 ac. Brushey fork Pine Swamp. Entry
              No. 1233.

4 Oct. 1779. WILLIAM FLETCHER e. 100 ac. above JOHN ROBERTS..including
              some waters main Hunting Creek and Craine Creek..(WM.
FLETCHER marked out..GEORGE SHAVER written in). Entry No. 1234.

4 Oct. 1779. JACOB CANNADY (KENNEDY) e. 100 ac. on waters Mitchels
              River..on Christians Creek at JOHN ROBERTSONS line on N
side..including improvement where THOMAS PORTER now lives. Entry No.
1235.

7 Oct. 1779. CHARLES GORDON e. 100 ac. E corner E & W line Mulberry
              Fields Tract joining DANIEL VANNOYS tract. Entry No. 1236.

7 Oct. 1779. BENJAMIN CUTHBEARD e. 100 ac. Rich Mountain opposite most
              N fork Elk Creek..towards N fork New River waters. Entry
No. 1237.

8 Oct. 1779. FRANCIS REYNOLDS e. 100 ac. on dividing Ridge of mountains
              between S & N forks New River..near Elk Mountain. Entry
No. 1238.

8 Oct. 1779. THOMAS GILBERT e. 100 ac. head Lewis Fork at JAMES TOMPKINS
              line..N to include CUTHBOARDS line. Entry No. 1239.

8 Oct. 1779. EDWARD FINCH e. 30 ac. head Halls Branch..including part of
              Rich Mountain. Entry No. 1240.

10 Oct. 1779. ALEXANDER GILREATH e. 60 ac. on Reddies River below the
               Bent..(ALEXANDER GILREATH marked out..JARVIS SMITH written
in). Entry No. 1241.

10 Oct. 1779. GEORGE CARPENTER e. 40 ac. S side Yadkin River at
               HUMPHRIES Camp. Entry No. 1242.

11 Oct. 1779. JOHN SALER e. 50 ac. head Stoney Fork..including the
               BARK Camp. Entry No. 1243.

13 Oct. 1779. WILLIAM TOLIVER e. 50 ac. waters Roaring River so as to
               assertain the good land as far as fifty ac. extends.
Entry No. 1244.

14 Oct. 1779.   THOMAS PURKINS e. 50 ac. S side Yadkin opposite to
                 WILLIAM BUNTONS. Entry No. 1245.

14 Oct. 1779.   SPENCER ADAMS e. 100 ac. on Osburns Creek at the County
                 line..(SPENCER ADAMS marked out..HENRY HAYS written in).
Entry No. 1246.

16 Oct. 1779.   WILLIAM FLETCHER e. 100 ac. first big branch of Mulberry
                 ..that runs into Mulberry Creek above CHARLES HICKERSONS
called the Hay or Mead Branch below improvement that the TOLIVORS made..
(WILLIAM FLETCHER marked out..AARON MASH written in). Entry No. 1247.

18 Oct. 1779.   DANIEL VANNOY e. 100 ac. branch New River called South
                 Beaver. Entry No. 1248.

18 Oct. 1779.   AMBROS CARLTON e. 100 ac. waters Kings Creek..(AMBROS
                 CARLTON & JOHN BARLOW written in..(also)..JOHN WM.
CROSTHWAIT marked out). Entry No. 1249.

NOTE: The edges of the next 16 entries are torn or frayed so that part
        of the entry is just not there..will abstract anything readable.

19 Oct. 1779.   WILLIAM (?) e. torn.... torn .... ac. Head N branch..torn
                 ..Creek S fork New River along Elk Ridge..(WM. (?) marked
out..DANIEL WHEATLEY written in). Entry No. 1251.

19 Oct. 1779.   JACOB KETCHAM e. ..torn..ac. on ..torn ..ridge one mile
                 from CUTHBEARDS near great fall of Lewis Fork..including
KETCHAMS improvement. Entry No. 1252.

19 Oct. 1779.   BENJAMIN CLEVELAND e. ..torn..ac... CLAUS TOMPSONS S line
                 on Lewis Fork..(BENJAMIN CLEVELAND marked out..JOHN
CLEVELAND written in). Entry No. 1253.

19 Oct. 1779.   1st enterer not readable..e...torn..ac...Ridge a mile
                 from CUTHBOARDS..near great falls Lewis Fork..including
the improvement..(JAMES FLETCHER written in). Entry No. 1254.

23 Oct. 1779.   1st enterer not readable..e...torn..hundred ac. little
                 below falls Moravian..below WILLIAM LOWS..(BENJAMIN JOHN-
SON written in). Entry No. 1255.

26 Oct. 1779.   JOHN WILLIAM CROSWAIT e. 150 ac. branch Kings..torn..
                 dividing ridge..Beaver Creek and Kings Creek..S from
THOMAS CARLTONS line..(JOHN WM. CROSTHWAIT marked out..JOHN BARLOW
written in). Entry No. 1256.

26 Oct. 1779.   JAMES SMITH e...torn..hundred ac. N side Mitchels River
                 at Christians Creek..joining JOHN ..torn.. (?) SCOTT &
BARNARD FRANKLIN..torn. Entry No. 1257.

torn..BARNARD FRANKLIN e. 100 ac......both sides Butler Creek..joining
      his own entry. Entry No. 1258.

torn..THOMAS PAYNE, SR. e. 50 ac. on Mitchels River..joining BARNARD
      FRANKLINS line. Entry No. 1259.

torn..GARRET HENDRICKS e. one..torn..ac Stoney fork at his lower line..
      (GARRET HENDRICK & ..torn..WHITAKER marked out..Transferred to
torn..THOMAS FARMER written in). Entry No. 1261.

torn.. GARRET HENDRICK e. 150 ac. top of Blue Ridge..including ..torn..
waters New River. Entry No. 1262.

torn.. GARRET HENDRICK e. 50 ac. on Chesnut Knob..including head of ..
torn.. Mill Branch. Entry No. 1263.

torn.. JOHN COX e. 100 ac. Beaver Branch Cranberry Creek. Entry No.
1264.

torn.. BENJAMIN JOHNSTON e. 100 ac. S side Brushey Mountain..including
some waters Hunting Creek. Entry No. 1265.

torn.. ..torn.. ..torn.. ..torn.. ..torn.. ..torn.. ..torn.. JOSEPH
SPARKS ..torn.. side of Brushey Mountain ..torn.. County line.
Entry No. 1266.

1 Nov. 1779. ALEXANDER GORDON e. 500 ac. adjoining BENJAMIN HERNDONS
line..(ALEX. GORDON marked out..BENJAMIN HERNDON written
in). Entry No. 1267.

1 Nov. 1779. JOB COAL e. 50 ac. S side Mill Creek below Cabbin..includ-
ing Mill Seate. Entry No. 1268.

2 Nov. 1779. JOHN TURNER e. 50 ac. fork N fork Readies River at Crooked
Branch. Entry No. 1269.

2 Nov. 1779. PHILIP DAVIS e. 100 ac. at WILLIAM BAYS line..branch Kings
Creek..(PHILIP DAVIS & BENJAMIN COFFEY marked out..THOMAS
WISDOM written in). Entry No. 1270.

4 Nov. 1779. JOHN SUTTON e. 100 ac. on Elledges Creek. Entry No. 1271.

5 Nov. 1779. JOHN WILLSON e. 200 ac. S side Yadkin..opposite the Bent
known by name MOSES BEE Branch..including his improvement..
(JOHN WILLSON marked out..(?) BRYANT written in). Entry No. 1272.

8 Nov. 1779. THOMAS PAYNE, JUNR. e. 100 ac. waters Big Bugaboe on
JONATHAN STAMPERS line. Entry No. 1273.

torn.. ..torn.. ..torn.. ..torn.. ..torn.. ..torn.. ..torn.. head spring
of S fork Lewis Fork at JAMES TOMPKINS plantation. Entry No.
1274.

8 Nov. 1779. BARNARD FRANKLIN e. 50 ac. head Ready fork of Mitchells
River. Entry No. 1275.

9 Nov. 1779. BARNARD FRANKLIN e. 100 ac. Mitchels River..adjoining his
other entry on Butlers Creek. Entry No. 1276.

9 Nov. 1779. JESSE FRANKLIN e. 100 ac. Mitchels River..upper end bottom.
Entry No. 1277.

10 Nov. 1779. DAVID AUSTIN e. 50 ac. Mitchels River on his other line..
joining BENJAMIN MAY & JONAS WALING. Entry No. 1278.

10 Nov. 1779. DAVID AUSTIN e. 70 ac. Butlers Creek..including his improvement. Entry No. 1279.

11 Nov. 1779. JOSEPH MCGLOCKLAND e. 50 ac. N fork Linvills Mill Creek.
Entry No. 1280.

11 Nov. 1779. WILLIAM NALL e. 200 ac. Cranberry Creek near MULCAYS
path..turns out of new road. Entry No. 1281.

11 Nov. 1779.   WILLIAM NALL e. 100 ac. lower end his line up New River.
                Entry No. 1282.

11 Nov. 1779.   JAMES BAKER e. 100 ac. dividing ridge between Cranberry
                and Peak Creek. Entry No. 1283.

11 Nov. 1779.   WILLIAM NALL e. 100 ac. on New River..near mouth Peak
                Creek..adjoining his own and HUGH SMITHS line..(WM. NALL
marked out..transfered to JOHN YOUNCE written in). Entry No. 1284.

13 Nov. 1779.   THOMAS PAYNE, JUNR. e. 250 ac. waters S fork Mitchels
                River..adjoining ROBERT HANKINS line..including SAMUEL
POUNDS improvement. Entry No. 1285.

13 Nov. 1779.   THOMAS PAYNE e. 100 ac. adjoining THOMAS GOINS lower
                entry on Big Elkin..(THOMAS PAYNE marked out..JAMES FIN-
LEY written in). Entry No. 1286.

13 Nov. 1779.   THOMAS PAYNE e. 100 ac. on or near Big Elkin..joining
                THOMAS GOINS..including part said GOINS upper improvement
..(THOMAS PAYNE marked out..JAMES FINLEY written in). Entry No. 1287.

13 Nov. 1779.   THOMAS PAYNE, JUNR. e. 100 ac. top mountain near some
                head waters Mitchels River..including entry made by JOHN
GARASON. Entry No. 1288.

13 Nov. 1779.   JOHN FARGUSON e. 150 ac. on Stoney fork adjoining his
                upper line. Entry No. 1289.

13 Nov. 1779.   THOMAS ELLEDGE e. 75 ac. on Warrior Creek..half mile be-
                low Mill..including the good land down the creek on both
sides. Entry No. 1290.

13 Nov. 1779.   THOMAS ELLEDGE e. 50 ac. near mouth Naked Creek..includ-
                ing great Shoals on Lewis Fork and Bad land on both sides.
Entry No. 1291.

13 Nov. 1779.   THOMAS ELLEDGE e. 100 ac. Stoney Fork of Yadkin River..
                below mouth Ready Branch..including all shoals and Good
Land on both sides..(THOMAS ELLEDGE marked out..JOHN GRAY written in).
Entry No. 1292.

13 Nov. 1779.   THOMAS ELLEDGE e. 100 ac. on Ruth's Branch on Sweet Laurel
                Hill..including good land joining NELLSON KELLEYS line..
(THOMAS ELLEDGE marked out..REUBEN HAYS written in). Entry No. 1293.

13 Nov. 1779.   SOLOMON CROSS e. 50 ac. joining shoals near mouth Fish
                Trap Branch. Entry No. 1294.

13 Nov. 1779.   JAMES SPARKS e. 150 ac. dividing ridge between Buffalow
                and Bever Creeks..waters New River..including both sides
path. Entry No. 1295.

13 Nov. 1779.   BARNET OWEN e. 100 ac. in Wilkes County in this State on
                Obids Creek near SAUNDERS Camp..taking both forks. Entry
No. 1296.

13 Nov. 1779.   HENRY MULLINS e. 100 ac. in this State at Rowlands Big
                Branch..down both forks. Entry No. 1297.

13 Nov. 1779.   SAMUEL SIMPSON e. 50 ac. Stuards Creek..upper end..down
                both sides. Entry No. 1298.

13 Nov. 1779. JAMES TOMPKINS e. 600 ac. near flat place Rich Mountain..
partly between Great Bald Mountain and Pinacle Mountain..
NW side Pine Swamp..on main branches N fork New River. Entry No. 1299.

14 Nov. 1779. ALEXANDER GILREATH e. 100 ac. N side New River..adjoining
his other entry..(Entry withdrawn). Entry No. 1300.

14 Nov. 1779. JOHN BAYS e. 50 ac. N fork Lewis Fork at JESSE GULLETS
upper line..down both sides. Entry No. 1301.

18 Nov. 1779. JOHN BYAS (BAYS?) e. 100 ac. Beaver Creek at a glade N
side..(JOHN BYAS marked out..ALEXANDER POOR written in).
Entry No. 1302.

18 Nov. 1779. ALEXANDER POOR e. 100 ac. branch that enters N fork Lewis
Fork..below JOHN WHITACRES (WHITAKER) line. Entry No.
1303.

18 Nov. 1779. MARK WHITACRE (WHITAKER) e. 100 ac. Osburns Creek below
the Rock House. Entry No. 1304.

18 Nov. 1779. WILLIAM GILREATH, SR. e. 250 ac. S side middle fork Little
Cub Creek at the foard where MONGOMERYS old foard crosses
the Creek..condt. line made by THOMAS LOW..including improvement whereon
SAMUEL WILLCOCKSON lives and the improvement that belongs to VOLENTINE
NUTTERVILL. Entry No. 1305.

18 Nov. 1779. PETER PEARSON e. 200 ac. little fork Mitchells River..
near his spring. Entry No. 1306.

18 Nov. 1779. WILLIAM WATTS e. 200 ac. fork Mitchels River called
ARCHIBALD LITCHFIELDS fork. Entry No. 1307.

18 Nov. 1779. WILLIAM WATTS e. 50 ac. S fork Mitchels River..said WATTS
E line. Entry No. 1308.

18 Nov. 1779. WILLIAM WATTS e. 100 ac. on Ambross's Branch that runs
into Mitchels River..above road leads to the Iron Works.
Entry No. 1309.

18 Nov. 1779. WILLIAM LEWIS e. 150 ac. N side Brushey Mountain..waters
of Hunting Creek between CORNELIOUS SALE & BOWMAN CASS'S.
Entry No. 1310.

18 Nov. 1779. JOEL LEWIS e. 100 ac. waters Big Elkin..including Great
Falls. Entry No. 1311.

19 Nov. 1779. LITTLEBERRY TONEY e. 200 ac. on Obeds Creek at the Nary
Pashed (narrow path?). Entry No. 1312.

19 Nov. 1779. LITTLEBERRY TONEY e. 100 ac. on New River at or nigh the
deep foard..both sides river. Entry No. 1313.

19 Nov. 1779. Entered by WILLIAM MCCLAIN & ANDREW BAKER e. 320 ac.
situated head drafts Beaver Dam..N fork New River. Entry
No. 1314.

19 Nov. 1779. JOHN SISK e. 100 ac. N fork Swan pond Creek..joining the
County line on PHILIP MASONS line..(JOHN SISK marked out..
NICHOLAS MITCHEL written in). Entry No. 1315.

19 Nov. 1779.   THOMAS SISK e. 100 ac. Sims fork on his own line..(THOMAS
                 SISK marked out..WILLIAM HENSON written in). Entry No.
1316.

19 Nov. 1779.   FRANCIS VANNOY e. 100 ac. Halls fork Roaring River..ad-
                 joining JOHN MORGANS upper line..both sides creek. Entry
No. 1317.

19 Nov. 1779.   PERON CARDWELL e. 100 ac. S branch Naked Creek..opposite
                 his Plantation..including a small improvement. Entry No.
1318.

19 Nov. 1779.   GEORGE ELMORE e. 50 ac. little fork Gullets branch..
                 (GEORGE ELMORE marked out..MOSES TOMPKINS written in).
Entry No. 1319.

19 Nov. 1779.   JOHN TURNBILL e. 200 ac. on road leads to the Fewege
                 (Forge?) at JOHN CARGILES corner and JOHN PARKS line.
Entry No. 1320.

19 Nov. 1779.   WILLIAM MCCUBBINS e. 50 ac. at MR. TURNBILLS corner..up
                 the mountain..(WM. MCCUBBINS marked out..JOHN CARGILE,
SENR. written in). Entry No. 1321.

20 Nov. 1779.   WILLIAM LEWIS e. 150 ac. N fork Hunting Creek..including
                 SOLOMON SPARKS improvement. Entry No. 1322.

23 Nov. 1779.   JAMES COFFEE SR. e. 300 ac. at his S corner..a condt. line
                 made between JAMES COFFEE, JR. & JAMES COFFEE, SENR.
Entry No. 1323.

23 Nov. 1779.   Name marked out completely..ISAAC MARTIN written in..e.
                 640 ac. on BENJAMIN HORNDOMS line near Wright Creek.
Entry No. 1324.

23 Nov. 1779.   Name marked out completely..ISAAC MARTIN written in..e.
                 640 ac. on BOWLINGS line..including vacant land between
GOOD & MITCHEL. Entry No. 1325.

23 Nov. 1779.   ISAAC MARTIN e. 640 ac. at GORDONS line..including vacant
                 land..(Entry withdrawn by the enterer). Entry No. 1326.

23 Nov. 1779.   JESSE LAY e. 100 ac. branch Elk Creek..including the
                 cabin..(JESSE LAY erased..EDWARD SMITH written in).
Entry No. 1327.

28 Nov. 1779.   RICHARD HANKINS e. 100 ac. little fork Mitchels River at
                 ROBERT HANKINS upper line of his lower entry. Entry No.
1328.

29 Nov. 1779.   WILLIAM COOK e. 400 ac. some waters New River near JAMES
                 TOMPKINS line that he made between Bald mtn. and Pinacle
mtn...including the good land. Entry No. 1329.

29 Nov. 1779.   CORNELIUS SALE e. 320 ac. at BENJAMIN HERNDONS line..in-
                 cluding vacant land between it and HANCH LIKEINGS line..
(CORNELIUS SALE marked out..JOHN MARTIN written in). Entry No. 1330.

29 Nov. 1779.   JAMES FOX e. 200 ac. middle prong Swan Creek on his own
                 line. Entry No. 1331.

1 Dec. 1779.   THOMAS ELLISTON e. 50 ac. long fork Beaver Creek above the
                 narrows. Entry No. 1332.

2 Dec. 1779.   JOHN NORRIS e. 50 ac. on branch Fishes Creek at EDWARD
                 HARRIS line. Entry No. 1333.

3 Dec. 1779.   WILLIAM LANDSDOWN e. 50 ac. fork Buffalow waters Yadkin
                 River..foot of mountain. Entry No. 1334.

4 Dec. 1779.   WILLIAM LEWIS, SR. e. 50 ac. drafts Littles Fork Hunting
               Creek at Forbushes Spring..up the Ridge..(WM. LEWIS marked
out..JAMES LOVE written in).   Entry No. 1335.

4 Dec. 1779.   WILLIAM LEWIS e. 50 ac. N side Hunting Creek..near head
               Pounding Mill Branch.   Entry No. 1336.

4 Dec. 1779.   MATTHEW MCCLAIN e. 100 ac. N fork New River at WM. MCCLAINS
               lower line..both sides river.   Entry No. 1337.

4 Dec. 1779.   REUBIN STANDLEY e. 50 ac. on Hunting Creek at Lazey hill..
               both sides creek..(REUBIN STANDLEY marked out..JAMES LOVE
written in).   Entry No. 1338.

4 Dec. 1779.   SILVERSTOR BAKER e. 50 ac. waters Bear Branch near EBEDNEGO
               BAKERS line..including the good land..(SILVESTOR BAKER
marked out..BENJAMIN CRABTREE written in).   Entry No. 1339.

6 Dec. 1779.   THOMAS NEWBERRY e. 100 ac. on Sams branch at BALLARDS line
               ..(Entry withdrawn).   Entry No. 1340.

6 Dec. 1779.   THOMAS NEWBERRY e. 100 ac. branch Fishes Creek.   Entry No.
               1340.

6 Dec. 1779.   GEORGE GORDON e. 100 ac. E side Sawmill tract.   Entry No.
               1341.

6 Dec. 1779.   THOMAS ELLEDGE, Esqr. e. 100 ac. on Naked Creek..between
               PEREN CARDWELL & JOHN WEB (WEBB)..both sides creek..in-
cluding the good land.   Entry No. 1342.

6 Dec. 1779.   THOMAS ELLEDGE, SR., Esqr. e. 200 ac. waters Warrier Creek
               joining ELISHA DYERS land..both sides creek.   Entry No.
1343.

6 Dec. 1779.   MICAEL KILBEY e. 100 ac. tumbling shoal branch below the
               foard.   Entry No. 1344.

6 Dec. 1779.   JOHN HOWARD e. 100 ac. waters Hunting Creek..(Entry with-
               drawn).   Entry No. 1345.

6 Dec. 1779.   RANDOLPH HOLDBROOK e. 100 ac. waters Roaring River..at or
               near his line.   Entry No. 1346.

6 Dec. 1779.   SIMION CARTER e. 100 ac. on said Carters Branch at his own
               line.   Entry No. 1347.

7 Dec. 1779.   BENJAMIN CLEVELAND e. 400 ac. forks Bugaboe Creek..(Crossed
               out with large cross-mark..no other name on entry).
Entry No. 1348.

7 Dec. 1779.   BENJAMIN CLEVELAND e. 400 ac. on Bugaboe & head Stuarts
               Creek.   Entry No. 1349.

7 Dec. 1779.   BENJAMIN CLEVELAND e. 100 ac. on Lewis Fork at MATTHEW
               FRANCIS'S line..down both sides of fork.   Entry No. 1350.

8 Dec. 1779.   BENJAMIN CLEVELAND e. 100 ac. Helton Creek..below WALLOMS
               (?) upper Camp.   Entry No. 1351.

8 Dec. 1779.   MICAJAH PENNINGTON e. 200 ac. on Helton Creek at Larel
               Cliff.   Entry No. 1352.

7 Dec. 1779.   BENJAMIN ELLEDGE e. 100 ac. branch Warrior Creek..commonly
               known by name Boonsfield Branch..joining line in Entry of
ELLEDGE, Esqr. and sold to JOHN FORBUS..Ruths mountain..(BENJAMIN
ELLEDGE marked out..GIDEON GILBERT written in).   Entry No. 1353.

7 Dec. 1779.   BENJAMIN ELLEDGE e. 200 ac. branch Warrior Creek..joining
               ELISHA DYER and an entry made by AQUILLA LOW above..both
sides said Creek..including PHILIP WALKERS improvement..(entry withdrawn).
Entry No. 1354.

7 Dec. 1779.   PHILIP WALKER e. 50 ac. Naked Creek at JOHN WEBS (WEBB)
               lower line..down both sides creek. Entry No. 1355.

7 Dec. 1779.   WILLIAM SMITH e. 100 ac. at his own N line on Cub Creek..
               both sides..(WM. SMITH marked out..JOHN R. JOHNSON written
in). Entry No. 1356.

7 Dec. 1779.   WILLIAM LAWS e. 100 ac. Lewis Branch on DYERS line..both
               sides branch..(WM. LAWS & JOEL HAMPTON marked out..JOHN
WILLSON written in). Entry No. 1357.

7 Dec. 1779.   JAMES MAHAN e. 150 ac. W side S fork New River..opposite
               mouth Praters Creek. Entry No. 1358.

7 Dec. 1779.   WILLIAM HOLLAND e. 25 ac. top of a mountain..including
               some waters Hunting Creek..a hundred yards below his
cabbin. Entry No. 1359.

7 Dec. 1779.   PETER PEARSON e. 150 ac. middle Bryshey fork Mitchels
               River. Entry No. 1360.

7 Dec. 1779.   JACOB HEDDEN e. 50 ac. both sides Bigg Elkin..joining his
               former entry made by GIBSON MAINORD..including a small
improvement.   Entry No. 1361.

7 Dec. 1779.   JOHN CLEVELAND, SR. e. 150 ac. waters Lewis Fork W side of
               entry that COLO. CLEVELAND purchased of LAWRENCE TOMPSON.
Entry No. 1362.

8 Dec. 1779.   JOHN GREER e. 100 ac. branch Cub Creek..joining GEORGE
               REAVES line..(JOHN GREER marked out..JACOB MADCALF written
in). Entry No. 1363.

8 Dec. 1779.   ISAAC PRESTON e. 50 ac. on Duchers Branch. Entry No. 1364.

8 Dec. 1779.   ISAAC PRESTON e. 100 ac. between head Buffalow and the
               Laurel fork of New River. Entry No. 1365.

8 Dec. 1779.   JAMES BAKER e. 200 ac. on Cranberry Creek..near mouth
               Cattail branch..E side creek..N down both sides. Entry No.
1366.

9 Dec. 1779.   JOSEPH KELLY e. 200 ac. branch Beaver Creek near WM. ELLI-
               SONS W line..(JOSEPH KELLY & WM. GRAY marked out..THOMAS
LAND written in). Entry No. 1367.

9 Dec. 1779.   JAMES HENDERSON e. 100 ac. on Beaver Creek..including
               vacant land between DAVID MCGEES & WILLIAM ELLISTON. Entry
No. 1368.

9 Dec. 1779.   JAMES HENDERSON e. 100 ac. branch Beaver Creek..line of
               WM. ELLISTON. Entry No. 1369.

9 Dec. 1779.   WILLIAM SMITH e. 50 ac. waters Hunting Creek..(WM. SMITH
               & EDWARD ROBERTS marked out..GEORGE ANDERSON written in).
Entry No. 1370.

9 Dec. 1779.   WILLIAM GRAY e. 100 ac. on JAMES GRAYS Creek..down creek
               to CAPT. HERNDSONS line. Entry No. 1371.

9 Dec. 1779.   PETER GOOD e. 25 ac. waters Hunting Creek at WILLIAM DAVIS
               corner near Good's spring. Entry No. 1372.

9 Dec. 1779. EDWARD BALL (BELL?) e. 100 ac. meadow branch on Sharpers Mountain. Entry No. 1373.

9 Dec. 1779. NATHANIEL BURDINE e. 400 ac. branch Readies River..N side by name Browns Branch..near three forks. Entry No. 1374.

10 Dec. 1779. WILLIAM LYON e. 100 ac. on Mitchels River at his S line. Entry No. 1375.

10 Dec. 1779. FRANCIS HILL e. 100 ac. branch Cane Creek. Entry No. 1376.

10 Dec. 1779. FRANCIS HILL e. 50 ac. on Roaring River..joining EDMOND DENNEY'S entry on Cane Creek. Entry No. 1377.

10 Dec. 1779. ROBERT CHANDLER e. 60 ac. S fork Roaring River..near mouth second creek above the forks. Entry No. 1378.

10 Dec. 1779. ROBERT CHANDLER e. 50 ac. on Fishes Creek. Entry No. 1379.

10 Dec. 1779. DANIEL AYERS e. 100 ac. waters Loving Creek at PHILIP MASONS line. Entry No. 1380.

15 Dec. 1779. MATTHEW FRANCIS e. 100 ac. N fork Lewis Fork near little branch below his improvement..(MATTHEW FRANCIS marked out ..JOPHS MOSS written in). Entry No. 1381.

15 Dec. 1779. DANIEL YARNELL e. 100 ac. E fork New River..in line of land bought from ABNER SMALLEY. Entry No. 1382.

15 Dec. 1779. JOHN WEBB e. 100 ac. Naked Creek..on his upper line. Entry No. 1383.

15 Dec. 1779. 1st enterer not readable and marked out..e. 200 ac. on SPENCER ADAMS line..both sides Osburns Creek..(BENJAMIN TAYLOR written in). Entry No. 1384.

15 Dec. 1779. JOSIAH CERTAIN (SERTAIN) e. 50 ac. middle fork Reddies River..on both sides above mouth Laurel fork. Entry No. 1385.

15 Dec. 1779. JOSIAH CERTAIN e. 50 ac. middle fork Reddies River..on both sides..above first location. Entry No. 1386.

15 Dec. 1779. JOSIAH CERTAIN e. 50 ac. middle fork Readies River among the mountains..both sides said fork. Entry No. 1387.

15 Dec. 1779. JOHN PITTMAN e. 100 ac. right hand fork of straight fork Fishes Creek..near foot of Brushey Mountain. Entry No. 1388.

15 Dec. 1779. ELISHA MOOR e. 50 ac. above falls Flat Branch..S side Yadkin River. Entry No. 1389.

15 Dec. 1779. WILLIAM T. LEWIS e. 100 ac. Hunting Creek..including BENET ROBERTS improvement. Entry No. 1390.

20 Dec. 1779. JAMES WARD e. 50 ac. waters N fork New River..head Branch opposite land he sold to Esqr. FLETCHER at mouth Glady branch. Entry No. 1391.

20 Dec. 1779. JOHN BAKER e. 100 ac. dividing ridge between Roans Creek and Bear Creek..including both sides ridge. Entry No. 1392.

20 Dec. 1779.   DEVEREUX BALLARD e. 300 ac. between Sams branch and Mill
                 Creek..joining BALLARDS other entry on Sams branch.   Entry
No. 1393.

20 Dec. 1779.   JOHN BAKER e. 100 ac. on Pine Creek..N fork New River..
                 near the Turkey Knob..(JOHN BAKER marked out..EDWARD
PENNINGTON written in).   Entry No. 1394.

20 Dec. 1779.   JOHN BAKER e. 150 ac. on Nathans Creek of New River..(JOHN
                 BAKER marked out..JAMES FLETCHER written in).   Entry No.
1395.

20 Dec. 1779.   JOHN BAKER e. 200 ac. waters New River on Buffaloe Creek..
                 near Clift of Rocks..fork creek between Paddy's Knob
mountain and Three Top Mountain..(JOHN BAKER marked out..JOHN SPARKES
written in).   Entry No. 1396.

20 Dec. 1779.   JOHN BAKER e. 150 ac. waters New River..including land he
                 bought NICHOLAS ANGEL..including head meadow branch..
(JOHN BAKER marked out..FREDERICK BLACK written in).   Entry No. 1397.

20 Dec. 1779.   JAMES WARD e. 300 ac. Beaver Dam Creek.   Entry No. 1398.

20 Dec. 1779.   JAMES WARD e. 200 ac. Silus's Creek..above forks and
                 running up both forks.   Entry No. 1399.

21 Dec. 1779.   JAMES WARD e. 50 ac. N fork New River.   Entry No. 1400.

21 Dec. 1779.   THOMAS WATKINS e. 100 ac. Bledsoes Gap..including waters
                 Nathans Creek and Long Shoal Creek..(THOMAS WATKINS marked
out..JAMES FLETCHER written in).   Entry No. 1401.

21 Dec. 1779.   BENJAMIN CLEVELAND e. 400 ac. waters Bugaboe and Long
                 Branch of Roaring River.   Entry No. 1402.

21 Dec. 1779.   BENJAMIN CLEVELAND e. 200 ac. waters on Horse Creek at
                 mouth branch..below HAYSES bottom.   Entry No. 1403.

21 Dec. 1779.   BENJAMIN CLEVELAND e. 200 ac. N fork New River..lower end
                 his other entry..(transfered to WILLIAM JONES).   Entry No.
1404.

21 Dec. 1779.   JOSEPH HERNDON e. 200 ac. Horse Creek known by name The
                 Old Fields..including improvement whereon WILLIAM SMITH
now lives.   Entry No. 1405.

21 Dec. 1779.   RICHARD ALLEN e. 100 ac. N fork New River..joining his
                 line at Cow Camp.   Entry No. 1406.

21 Dec. 1779.   RICHARD ALLEN e. 100 ac. on branch runs into Beaver Dam
                 Bottom..(RICHARD ALLEN marked out..SPRUCE MACAY written
in).   Entry No. 1407.

21 Dec. 1779.   JAMES WARD e. 150 ac. N fork New River..Pine Creek right
                 hand fork.   Entry No. 1408.

21 Dec. 1779.   JAMES WARD e. 100 ac. N fork New River..above mouth Silus
                 creek.   Entry No. 1409.

21 Dec. 1779.   JOHN BAKER e. 200 ac. head waters Horse Creek on Pond
                 Mtn...(JOHN BAKER marked out..SOLOMON BAKER written in).
Entry No. 1410.

21 Dec. 1779.   DAVID MACKENZIE e. 100 ac. waters Dog Creek of New River..
                 Ridge leads Mill to Forks creek..including good land on
said ridge.   Entry No. 1411.

21 Dec. 1779. 1st enterer marked out completely..e. 250 ac. on New River
above mouth Nathans Creek..(CHARLES VICKAS & JAMES
FLETCHER written in). Entry No. 1412.

21 Dec. 1779. JOHN BAKER e. 50 ac. lower fork Nathans Creek of New
River..(JOHN BAKER & NICKLUS ANGEL marked out..PHILLIP
SIGLER written in). Entry No. 1413.

21 Dec. 1779. JAMES WARD e. 100 ac. on New River..N fork near Lewis
Path..including the good land. Entry No. 1414.

21 Dec. 1779. DAVID MACKENSY e. 100 ac. head N fork Naked Creek of New
River at a big crab orchard..including the good land
thereabouts. Entry No. 1415.

21 Dec. 1779. JOHN BAKER e. 100 ac. Bear Creek of New River against
upper end of Blue hill below mouth of branch..(entry
withdrawn by enterer). Entry No. 1416.

21 Dec. 1779. JOHN BAKER e. 100 ac. on New River..dividing ridge between
little Naked Creek and the River..including all the good
land on Ridge. Entry No. 1417.

22 Dec. 1779. JAMES WARD e. 100 ac. on New River..waters on branch
Willson Creek..heads up from PENNINGTONS Mill..near the
Virginia line. Entry No. 1418.

22 Dec. 1779. JAMES WARD e. 100 ac. on New River..waters on branch near
Virginia line..leading up ridge leading from ZACHARIAH
WELLS. Entry No. 1419.

23 Dec. 1779. GEORGE SHOREFIELD e. 100 ac. Big Branch of Mulberry into
creek below JOHN ROBINS. Entry No. 1420.

23 Dec. 1779. FRANCIS VANNOY e. 100 ac. Yadkin River..lower end entry
where he now lives..(Entry withdrawn and cross-marked
out). Entry No. 1421.

23 Dec. 1779. BENJAMIN HERNDON e. 280 ac. N fork Caleys Creek..waters
Hunting Creek..above improvement where JOHN ROBERTS,
SENR. lives..(BENJ. HERNDON marked out..ELIZABETH ROBERTS written in).
Entry No. 1422.

23 Dec. 1779. BENJAMIN HERNDON e. 200 ac. on Swan Creek near upper end
falls above BOURLANDS..(BENJ. HERNDON marked out..WILLIAM
BROWN written in). Entry No. 1423.

23 Dec. 1779. BENJAMIN HERNDON e. 200 ac. Brushey Mountain below the
old camp where the PENSONS (?) Camped. Entry No. 1424.

23 Dec. 1779. BENJAMIN HERNDON e. 200 ac. Brushey Mountain near head
Sales Creek..top of mountain..back of Cove. Entry No.
1425.

23 Dec. 1779. JAMES FLETCHER e. 100 ac. on Stoney Branch that runs into
Elk Creek..opposite plantation HUGH MONTGOMERY had of
BENJAMIN ANGEL. Entry No. 1426.

23 Dec. 1779. JAMES FLETCHER e. 400 ac. head Larel fork..N fork New
River..on ridge leads Pond Mountain. Entry No. 1427.

23 Dec. 1779. JAMES FLETCHER e. 300 ac. on Syluses Branch of New River..
near the falls. Entry No. 1428.

23 Dec. 1779. JAMES FLETCHER e. 100 ac. head waters Horse Creek of New
River..dividing ridge between head little Horse Creek &
some head waters Laurel fork known by name of Nalls Elk Garden..includ-
ing the gardain..(JAMES FLETCHER marked out..RUBEN WOOD written in).
Entry No. 1429.

23 Dec. 1779. JAMES FLETCHER e. 300 ac. on three top fork New River..
above end Three Top Mountain. Entry No. 1430.

23 Dec. 1779. JAMES FLETCHER e. 150 ac. long shoal creek on New River..
above small bridge..(Duplicate May 19th AD 1806 written
in margin). Entry No. 1431.

23 Dec. 1779. JAMES FLETCHER e. 200 ac. some waters Obeds Creek..near
main road on both sides branch that OWENS camp is at..
(JAMES FLETCHER marked out..ROBERT NALL written in). Entry No. 1432.

23 Dec. 1779. JAMES FLETCHER e. 100 ac. W fork New River..(JAMES FLET-
CHER & MICAJAH PENNINGTON marked out..WILLIAM PENNINGTON
written in). Entry No. 1433.

23 Dec. 1779. JAMES FLETCHER e. 400 ac. waters New River..near road
from SQUIRE MORRISES to PENNINGTONS Mill..including some
head waters Silus branch and Dog Creek. Entry No. 1434.

23 Dec. 1779. JAMES FLETCHER e. 150 ac. Nathans Creek. Entry No. 1435.

29 Dec. 1779. JAMES FLETCHER, JUNR. e. 150 ac. Cranes Creek near his
other line..including the good land. Entry No. 1436.

20 Dec. 1779. JAMES FLETCHER e. 150 ac. left fork Dog Creek at JOHN
BAKERS path..(JAMES FLETCHER marked out..HENRY SHUTE
written in). Entry No. 1437.

29 Dec. 1779. JAMES FLETCHER e. 50 ac. S side Old Field Creek of New
River..(JAMES FLETCHER marked out..ROBERT NALL written
in). Entry No. 1438.

29 Dec. 1779. BENJAMIN HERNDON e. 300 ac. ridge called Deep Gap near
old camp..including some of head waters Deep Gap Creek &
Stoney fork..(entry taken away by second entry..entry cross-marked out).
Entry No. 1439.

29 Dec. 1779. JAMES FLETCHER e. 400 ac. near his other line..both sides
main road..including some waters Cub Creek and (?) branch
and part of Cranes path where it leaves main road. Entry No. 1440.

29 Dec. 1779. THOMAS WATKINS e. 100 ac. Bledsoes gap..including waters
Nathans Creek and Long Shoal Creek..(entry crossed out
and word False written in). No entry no.

29 Dec. 1779. BENJAMIN CLEVELAND e. 400 ac. waters Bugaboe and long
branch Roaring River..(entry is crossed and word false
written in). No entry no.

29 Dec. 1779. BENJAMIN CLEVELAND e. 200 ac. waters New River on Horse
Creek..(entry crossed out and word false written in).
No entry no.

29 Dec. 1779. RICHARDSON OWENS e. 640 ac. on (?) fork being S fork
Little River. Entry No. 1441.

29 Dec. 1779. SAMUEL WILCOXSON e. 100 ac. N side New River..near COUCHES
entry..(SAMUEL WILCOXSON and JAMES FLETCHER marked out..
JOSEPH COUCH written in). Entry No. 1441.

29 Dec. 1779. JOHN BAKER e. 200 ac. S fork New River..joining DANIEL
RICHARDSONS line..including vacant land..(JOHN BAKER
marked out..DANIEL RICHARDSON sold by the Sheriff written in). Entry
No. 1442.

29 Dec. 1779.   WILLIAM DAVIS e. 100 ac. waters (?)..joining THOMAS
                PAYNE entry on top of Ridge. Entry No. 1443.

29 Dec. 1779.   WILLIAM DAVIS e. 100 ac. on top of ridge near head waters
                ..S fork Mitchels River. Entry No. 1444.

29 Dec. 1779.   JAMES TATE e. 50 ac. path from HUGH SMITHS to Cranberry
                Creek..end of Chesnut Knob..including said Knob..(JAMES
TATE marked out..FANNEY VICKAS written in). Entry No. 1445.

29 Dec. 1779.   STEVEN AUSTIN e. 50 ac. on Christians Creek..fork Mitchels
                River at his other line he bought of ROBINSON..(STEVEN
AUSTIN marked out..WILLIAM AUSTIN written in). Entry No. 1446.

29 Dec. 1779.   JOHN ROBINSON e. 100 ac. on Christians Creek of Mitchels
                Riverfork..said creek near big falls. Entry No. 1447.

29 Dec. 1779.   HENRY REED e. 100 ac. waters Hunting Creek..W side of N
                BARNES line. Entry No. 1448.

29 Dec. 1779.   SAMUEL WILLCOXSON e. 100 ac. small branch of Cub Creek..
                including ridge between Hunting Creek and Cub Creek..
(SAMUEL WILLCOXSON marked out..SAMUEL ANDERSON written in). Entry No.
1449.

29 Dec. 1779.   MEMUCAN HUNT e. 250 ac. head Old Field Creek of New River
                ..near ridge between said creek and Buffaloe..including
some of water of Beaver Creek. Entry No. 1450.

29 Dec. 1779.   MEMUCAN HUNT e. 250 ac. in Bledsoes Gap..adjoining WATKINS
                line..including some of water Long Shoal Creek or Nathans
Creek. Entry No. 1451.

29 Dec. 1779.   BENJAMIN HERNDON e. 320 ac. on JAMES FLETCHERS lower line
                ..down main road both sides..including some waters Fishes
Creek..(entry withdrawn by the entyer). Entry No. 1452.

29 Dec. 1779.   BENJAMIN HERNDON e. 150 ac. joining S & W forks HAUNCH
                LICANS line..on side Brushey Mountain..(BENJ. HERNDON
marked out..WM. MATHIS written in). Entry No. 1453.

29 Dec. 1779.   JOHN OREAR e. 150 ac. between little River and Noheaded
                branch..S side Peak Mountain..(JOHN OREAR, CLIZBEY COBB,
JONATHAN HAINES marked out..WILLIAM LENOIR written in). Entry No. 1454.

29 Dec. 1779.   JOHN BAKER e. 640 ac. head waters Chesnut Creek..New
                River..near Fishes Gap and some head waters Meadow Creek..
including OSBURNS Camp..(JOHN BAKER marked out..WILLIAM DAVIDSON written
in). Entry No. 1455.

31 Dec. 1779.   JOHN BAKER e. 300 ac. head Praters Creek..near old path
                goes from Elk Creek Ridge to DANIEL RICHARDSONS..(JOHN
BAKER marked out..JACOB SIGLER written in). Entry No. 1456.

31 Dec. 1779.   JOHN BAKER e. 200 ac. fork of Cranberry on N side branch..
                runs into creek..N side Turkey Knob..including the good
land..(JOHN BAKER & SOLLOMON BAKER marked out..JONATHAN STAMPER written
in). Entry No. 1457.

31 Dec. 1779.   JOHN BAKER e. 200 ac. on Peak Creek..joining WM. NALLS
                line. Entry No. 1458.

31 Dec. 1779.   JOHN BAKER e. 200 ac. N side S fork New River..(JOHN
                BAKER & GEORGE BAKER marked out..CHRISTIAN BURKETT
written in). Entry No. 1459.

31 Dec. 1779.   JOHN BAKER e. 100 ac. waters Mitchels River..fork runs
                between JAMES WALLENS..(JOHN BAKER marked out..ANDREW
BAKER written in). Entry No. 1460.

31 Dec. 1779.   JOHN BAKER e. 200 ac. waters Cranberry Creek of New River
                ..N side Elk Hill..including the rich land..(JOHN BAKER
marked out..THOS. JOHNSON written in). Entry No. 1461.

31 Dec. 1779.   JAMES WARD e. 150 ac. main fork New River..including
                JOHN LEERAYS improvement. Entry No. 1462.

31 Dec. 1779.   JAMES WARD e. 100 ac. New River..near ridge between two
                branches. Entry No. 1463.

31 Dec. 1779.   JAMES WARD e. 100 ac. N fork New River above seven islands.
                Entry No. 1464.

31 Dec. 1779.   JAMES WARD e. 50 ac. on New River below the fork. Entry
                No. 1465.

31 Dec. 1779.   JOHN OLIVER e. 100 ac. Rockey branch. Entry No. 1466.

31 Dec. 1779.   THOMAS TERRY, son of JOSEPH TERRY..e. 200 ac. N side New
                River below Ilk Shoals and Island..(THOMAS TERRY, ROBERT
NALL marked out..JUSTICE BOLLINS written in). Entry No. 1467.

1 Jan. 1780.   THOMAS TERRY..son of JOSEPH TERRY..e. 100 ac. on Beaver
               Creek..N side New River on BENJAMIN CLEVELANDS upper line.
Entry No. 1468.

1 Jan. 1780.   JAMES FLETCHER e. 600 ac. head waters Crab fork Little
               River..joining the Virginia line..near path that goes from
CAPT. HARDINS to Fishers Gapp. Entry No. 1469.

1 Jan. 1780.   JAMES FLETCHER e. 200 ac. waters Mitchels River on fork
               Taylors branch known by name of Rich Cove..including the
Cove with SOLOMON HIX'S improvement. Entry No. 1470.

1 Jan. 1780.   JAMES FLETCHER e. 300 ac. on his E line..both sides main
               road that goes to Wilkes Court House..including some of
waters of Cub Creek. Entry No. 1471.

1 Jan. 1780.   JAMES FLETCHER e. 400 ac. on waters Bear Creek of New
               River..near the waggon road..including the good land
thereabouts. Entry No. 1472.

1 Jan. 1780.   JOHN PARKS, CAPT...e. 100 ac. N fork Roaring River. Entry
               No. 1473.

1 Jan. 1780.   REUBEN PARKS e. 400 ac. waters Roaring River. Entry No.
               1474.

1 Jan. 1780.   WILLIAM CANADY e. 200 ac. on creek that PETER PEARSON
               lives on..at COLEYS line. Entry No. 1475.

1 Jan. 1780.   WILLIAM CANADY e. 200 ac. Fans branch at WM. WATSONS line..
               (WM. CANADY & ELKANEY LEWIS marked out..WM. WATSON (?)
written in). Entry No. 1476.

1 Jan. 1780.   WILLIAM CANADY e. 100 ac. joining THOMAS MAYS line and
               JAMES WALINGS line..(Entry withdrawn by the entryer).
Entry No. 1477.

1 Jan. 1780.   WILLIAM CANADY e. 100 ac. on Big Elkin..in his own line.
               Entry No. 1478.

1 Jan. 1780.   MARTIN ADAMS e. 50 ac. Beaver Creek..adjoining WM. COLVARDS
               line..including the improvement. Entry No. 1479.

1 Jan. 1780.   ROWLAND JUDD e. 400 ac. at W end Buck Mountain..S down
               Old Field Creek. Entry No. 1480.

1 Jan. 1780.   MEMUCAN HUNT e. 200 ac. Rich Gap of Buck Mountain..near
               path leads from WM. SCOTTS to Three Top Mountain..includ-
ing good land on both sides path. Entry No. 1481.

1 Jan. 1780.   MEMUCAN HUNT e. 100 ac. on New River..N fork on Staggs
               Creek..below WM. HENSONS improvement..including said
improvement. Entry No. 1482.

4 Jan. 1780.   JAMES HAGOOD e. 200 ac. on waters Hunting Creek..on top of
               mountain..(JAMES HAGOOD marked out..JAMES FLETCHER written
in). Entry No. 1483.

4 Jan. 1780.   JAMES HAGOOD e. 50 ac. waters Bryer Creek on TURNBILLS
               line..(JAMES HAGOOD marked out..JAMES FLETCHER written in).
Entry No. 1484.

5 Jan. 1780.   WILLIAM HARRISON e. 100 ac. N side Reddies River..second
               foard where he now lives. Entry No. 1485.

5 Jan. 1780.   WILLIAM LENOIR e. 200 ac. joining his other survey whereon
               JOHN SUTTON now lives..including some waters of Saw Mill
Creek. Entry No. 1486.

5 Jan. 1780.   WILLIAM LENOIR e. 150 ac. joining an entry he sold to
               SAMUEL STALLING..including some waters of Fishes Creek and
others..(WM. LENOIR marked out..ANDREW YERGAIN written in). Entry No.
1487.

5 Jan. 1780.   ISAAC NORMAN e. 250 ac. on Pine Creek on N side. Entry No.
               1488.

6 Jan. 1780.   WILLIAM LENOIR e. 200 ac. E fork Little Elk Creek of New
               River..joining E side BEVERLY WATKINS entry. Entry No.
1489.

6 Jan. 1780.   WILLIAM LENOIR e. 200 ac. W fork Little Elk Creek..joining
               W side BEVERLY WATKINS entry. Entry No. 1490.

6 Jan. 1780.   WILLIAM LENOIR e. 640 ac. both sides Pine Creek that runs
               in E side New River..below path leads from -----cocks (?)
improvement to MICAJAH PENNINGTONS..(In margin..Deeded to JOHN LATIMER).
Entry No. 1491.

6 Jan. 1780.   WILLIAM LENOIR e. 200 ac. between New River & Fighting
               Creek..(WM. LENOIR marked out..transfared to PETER WHITAKER
written in). Entry No. 1492.

6 Jan. 1780.   WILLIAM LENOIR e. 200 ac. both sides little Helton Creek.
               Entry No. 1493.

6 Jan. 1780.   WILLIAM LENOIR e. 200 ac. both sides little Helton Creek..
               joining the Virginia line below BENAJAH PENNINGTONS im-
provement that lies in Virginia. Entry No. 1494.

6 Jan. 1780.   JOHN OREAR e. 250 ac. on Pine Swamp above MARTIN GAMBILLS
               line..(JOHN OREAR and JAMES HARTE (?) marked out..JOHN
COX written in). Entry No. 1495.

6 Jan. 1780.   WILLIAM STURDIE e. 200 ac. N side New River..opposite
               mouth Brushey Creek. Entry No. 1496.

6 Jan. 1780. WILLIAM STURDIE e. 200 ac. Grassy fork of Obeds Creek. Entry No. 1497.

7 Jan. 1780. BAILEY CHANDLOW e. 50 ac. on EDWARD CROSSES line..joining CHANDLOWS other entry. Entry No. 1498.

10 Jan. 1780. CHARLES CRANSHAW e. 200 ac. joining his entry upper N & S line..including both sides road. Entry No. 1499.

10 Jan. 1780. ALEXANDER GILREATH e. 100 ac. head two little branches that makes into branch THOMAS HOPPER lives on..(ALEX. GILREATH marked out..entry withdrawn). Entry No. 1500.

10 Jan. 1780. ALEXANDER GILREATH e. 150 ac. Branch Hunting Creek.. opposite REUBIN STANDLEYS entry below where SAMUEL LANS-DOWNS house (??). Entry No. 1501.

10 Jan. 1780. ALEXANDER GILREATH e. 150 ac. near JOSHUA MORGANS line.. including some of branches Little Cub Creek. Entry No. 1502.

10 Jan. 1780. WILLIAM FLETCHER e. 100 ac. on Stoney Fork of Yadkin River..at JOHN FARGUSONS line..(Entry withdrawn by the enterer). Entry No. 1503.

10 Jan. 1780. WILLIAM FLETCHER e. 100 ac. Stoney Fork of Yadkin River.. at JOHN FARGUSONS line..(Entry withdrawn by the enterer). Entry No. 1504.

10 Jan. 1780. MEMUCAN HUNT e. 150 ac. some waters of Hunting Creek at HARRIS STANDLEYS branch. Entry No. 1505.

10 Jan. 1780. MEMUCAN HUNT e. 300 ac. Bugaboe Creek. Entry No. 1506.

10 Jan. 1780. MEMUCAN HUNT e. 250 ac. near top of Blue Ridge on road leads from Stoney Fork to Bent of New River..including Osburns Springs. Entry No. 1507.

8 Jan. 1780. MEMUCAN HUNT e. 320 ac. on Pine Swamp..branch New River.. below COLO. GORDONS entry. Entry No. 1508.

8 Jan. 1780. MEMUCAN HUNT e. 250 ac. on big Bugahoe Creek. Entry No. 1509.

8 Jan. 1780. MEMUCAN HUNT e. 300 ac. E fork Little Elkin. Entry No. 1510.

11 Jan. 1780. MEMUCAN HUNT e. 320 ac. adjoining the tract called Hughes Bottom. Entry No. 1511.

11 Jan. 1780. MEMUCAN HUNT e. 300 ac. waters Little Elkin. Entry No. 1512.

11 Jan. 1780. HENRY REED e. 50 ac. E line his own tract. Entry No. 1513.

11 Jan. 1780. RICHARD ALLEN e. 100 ac. on Little Bugaboe above his own line where he lives. Entry No. 1514.

11 Jan. 1780. RICHARD ALLEN e. 40 ac. his line..including Maple Swamp. Entry No. 1515.

11 Jan. 1780. ABEL CARTER e. 100 ac. waters Big Elkin above HUMPHREY NIECES'S. Entry No. 1516.

15 Jan. 1780. WILLIAM LENOIR e. 60 ac. on Fishes Creek..including waters of branch at his other line. Entry No. 1517.

15 Jan. 1780. BENJAMIN HERNDON e. 240 ac. Cranberry Creek of New River
..at lower end Great Meadows of Cranberry Creek where the
hills makes (meets?) near the Creek on both sides..including an old Ax
entry made by BARRY BRUMLY. Entry No. 1518.

11 Jan. 1780. BENJAMIN HERNDON e. 200 ac. mile and a half above fork
Elk Creek of New River. Entry No. 1519.

13 Jan. 1780. SAMUEL SUMNER e. 50 ac. top of Blue Ridge..including some
waters of Brushey fork of New River. Entry No. 1520.

13 Jan. 1780. THOMAS CALLAWAY e. 200 ac. Slide fork Obeds Creek..adjoin-
ing JOHN BROWNS or THOMAS PAYNE, JUNR. S line..(THOMAS
CALLAWAY marked out..JOHN JOHNSON written in). Entry No. 1521.

13 Jan. 1780. THOMAS CALLAWAY e. 200 ac. little Fork of Obeds Creek..
(THOMAS CALLAWAY marked out..JOHN JOHNSON written in).
Entry No. 1522.

13 Jan. 1780. THOMAS CALLAWAY e. 50 ac. line his former entry..S side
New River..(THOMAS CALLAWAY & NEMIATH BLUHMER (?) marked
out..SAMUEL CARTER written in). Entry No. 1523.

23 Jan. 1780. MEMUCAN HUNT e. 300 ac. waters Beaver Creek on New River.
Entry No. 1524.

13 Jan. 1780. BENJAMIN CUTHBERTH e. 100 ac. on Deep Gap Creek near mouth
little fork below COLO. CLEVELANDS. Entry No. 1525.

16 Jan. 1780. JAMES BROWN e. 50 ac. waters Hunting Creek at PETER GOODS
N corner..his N line to MITCHELS line. Entry No. 1526.

16 Jan. 1780. DAVID HARVIL e. 100 ac. long Branch at lower end his old
survey..(DAVID HARVIL marked out..BENJAMIN HERNDON
written in). Entry No. 1527.

16 Jan. 1780. DAVID HARVIL e. 50 ac. head long Branch..(DAVID HARVIL
marked out..BENJAMIN HERNDON written in). Entry No. 1528.

16 Jan. 1780. NATHAN BARNETT e. 75 ac. on fork Bear Branch. Entry No.
1529.

17 Jan. 1780. MUMUCAN HUNT e. 250 ac. Big Bald Mountain..adjoining line
of WILLIAM LENOIR. Entry No. 1530.

17 Jan. 1780. MEMUCAN HUNT e. 250 ac. Big Bald Mountain on or near his
own line. Entry No. 1531.

17 Jan. 1780. MEMUCAN HUNT e. 150 ac. S side Howards Creek on New River
..below path goes from Camp Creek..path head fork of Cove
Creek. Entry No. 1532.

17 Jan. 1780. MEMUCAN HUNT e. 300 ac. waters Little River..S side
Chesnut Ridge. Entry No. 1533.

17 Jan. 1780. MEMUCAN HUNT e. 300 ac. waters Beaver Dam Creek..both
sides path..at the rich mountain. Entry No. 1534.

17 Jan. 1780. MEMUCAN HUNT e. 300 ac. right hand fork Beaver Dam Creek.
Entry No. 1535.

17 Jan. 1780. BENJAMIN HERNDON e. 500 ac. on OSBURNS line on ridge
between Rock Creek & Elk Creek..including improvement
MICAJAH BUNCH made on the rich mountain. Entry No. 1536.

17 Jan. 1780. MARY GORDON e. 100 ac. at JOSEPH HOLDMANS corner on main
road..both sides said road including some waters of Cub
Creek..(entry withdrawn). Entry No. 1537.

20 Jan. 1780. 1st enterer marked out completely..e. 100 ac. branch
called SIMON CARTERS Branch..waters Little Elkin..(WM.
TERREL LEWIS marked out..GABRIEL PHILIPS written in). Entry No. 1538.

21 Jan. 1780. MOSES JOHNSTON e. 100 ac. Little Elkin below big falls.
Entry No. 1539.

21 Jan. 1780. JOHN HOWARD e. 200 ac. S side Hunting Creek at JAMES
BROWNS line. Entry No. 1540.

21 Jan. 1780. JOHN HOWARD e. 100 ac. Little fork Hunting Creek on SAIL
BAKERS upper line..(JOHN HOWARD marked out..JAMES REAVES
written in). Entry No. 1541.

21 Jan. 1780. WILLIAM SMITH e. 300 ac. waters Cub Creek at his W line..
both sides main road..including some waters Moravian
Creek..(WM. SMITH marked out..BEN JOHNSON written in). Entry No. 1542.

21 Jan. 1780. WILLIAM MITCHEL e. 100 ac. on Dausons branch..on his W
line..(WM. MITCHEL marked out..ISAAC ELLEDGE written in).
Entry No. 1543.

22 Jan. 1780. JOHN JOHNSTON e. 100 ac. side Roaring River on Great
Branch..near great falls..(entry withdrawn). Entry No.
1544.

21 Jan. 1780. JOHN JOHNSTON e. 400 ac. falling branch..some waters
Yadkin River..including head of Sebastiams branch..(JOHN
JOHNSTON marked out..JOHN SHUMATE written in). Entry No. 1545.

22 Jan. 1780. REUBEN FLETCHER e. 50 ac. waters Hunting Creek..at his
own corner..N with MITCHELS line. Entry No. 1546.

22 Jan. 1780. ELISHA REYNOLDS e. 200 ac. S side Roaring River..near
mouth Camp branch..(entry withdrawn). Entry No. 1547.

22 Jan. 1780. LEONARD SALES e. 320 ac. Duggars Branch near where Adams
Spring branch runs. Entry No. 1548.

24 Jan. 1780. ELISHA REYNOLDS e. 200 ac. fork Roaring River..right hand
fork Camp Branch. Entry No. 1549.

24 Jan. 1780. LEONARD SALES e. 370 ac. on Duggars branch at MISAS
(MIZES) upper line. Entry No. 1550.

24 Jan. 1780. JEFFREY JOHNSTON (JOHNSON) e. 300 ac. where his own line
joins MR. DENNEYS line..including Indiams Branch and Rock
Branch. Entry No. 1551.

24 Jan. 1780. FRANCIS REYNOLDS e. 200 ac. Rockey fork Branch of Mulberry
Creek..including head Little fork Rock Creek. Entry No.
1552.

24 Jan. 1780. FRANCIS REYNOLDS e. 100 ac. S side Roaring River on Camp
Branch..at his own lower line. Entry No. 1553.

24 Jan. 1780. HENRY CARTER e. 100 ac. on Peak Creek at E line of Land
he bought of JAMES REYNOLDS..up said creek to Yadkin
River. Entry No. 1554.

24 Jan. 1780. JOSEPH HERNDON e. 200 ac. upper long branch Mulberry
Creek..above path leads from Mulberry Fields to CHARLES
HICKERSONS. Entry No. 1555.

24 Jan. 1780. BOMAN CASS e. 100 ac. little fork Hunting Creek..joining
said CASS'S entry at upper end. Entry No. 1556.

24 Jan. 1780. BOMAN CASS e. 200 ac. Duggars Mountain big branch little
fork Hunting Creek..(BOMAN CASS marked out..JOHN MIZE
written in). Entry No. 1557.

24 Jan. 1780. JOHN FORBUSH e. 100 ac. little fork Hunting Creek at JOHN
HOWARDS lower line..(JOHN FORBUSH marked out..JOHN HOWARD
written in). Entry No. 1558.

27 Jan. 1780. JOSEPH HERNDON e. 200 ac. S side Yadkin River at mouth of
Moravian Creek at JOSEPH WILSONS upper corner..S side
River & Moravian Creek to JOSHUA SCURLOCKS line. Entry No. 1559.

28 Jan. 1780. BEN PERKINS..(entry withdrawn..no other writing). Entry
No. 1560.

28 Jan. 1780. JOHN BROWN e. 200 ac. on waters N fork Lewis Fork..upper
line entry made where JOHN ADAMS cabbin is. Entry No.
1561.

28 Jan. 1780. JOHN FORBUSH e. 50 ac. on condt. line between JOHN HOWARD
and said FORBUSH..including the good land between that
line and FORBUSHS lower line. Entry No. 1562.

28 Jan. 1780. JOHN BROWN e. 200 ac. Reedy Branch of Readys River above
entry made on SHARPERS improvement. Entry No. 1563.

28 Jan. 1780. JAMES BROWN e. 100 ac. N side New River..joining his
other entry. Entry No. 1564.

28 Jan. 1780. HENRY HAND e. 200 ac. three forks big Glades..W side his
other entry. Entry No. 1565.

28 Jan. 1780. HENRY HAND e. 320 ac. Brushey fork New River..a little
Knob..(HENRY HAND marked out..CHRISTEFOR MANARD written
in). Entry No. 1566.

29 Jan. 1780. DEVOREUX BALLARD e. 120 ac. said BALLARDS line below his
Mill down both sides his Mill Creek..(DEVEREAUX BALLARD
marked out..STEPHEN HARRIS marked out..SILAS TOMKINS written in).
Entry No. 1567.

29 Jan. 1780. DEVEREUX BALLARD e. 150 ac. N fork Fishes Creek..above an
old Cabbin on Hunting Creek..path where READDEN TOMPSON
once lived. Entry No. 1568.

29 Jam. 1780. DEVEREUX BALLARD e. 50 ac. head Ballards Mill Creek.
Entry No. 1569.

29 Jan. 1780. WILLIAM LENOIR e. 300 ac. between Moravian Creek & Cub
Creek joining LENOIR & JOSHUA SCURLOCKS lines..including
part of the main road..(WM. LENOIR & WILLIAM JOHNSON marked out..GEORGE
LANSDOWN written in). Entry No. 1570.

29 Jan. 1780 JOHN MORRIS e. 100 ac. waters Fishes Creek at CARLTON
KEELINGS line..including head WM. HOLDERS Creek. Entry
No. 1571.

29 Jan. 1780. THOMAS JONES e. 100 ac. both sides Fishes Creek at JAMES
               JONES line. Entry No. 1572.

29 Jan. 1780. WILLIAM JONES e. 100 ac. some waters Fishes Creek at
               THOMAS JONES E line. Entry No. 1573.

29 Jan. 1780. JOSEPH HORTON e. 50 ac. at his former survey..branch
               called the Tan-Trough Branch. Entry No. 1574.

29 Jan. 1780. JOHN DARNALL e. 80 ac. at WM. FRAZERS N Corner. Entry
               No. 1575.

29 Jan. 1780. JOHN DARNALL e. 80 ac. at WM. FRAZERS..S up Brushey Mtn.
               Entry No. 1576.

29 Jan. 1780. BENJAMIN BRIMER e. 100 ac. fork Elk Creek..adjoining his
               former entry..(BENJ. BRIMER marked out..BENJAMIN DUGGAR
written in).   Entry No. 1577.

1 Feb. 1780.   JOHN DOYLE e. 100 ac. Pipe Camp Branch..waters Hunting
               Creek on WM. HULINS line..including a mill seat. Entry
No. 1578.

1 Feb. 1780.   GEORGE PAYNE e. 200 ac. main fork Roaring River..point of
               a mtn...two hundred yards of Orears foard. Entry No. 1579.

1 Feb. 1780.   BIRD HAYGOOD e. 50 ac. E fork Fishes Creek..head said
               creek on Brushey Mountain..(BIRD HAGOOD marked out..JOHN
BULLEN written in). Entry No. 1580.

2 Feb. 1780.   THOMAS TOMSON e. 50 ac. on Hunting Creek..above his im-
               provement..(THOMAS TOMSON & JOHN CHANDLOW marked out..
JOHN LOVE written in). Entry No. 1581.

2 Feb. 1780.   DAVID WITHERSPOON e. 200 ac. N fork Beaver Creek on JAMES
               HENDERSONS line. Entry No. 1582.

2 Feb. 1780.   JAMES WILSON e. 150 ac. E side Cub Creek on JOHN WHITAKERS
               corner. Entry No. 1583. -

2 Feb. 1780.   CHARLES RUNNALDS (REYNOLDS) e. 100 ac. on E side Cub Creek
               ..on JAMES WILSONS line. Entry No. 1584.

2 Feb. 1780.   THOMAS BENGE e. 100 ac. Brushey Mountain..joining said
               BENGE & MR. BURROS line. Entry No. 1585.

4 Feb. 1780.   JOHN BAKER e. 400 ac. Praters Creek of New River..joining
               RICHARD ALLENS line..(JOHN BAKER, JACOB SIGLER & WILLIAM
NALL marked out..ELISHA BALDWIN written in). Entry No. 1586.

4 Feb. 1780.   JOSEPH SOUTH..(entry withdrawn..no other writing). Entry
               No. 1587.

4 Feb. 1780.   ROSANAH ROBERTS e. 250 ac. on Duggars Creek on JOHN EVANS
               former line..including her improvement. Entry No. 1588.

4 Feb. 1780.   JAMES MCBRIDE e. 120 ac. middle fork Hunting Creek..head
               Bear Branch. Entry No. 1589..

4 Feb. 1780.   JAMES GARRISON e. 50 ac. Pipe Camp branch of Hunting Creek.
               Entry No. 1590.

4 Feb. 1780.   JOHN ADAMS e. 50 ac. N fork Lewis Fork. Entry No. 1591.

4 Feb. 1780. WILLIAM ADAMS e. 50 ac. N side Lewis Fork somewhere in his other line to JOHN ADAMS line. Entry No. 1592.

4 Feb. 1780. JOHN BAKER e. 50 ac. on New River joining ALEXANDER GORDONS ..near Rockey fork..(JOHN BAKER marked out..WILLIAM HUMPHRIES marked out..JAMES BUNYARD written in). Entry No. 1593.

4 Feb. 1780. CHARLES CRENSHAW e. 300 ac. joining CHARLES WALKER & JOHN WHITAKERS..including the Hollows & head of big branch. Entry No. 1594.

5 Feb. 1780. THOMAS GOINS e. 50 ac. near Big Elkin Creek..adjoining his old entry..contrary to THOMAS PAYNES entry. Entry No. 1595.

5 Feb. 1780. THOMAS GOINS e. 100 ac. near SAMUEL SCRITCHFIELDS line.. towards JOHN FIDDLERS. Entry No. 1596.

5 Feb. 1780. THOMAS GOINS e. 100 ac. near ELISHA HEDDINS line..down Big Elkin Creek..(THOMAS GOINS marked out..TIMOTHY IZELL written in). Entry No. 1597.

5 Feb. 1780. THOMAS GOINS e. 50 ac. near Big Elkin Creek..adjoining his lower entry..near to THOMAS PAYNES entry. Entry No. 1598.

5 Feb. 1780. WILLIAM LENOIR e. 300 ac. N fork Fishes Creek..waters Cub Creek..joining ISAAC WALKERS land..including some part of CRANES path. Entry No. 1599.

5 Feb. 1780. THOMAS GILBERT e. 50 ac. Deep Gap Creek where STRINGERS path crosses the creek. Entry No. 1600.

7 Feb. 1780. JOSHUA TOMSON e. 200 ac. N side Hunting Creek at REUBEN STANDLEYS land that he sold to JAMES LOVE. Entry No. 1601.

7 Feb. 1780. JACOB PATE e. 100 ac. N side Hunting Creek..near his other line. Entry No. 1602.

7 Feb. 1780. JOHN WHITAKER e. 50 ac. waters Cub Creek..(JOHN WHITAKER, BENJAMIN PARKER marked out..CHARLES GORDON, JUNR. written in). Entry No. 1603.

7 Feb. 1780. ISAAC DARNALL e. 100 ac. on Fishes Creek..joining said DARNALLS improvement. Entry No. 1604.

7 Feb. 1780. WILLIAM GILREATH e. 290 ac. Rock Creek..a half-mile above JEFFREY JOHNSONS line..(WM. GILREATH marked out..ELIAS MASSEY written in). Entry No. 1605.

7 Feb. 1780. JAMES BROWN e. 100 ac. Hunting Creek..near his giving (?) line of survey he now lives on..including the various line between his two surveys. Entry No. 1606.

8 Feb. 1780. FRANCIS VANNOY e. 320 ac. S fork Rock Creek..mouth of ELISHA REYNOLDS Branch. Entry No. 1607.

8 Feb. 1780. FRANCIS VANNOY e. 150 ac. near main Rick Creek..including good land. Entry No. 1608.

8 Feb. 1780. FRANCIS VANNOY e. 100 ac. S Beaver..at his other line on said creek..(FRANCIS VANNOY, JASPER BILLINGS & GEORGE BAKER marked out..CATTREN RITTER written in). Entry No. 1609.

10 Feb. 1780. THOMAS STUBBLEFIELD e. 150 ac. on GEORGE STUBBLEFIELDS improvement..on his back line. Entry No. 1610.

10 Feb. 1780. WILLIAM VIARS e. 50 ac. waters Reddies River at a condt.
line made between WM. TIREY and WM. VIARS. Entry No. 1611

10 Feb. 1780. WILLIAM VIARS e. 50 ac. on Rackcoon Branch. Entry No.
1612.

10 Feb. 1780. JOEL STAMPER e. 250 ac. path goes from the bullhead to
JACOB MINERS..S side Chesnut Ridge near the spring on
waters Little River..(JOEL STAMPER & MORGAN BRYANT marked out..FRANCIS
BRYANT written in). Entry No. 1613.

10 Feb. 1780. ANDREW CANADY e. 250 ac. on Mockasan Creek. Entry No.
1614.

11 Feb. 1780. NATHANIEL JUDD e. 200 ac. near a pond between Lewis Fork
and Reddies River waters. Entry No. 1615.

11 Feb. 1780. NATHANIEL JUDD e. 100 ac. S fork Reddies River. Entry No.
1616.

14 Feb. 1780. TIMOTHY SISK e. 100 ac. on his own corner. Entry No.
1617.

14 Feb. 1780. CHARLES PARKS e. 100 ac. waters Swan Creek..joining his
own line. Entry No. 1618.

14 Feb. 1780. WILLIAM LOVEING e. 100 ac. on corner on River bank.
Entry No. 1619.

14 Feb. 1780. GABRIEL LOVING, JUNR. e. 300 ac. on creek called JOHN
PARKS..Creek on the County line. Entry No. 1620.

15 Feb. 1780. DANIEL HOLDMAN e. 100 ac. branch of Hunting Creek. Entry
No. 1621.

15 Feb. 1780. DANIEL HOLDMAN e. 100 ac. on Hunting Creek waters..at MR.
CRANES lower line..including some of waters of branches
that runs through said HOLDMANS plantation..(DANIEL HOLDMAN marked out..
JOHN LOVE written in). Entry No. 1622.

15 Feb. 1780. DANIEL HOLDMAN e. 50 ac. on Hunting Creek..condt. line
between AMBROS CRANE and ---TUSBURN CULLERS (?)..(Entry
withdrawn). Entry No. 1623.

16 Feb. 1780. RODDEN TOMPSON e. 100 ac. S side Hunting Creek..both
sides Rockey Creek..above a rich cove..including his improvement. Entry No. 1624.

16 Feb. 1780. EDMOND DEMMEY e. 300 ac. at his line where he lives..up
Roaring River to his Mill survey..including 300 ac. land
between the two lines. Entry No. 1625.

16 Feb. 1780. EDMOND DENNEY e. 150 ac. S side his entry on Cane Creek.
Entry No. 1626.

16 Feb. 1780. JOSEPH HAMRICK e. 100 ac. at JOSHUA MORGANS lower corner..
including vacant land between THOMAS WILSONS line and
MORGANS survey. Entry No. 1627.

16 Feb. 1780. THOMAS HAMRICK e. 100 ac. on Moravian Creek at his line
on both sides of said creek. Entry No. 1628.

16 Feb. 1780. STEPHEN SOUTHER e. 100 ac. waters Hunting Creek on OSBURN
KEELINGS line..along SOUTHERS other line. Entry No. 1629.

16 Feb. 1780. EDMOND DENNEY e. 200 ac. on Round Mountain Branch.
Entry No. 1630.

18 Feb. 1780.   THOMAS NEWBERRY, JUNR. e. 100 ac. between Sams Branch &
                Fishes Creek at old JONES E corner. Entry No. 1631.

18 Feb. 1780.   JOHN STANDLEY e. 100 ac. on Mill Creek at said STANDLEYS
                other line up creek on both sides..(JOHN STANDLEY marked
out..GEORGE COMBS written in). Entry No. 1632.

18 Feb. 1780.   ELISHA REYNOLDS e. 100 ac. S side Roaring River on head
                Camp Branch at his own upper line..(ELISHA REYNOLDS marked
out..MASON WHITLEY (WHEATLEY) written in). Entry No. 1633.

19 Feb. 1780.   ELISHA REYNOLDS e. 100 ac. S side Roaring River on Rockey
                fork at Camp Branch..including the meadow..(entry with-
drawn). Entry No. 1634.

21 Feb. 1780.   WILLIAM WILLCOCKS e. 100 ac. N fork Hunting Creek. Entry
                No. 1635.

22 Feb. 1780.   CHARLES GORDON e. 100 ac. Pine Swamp at his lower entry
                of his old entry. Entry No. 1636.

22 Feb. 1780.   JOHN PROPHET e. 50 ac. on New River..at his E line.
                Entry No. 1637.

22 Feb. 1780.   BENJAMIN CLEVELAND e. 500 ac. N side N fork Lewis Fork..
                joining his other survey..it being part improvement LAU-
RANCE TOMPSON claims. Entry No. 1638.

22 Feb. 1780.   ISHAM HARVIL e. 100 ac. at his other N line..including
                some waters of Duggars Creek. Entry No. 1639.

23 Feb. 1780.   WILLIAM JOHNSTON e. 100 ac. on small branch of Osburns
                Creek..N side HOWARDS line. Entry No. 1640.

23 Feb. 1780.   JAMES NORMAN e. 150 ac. at JOHN HOWARDS E & W lines..
                including NORMANS improvement. Entry No. 1641.

23 Feb. 1780.   JAMES NORMAN e. 150 ac. on W side Pine Mountain. Entry
                No. 1642.

23 Feb. 1780.   JACOB NICHOLS e. 120 ac. S side Yadkin River..at his
                upper corner on said river. Entry No. 1643.

25 Feb. 1780.   SAMUEL STALINGS e. 50 ac. S side Yadkin River on his E
                line. Entry No. 1644.

25 Feb. 1780.   REUBEN STANDLEY e. 100 ac. S side Hunting Creek at JAMES
                LOVES line..so as to asurtain various land between JOHN
STANDLEYS line and THOMAS TOMSONS line..(REUBEN STANDLEY marked out..WM.
COMBS written in). Entry No. 1645.

25 Feb. 1780.   WILLIAM KILBY e. 600 ac. some of waters of Reddies River
                ..at his other line. Entry No. 1646.

25 Feb. 1780.   CHARLES ADAMS e. 50 ac. N side Readies River at his other
                line. Entry No. 1647.

28 Feb. 1780.   JOHN HOWARD e. 50 ac. Pipe Camp Creek..below the head..
                (JOHN HOWARD marked out..RACHEL YOUNG written in). Entry
No. 1648.

Entry No. 1649 skipped.

28 Feb. 1780. THOMAS PAYNE, JUNR. e. 100 ac. on branch Obeds Creek of New River..joining his W line. Entry No. 1650.

28 Feb. 1780. RICHARD GWIN e. 320 ac. N side Yadkin River at EDWARD HUGHES upper line..down river..including said HUGHES old survey together with improvement where THOMAS PAYNE & WILLIAM PAYNE now lives. Entry No. 1651.

1 March 1780. ISAAC GARRISON e. 100 ac. on his own line..near the creek. Entry No. 1652.

1 March 1780. WILLIAM TOLBY e. 640 ac. on road that goes from COXES settlement to mouth Cranberry..upon waters Fighting Creek ..(WM. TOLBY marked out..PETER WHITEKER written in). Entry No. 1653.

1 March 1780. WILLIAM TOLBY e. 150 ac. at foot Peach Bottom Mountain.. including the cabbin made by JULIUS BUNCH..a little above the house..(WM. TOLBY marked out..JOHN CARRELL written in). Entry No. 1654.

1 March 1780. ANDREW CANADY e. 640 ac. on S side little River..laying on both sides road that goes from TAYLORS Camp to Little River below foard. Entry No. 1655.

1 March 1780. MARY GORDON e. 150 ac. Cub Creek..joining JOHN WHITAKER, JAMES WILSON, WILLIAM GILREATH and JAMES FREEMAN. Entry No. 1656.

1 March 1780. ENOCH OSBURN e. 200 ac. near GEORGE REAVES line below Rock Creek. Entry No. 1657.

1 March 1780. ENOCH OSBURN e. 200 ac. at MICAJAH PENNINGTONS line on Elk Creek. Entry No. 1658.

1 March 1780. WILLIAM MCCLAIN e. 200 ac. at MICAJAH PENNINGTONS line.. E crossing Elk Creek. Entry No. 1659.

1 March 1780. WILLIAM MCCLAIN and JOHNATHAN SMITH e. 100 ac. mouth of a spring branch..both sides River..(WM. MCCLAIN & JOHNATHAN SMITH marked out..LEVEY PENNINGTON written in). Entry No. 1660.

8 March 1780. WILLIAM MCCLAIN and JONATHAN SMITH e. 100 ac. mouth Old Field Creek..both sides of River..(WM. MCCLAIN & JONATHAN SMITH marked out..MICAJAH PENNINGTON written in). Entry No. 1661.

23 Feb. 1780. WILLIAM WHITAKER e. 200 ac. N side Yadkin River..above mouth Lewis Fork on HOLEMANS line. Entry No. 1662.

7 March 1780. ISAAC ELLEDGE e. 200 ac. waters Warriors Creek..joining line his former entry whereon he now lives..extending between line of THOMAS ELLEDGE, ELISHA DYER & PHILLIP WALKER..(ISAAC ELLEDGE marked out..WILLIAM JOHNSON written in). Entry No. 1663.

7 March 1780. BENJAMIN ELLEDGE e. 5 ac. on an Island in the Yadkin River..near Old MR. EALLISONS (?) & MEREDY DENINSONS.. including the whole. Entry No. 1664.

7 March 1780. BENJAMIN ELLEDGE e. 150 ac. near head of Yadkin River.. known by name the Rich Lands..including improvement whereon JOHN BATES lives..(BENJAMIN ELLEDGE marked out..JOHN L. JONES written in). Entry No. 1665.

7 March 1780. JONAS WIGGINS e. 50 ac. long Branch Lewis Fork at EBENEZER FAIRCHILDS upper line of said FAIRCHILDS entry..(Entry withdrawn). Entry No. 1666.

7 March 1780. ISAAC ELLEDGE e. 50 ac. Beaver Creek..joining THOMAS
ELLEDGE, BENJAMIN BROWN, FRANCIS ELLEDGE..including the
Bridge..both sides waggon road near the graveyard..(ISAAC ELLEDGE marked
out..JOHN BRUMLEY written in). Entry No. 1667.

7 March 1780. WILLIAM NALL e. 200 ac. Peak Creek..New River below the
Mill Seat. Entry No. 1668.

7 March 1780. ROWLAND JUDD e. 25 ac. S fork Reddies River on JOHN TIREYS
line..down both sides river. Entry No. 1669.

7 March 1780. GEORGE MORRIS e. 150 ac. waters Grassey Creek..N fork New
River on WILLIAM LENOIRS line. Entry No. 1670.

8 March 1780. MEREDITH MINTON e. 100 ac. at branch Lewis Fork where runs
between JOHN COOLEYS & MEREDITHS field..including his
field. Entry No. 1671.

8 March 1780. JOHN COLLIER, JUNR. e. 100 ac. N fork Roaring River..down
Hightowers Branch..including his improvement. Entry No.
1672.

8 March 1780. JAMES BUNYARD e. 100 ac. upper line where it crosses the
creek..including his improvement. Entry No. 1673.

8 March 1780. JAMES BUNYARD e. 100 ac. E fork Roaring River near his
line that runs up creek of Roaring River..including his
improvement. Entry No. 1674.

8 March 1780. NATHANIEL VANNOY e. 100 ac. E fork Crab fork joining his
back line. Entry No. 1675.

8 March 1780. NATHANIEL JUDD e. 100 ac. on waters Reddies River at
ROWLAND JUDDS line..including NATHANIEL JUDDS improvement.
Entry No. 1676.

8 March 1780. NATHANIEL JUDD e. 150 ac. waters Reddies River at BARNET
OWENS line near head Potato hill Branch..(NATHANIEL JUDD
marked out..WILLIAM KILBY written in). Entry No. 1677.

8 March 1780. BARNET OWENS e. 100 ac. waters Reddies River..near head
Tumbling Shoal Branch. Entry No. 1678.

8 March 1780. JOHN DOYAL e. 290 ac. between JAMES BROWNS & WILLIAMS
KELLINGS line on waters Hunting Creek..including the
vacant land between said lines..(JOHN DOYAL marked out..DAVID GRANT
written in). Entry No. 1679.

8 March 1780. CHRISTOPHER MAINARD e. 50 ac. N fork Roaring River near
lower end of the Roundabout. Entry No. 1680.

8 March 1780. JOSEPH GOUGE e. 100 ac. Big Falls Sandy Creek..Roaring
River. Entry No. 1681.

8 March 1780. MARTIN GAMBILL e. 150 ac. S side N fork New River at
Horesfoard below mouth Horse Creek..(MARTIN GAMBILL &
RICHARD ---- (?) marked out..transfered to ABRAHAM MAY written in).
Entry No. 1682.

8 March 1780. MARTIN GAMBILL e. 100 ac. on Horse Creek at CAPT. OSBORNS
line..(MARTIN GAMBILL & RICHARD ---- (?) marked out..
GUIDEAN LEWIS written in). Entry No. 1683.

9 March 1780. WILLIAM MCCUBBINS e. 100 ac. at his other line..down Byer
Creek..(WM. MCCUBBINS marked out..PARTIN HAGOOD written
in). Entry No. 1684.

9 March 1780. WILLIAM P. MCCUBBINS (?) e. 60 ac. land in Wilkes County
..(entry crossmarked out..no other wording on it). Entry
No. 1685.

9 March 1780. BENJAMIN ELLEDGE e. 150 ac. near head Yadkin River..name
of Rich Lands..including improvement where BENJAMIN
ELLEDGE now lives..(BENJ. ELLEDGE marked out..JOHN L. JONES written in).
Entry No. 1686.

9 March 1780. EMANUEL ROSE e. 200 ac. top Blue Ridge on dividing waters
New River & Roaring River..near a good spring..(EMANUEL
ROSE marked out..JOHN ALLEN WOODRUFF written in). Entry No. 1687.

9 March 1780. WILLIAM ORASTUS e. 60 ac. beginning at JOSEPH HORTONS W
line on Fishes Creek. Entry No. 1688.

9 March 1780. JACOB ROBERTS e. 50 ac. branch N fork Lewis Fork..joining
WILLIAM ROBERTS line. Entry No. 1689.

10 March 1780. JOSEPH THOMPSON e. 100 ac. on creek leads to AUSTINS gap
..joining said TOMPSONS other entry. Entry No. 1690.

10 March 1780. JOSEPH TOMPSON e. 100 ac. on Mitchels River..joining his
other entry. Entry No. 1691.

10 March 1780. JAMES BROWN, JUNR. e. 100 ac. on waters Reddies River.
Entry No. 1692.

10 March 1780. EPHRAIM NORRIS e. 50 ac. fork Beaver Creek..joining JOHN
NORRIS upper line on both sides creek. Entry No. 1693.

10 March 1780. EPHRAIM NORRIS e. 50 ac. Big Branch Beaver Creek..(EPH-
RAIM NORRIS marked out..WILLIAM ELLOSON written in).
Entry No. 1694.

10 March 1780. WILLIAM PENNINGTON e. 50 ac. N fork New River on condt.
line between JOSHUA WEAVER..(WM. PENNINGTON marked out..
SAMUEL TIN---(?) written in). Entry No. 1695.

10 March 1780. CLEVELAND COFFEE e. 50 ac. N fork Kings Creek near head
said creek. Entry No. 1696.

10 March 1780. WILLIAM TERREL LEWIS e. 400 ac. bounded by his own line..
THOMAS BECKNELLS line..JOHN BOURLANDS line..BENJAMIN
HERNDONS line..THOMAS BENGES line..JAMES FOXES line..including the vacant
land. Entry No. 1697.

10 March 1780. CORNELIUS SALE e. 100 ac. near his line top of mountain
..(CORNELIUS SALE marked out..WILLIAM SALE written in).
Entry No. 1698.

10 March 1780. CORNELIOUS SALE e. 100 ac. Top of mountain upon waters
of Hunting Creek. Entry No. 1699.

10 March 1780. JOHN BAKER e. 200 ac. S fork New River..lower end his
plantation opposite the plantation whereon HUGH SMITH
now lives..including said BAKERS improvement. Entry No. 1700.

10 March 1780. ANDREW BAKER e. 150 ac. head branch Three Top fork New
River at a Camp of said BAKERS..including the Duck Elk
Cove. Entry No. 1701.

10 March 1780. ANDREW BAKER e. 200 ac. on Roans Creek..N side New River
near upper foarding. Entry No. 1702.

10 March 1780. ANDREW BAKER e. 150 ac. on waters Roans Creek..above
upper foard..including the rich Timberlands at foot of
the big ridge..(ANDREW BAKER, JOHN SUMMONS & FREDERICK (?) marked out..
PETER ELLER written in). Entry No. 1703.

10 March 1780. MUMUCAN HUNT e. 200 ac. S fork New River..near mouth
branch runs into River below JOHN COUCHS..track leading
from WM. NALLS to JOHN COUCHES. Entry No. 1704.

10 March 1780. MEMUCAN HUNT e. 150 ac. S fork New River at COLO. CLEVE-
LANDS entry at JOHN COUCHS improvement. Entry No. 1705.

10 March 1780. MEMUCAN HUNT e. 200 ac. waters Long Shoal Branch and
Phenix Creek..on his former line. Entry No. 1706.

10 March 1780. ANDREW BAKER e. 150 ac. on path leads from Naked Creek
to GEORGE MORRIS'S Mill at place where MATTHEW SPARKS
survey ended. Entry No. 1707.

14 March 1780. SAMUEL WILCOXSON e. 50 ac. head S fork Fishes Creek.
Entry No. 1708.

14 March 1780. ROBERT HAND e. 200 ac. Glad fork Little River..E end
HENRY HANDS line..joining JACOB MANERS line..(ROBERT
HAND marked out..CHARLES CATE written in). Entry No. 1709.

16 March 1780. MEREDITH MINTON e. 50 ac. Yadkin River at his own line.
Entry No. 1710.

16 March 1780. THOMAS PAYNE e. 320 ac. waters Hughes Creek..including
some waters of both forks. Entry No. 1711.

16 March 1780. MEMUCAN HUNT e. 300 ac. Stags Creek..including WM. HEN-
SONS Cabbin. Entry No. 1712.

16 March 1780. MEMUCAN HUNT e. 300 ac. Big Helton Creek above KEES
Camp. Entry No. 1713.

16 March 1780. MEMUCAN HUNT e. 300 ac. on Little Helton Creek..joining
the Virginia line..(entry withdrawn..the land taken by
WM. ADKINS written in). Entry No. 1714.

16 March 1780. MEMUCAN HUNT e. 100 ac. Little Helton Creek..above the
mouth Long Branch. Entry No. 1715.

16 March 1780. MEMUCAN HUNT e. 100 ac. Heltons Creek below Low Notch.
Entry No. 1716.

16 March 1780. WILLIAM LENOIR (of Brunswick County, Virginia..this is
written in the entry in a different handwriting & ink)..
e. 640 ac. N side N fork New River on waters Rich Bent Creek..including
WALLINGS long ridge. Entry No. 1717.

16 March 1780. HENRY HAYS e. 150 ac. at WM. MORGANS line..S side little
fork Hunting Creek. Entry No. 1718.

16 March 1780. BENJAMIN HOWARD e. 50 ac. S side Yadkin River somewhere
in upper line of BENJAMIN BIRD. Entry No. 1719.

21 March 1780. ANDREW YEARGAIN e. 200 ac. S fork Fishes Creek at his
upper line. Entry No. 1720.

21 March 1780. DAVID OWINS e. 50 ac. Joining on W side WM. OWENS, SENR.
entry. Entry No. 1721.

21 March 1780. DAVID OWENS e. 50 ac. at the Gap between WM. OWENS, SENR.
& JOHN ROBINS. Entry No. 1722.

21 March 1780 BARNET OWEN e. 50 ac. near WM. OWENS, JUNRS. upper corner
..(BARNET OWEN marked out..WILLIAM KILBEY written in).
Entry No. 1723.

23 March 1780. CHRISTOPHER ------- (?) e. 50 ac. at THOMAS HAMRICKS
upper corner..including the vacant land..(CHRISTOPHER
(?) marked out..JOHN GILREATH written in). Entry No. 1724.

23 March 1780. JOHN WM. CROSTHWAIT e. 75 ac. Mouth branch runs into
Kings Creek..below said CROSTHWAITS. Entry No. 1725.

23 March 1780. ENOCH OSBURN e. 300 ac. Elk Creek..including a Mill Seat.
Entry No. 1726.

23 March 1780. ENOCH OSBURN e. 200 ac. path between his house & BUNCHES.
Entry No. 1727.

23 March 1780. BENJAMIN YEARGAIN e. 400 ac. on a Crean (?) that runs
into his branch of Cub Creek..joining JOHN WHITAKERS 50
ac. entry. Entry No. 1728.

23 March 1780. BENJAMIN YEARGAIN e. 100 ac. N side tract land whereon
JOHN WHITAKER now lives. Entry No. 1729.

25 March 1780. JOHN BROWN e. 200 ac. joining upper end his other survey
that lyeth against the Bent. Entry No. 1730.

27 March 1780. WILLIAM SMITH e. 150 ac. near his E & W line. Entry No.
1731.

28 March 1780. WILLIAM LYON e. 100 ac. middle fork Roaring River at
JOHN GAMBILLS lower line. Entry No. 1732.

28 March 1780. CHARLES CRENSHAW e. 50 ac. N side Yadkin River at HUGH
MONTGOMERYS lower line of entry that JOHN BROWN now
lives on..(entry withdrawn by enterer). Entry No. 1733.

30 March 1780. WILLIAM GILREATH, SENR. e. 400 ac. on Crab fork Little
River..at or near Virginia line. Entry No. 1734.

Entry No. 1735 skipped.

30 March 1780. WILLIAM FLETCHER e. 400 ac. fork between Crab fork and
Little River near Virginia line..(WM. FLETCHER marked
out..BLADSHAW HARDEN written in). Entry No. 1736.

30 March 1780. JOB COAL (COLE) e. 50 ac. Mirey branch Hunting Creek
between road goes from THOMAS TOMSONS to JOHN STANDLEYS.
Entry No. 1737.

30 March 1780. BENJAMIN HERNDON e. 200 ac. Great Elkin..upper end
ELISHA HEDDENS entry of 200 ac. Entry No. 1733.

1 April 1780. THOMAS HENDERSON e. 60 ac. on Beaver Creek..joining JOEL COFFEE & JOHN BARKER. Entry No. 1739.

1 April 1780. THOMAS HENDERSON e. 60 ac. N fork Beaver Creek..joining JAMES HENDERSON. Entry No. 1740.

1 April 1780. JOHN HAND e. 300 ac. Little Glade Creek..some of waters New River..(JOHN HAND marked out..THOMAS YAIRS (AYERS) written in. Entry No. 1741.

1 April 1780. THOMAS HOLDMAN e. 50 ac. upon Glade Creek..joining Entry of DANIEL SUTHERLAND at old improvement..(THOMAS HOLDMAN marked out..DAN'L. SOUTHERLIN written in). Entry No. 1742.

1 April 1780. THOMAS CALLAWAY, JUNR. e. 100 ac. S fork New River above mouth Beaver Creek. Entry No. 1743.

1 April 1780. WILLIAM STURDIE e. 100 ac. S side Enchanted Ridge near Prathers Creek..a branch of New River..a claim of JAMES MULKEY formerly. Entry No. 1744.

1 April 1780. WILLIAM STURDIE e. 300 ac. Praters Creek..S fork New River..below JAMES MULKEY Camp. Entry No. 1745.

3 April 1780. JAMES MULKEY e. 100 ac. S fork New River..below his survey..(JAMES MULKEY marked out..JOSEPH COLWILL written in). Entry No. 1746.

3 April 1780. MORRIS BAKER e. 50 ac. S side S fork New River..top ridge divides his and ANDREW BAKERS land. Entry No. 1747.

3 April 1780. DANIEL RICHARDSON e. 150 ac. S fork New River at corner his former entry to a condt. line of JAMES MULKEY. Entry No. 1748.

3 April 1780. NATHANIEL BURDINE e. 100 ac. S side Mulberry Creek. Entry No. 1749.

5 April 1780. THOMAS HIGHSMITH e. 150 ac. joining JOHN PROPHETS entry.. (THOMAS HIGHSMITH marked out..GIDEN WOODRUFF written in). Entry No. 1750.

6 April 1780. ZEADOCK RIGGS e. 100 ac. branch Mitchels River known by name Big Branch..including JAMES CHILDERS improvement. Entry No. 1751.

6 April 1780. BENJAMIN ELLEDGE e. 100 ac. N side Yadkin River joining JOHN SMITHER & MEREDY MINTON. Entry No. 1752.

6 April 1780. BEN ELLEDGE e. 150 ac. Moravian Creek..joining entry made by SUMMERLING now belonging to REES & WM. MCGILL..entry sold to JOHN PARSONS..extending up the waters towards the mountains.. (BEN ELLEDGE marked out..JOSHUA MORGAN written in). Entry No. 1753.

6 April 1780. JAMES ISBELL e. 100 ac. on Brushey Mountain in BEN ELLEDGE line of PLEASENT GARDIN tract extending towards rocks called Garden Ground. Entry No. 1754.

6 April 1780. JAMES ISBELL e. 100 ac. joining BEN ELLEDGES Pleasant Garden tract..ISBELLS line down branches of Garrels fork. Entry No. 1755.

6 April 1780. JOHN OREAR e. 200 ac. Little River S fork. Entry No. 1756.

6 April 1780. OSBURN KEELING e. 100 ac. at his & AMBROS CRANES corner.
              Entry No. 1757.

10 April 1780. JOSEPH THOMPSON e. 200 ac. Reedy fork Mitchels River..
               adjoining JESSE FRANKLINGS entry. Entry No. 1758.

10 April 1780. SAMUEL SCRITCHFIELD e. 100 ac. head Brushey fork Branch
               ..including a little improvement JOHN COOLY made. Entry
No. 1759.

13 April 1780. JOEL COFFEE e. 50 ac. both sides Beaver Creek between his
               former line & THOMAS HENDERSON, JUNR. Entry No. 1760.

13 April 1780. JOHN PARKER e. 50 ac. fork Beaver Creek in his former
               line..both sides a little branch comes by his spring.
Entry No. 1761.

14 April 1780. SOLOMON HICKS e. 200 ac. both sides Grassey Creek..
               waters Big Elkin..including head of said creek. Entry
No. 1762.

14 April 1780. FRANCIS VANNOY e. 100 ac. W side land he bought of DUKE
               FIELDS and joining said land. Entry No. 1763.

22 March 1780. WILLIAM NALL e. 400 ac. at lower end his own line..down
               New River on S side..(WM. NALL marked out..transfared
by Sherriff to ROBERT NALL written in). Entry No. 1764.

30 March 1780. BENJAMIN CLEVELAND e. 640 ac. S fork New River..SW corner
               his other survey made at mouth Cranberry Creek. Entry
No. 1765.

30 March 1780. BENJAMIN CLEVELAND e. ..torn.. ..torn.. Hundred & twenty
               ac. waters Cranberry Creek..joining his other survey on
E side..(BENJAMIN CLEVELAND marked out..transfered to ROBERT NALL written
in). Entry No. 1766.

No date. ANDREW BAKER e. 100 ac. Naked Creek on CHARLES GORDONS line.
          Entry No. 1767.

No date. JAMES BAKER e. 250 ac. on ridge divides waters Silvans Branch
          and the River branches above..(JAMES BAKER marked out..ALEXAN-
DER SMITH written in). Entry No. 1768.

15 April 1780. GEORGE MCNIEL e. 100 ac. S side S fork Reddeys River
               at his & ROBERT SHEPHERDS corner. Entry No. 1769.

15 April 1780. LEWIS DEMOSS e. 60 ac. N side Yadkin..adjoining his line.
               Entry No. 1770.

18 April 1780. BENJAMIN ROSE e. 200 ac. at (?) mountain..down the
               Cranberry Glades on waters Little River..including head
of the Cranberry Glades. Entry No. 1771.

20 April 1780. SAMUEL SIMPSON, JUNR. e. 150 ac. waters New River in Gap
               Rich Mountain where path crosses the mountain. Entry
No. 1772.

20 April 1780. SAMUEL SIMPSON e. 300 ac. Howards Creek on ridge..in-
               cluding small clearing made by CHARLES WILLIAMS. Entry
No. 1773.

22 April 1780. HILLIAR RUSSAU e. 200 ac. on Mulberry on ANDREW VANNOYS
               E & W line..(HILLIAR RUSSAU marked out..BENJAMIN RAY
written in). Entry No. 1774.

-No date. WILLIAM FLETCHER transfers to JAMES FLETCHER e. 200 ac. S
       fork New River near JOSEPH COUCHES lower line or claim.
(FLETCHERS marked out..transfered to JOSEPH COUCH written in). Entry
No. 1775.

22 April 1780. JOHN HALL e. 100 ac...a big branch Mulberry Creek at
       JOHN HALL, SENRS. upper line. Entry No. 1776.

22 April 1780. JOHN HALL, JUNR. e. 100 ac. N side Mulberry Creek on
       small branch down a ridge..including some waters Cain
Creek. Entry No. 1777.

22 April 1780. WILLIAM FLETCHER e. 100 ac. on Mulberry Creek..joining
       ANDREW VANNOYS upper line..up a big branch runs through
said VANNOYS plantation. Entry No. 1778.

(Top of this page torn completely away..will abstract what is left)..
       on Hunting ---------- that I bought of EDWARD FINCH in my E line.
Entry No. 1779.

No date. BENJAMIN YEARGAIN e. 120 ac. head Hawkins Creek Branch..at
       his corner. Entry No. 1780.

No date. BENJAMIN YEARGAIN e. 80 ac. joining EDWARD FINCHES land..fork
Mulberry Creek in his N line. Entry No. 1781.

No date. BENJAMIN YEARGAIN e. 50 ac. on one of waters of Darnals Branch.
       Entry No. 1782.

No date. ANDREW YEARGAIN, SR. e. 100 ac. near head Andrew's Branch..
       including a cove. Entry No. 1783.

22 April 1780. WILLIAM LENOIR e. 400 ac. on Naked Creek of New River..
       E side his other survey..including the vacant land.
Entry No. 1784.

22 April 1780. WILLIAM LENOIR e. 200 ac. waters Elk Creek..joining his
       own and ENOCH OSBURNS surveys..(WM. LENOIR marked out..
WM. MAXWELL written in). Entry No. 1785.

(Other side page carrying Entry #1779 completely torn away..the waters
       of Rockey Creek..joining E side his other survey. Entry No. 1786.

22 April 1780 WILLIAM LENOIR e. 200 ac. waters Little Elk Creek of New
       River..joining S side his other survey..(WM. LENOIR marked
out..THEOPHELUIS EVENS written in). Entry No. 1787.

22 April 1780. WILLIAM LENOIR e. 250 ac. waters Rockey Creek of New
       River..joining S side his other survey..(WM. LENOIR
marked out..JOHN LATIMER written in). Entry No. 1788.

No date. BENJAMIN YEARGAIN e. 640 ac. waters Rockey Creek known as
       Cranes Creek..N side WM. FLETCHERS entry on Grassy branch..
joining E side JOHN ROBERTS. Entry No. 1789.

No date. BENJAMIN YEARGAIN e. 200 ac. joining E side JAMES FLETCHERS
       line. Entry No. 1790.

No date. BENJAMIN YEARGAIN e. 100 ac. S side Craines Creek at WM.
       FLETCHERS line..on N side JAMES FLETCHERS line. Entry No.
1791.

24 April 1780. BENJAMIN DUGGER e. 100 ac. Elk Creek on JOSEPH JONES
       line. Entry No. 1972.

No date. BENJAMIN DUGGER e. 20 (?, worn) ac. on Elk Creek..JOSEPH JONES
line..on both sides creek..including Long Bottom. Entry No.
1793.

24 April 1780. THOMAS EVANS e. 50 ac. on Elk Creek..joining his other
entry..(THOMAS EVANS marked out..MOSES STANBERRY written
in). Entry No. 1794.

No date. ALEXANDER GILREATH e. 50 ac. on Elk Creek..(entry withdrawn).
Entry No. 1795.

25 April 1780. SAMUEL STALLINGS e. 50 ac. on S side Yadkin River at
said STALLINGS upper line..(SAMUEL STALLINGS marked out..
WILLIAM TRIBBLE written in). Entry No. 1796.

26 April 1780. DEVEROUX BALLARD e. 100 ac. Middle fork Hunting Creek.
Entry No. 1797.

26 April 1780. DEVEROUX BALLARD e. 100 ac. on his other line. Entry
No. 1798.

1 May 1780. JAMES FLETCHER e. 200 ac. Mitchels River at said FIELDERS
upper line of land that he bought of NATHANIEL SCRITCHFIELD
..(JAMES FLETCHER (FIELDER) marked out..JOHN JINNINGS written in).
Entry No. 1799.

29 April 1780. JAMES FIELDER e. 100 ac. branch Mitchels River in walnut
bottom..joining upper line of his other entry..(JAMES
FIELDER marked out..JAMES JINNINGS written in). Entry No. 1800.

1 May 1780. DANIEL FULLER e. 50 ac. draughts Bryer Creek at his other
line on JOHN TURNBILLS line..including some of the mountains.
Entry No. 1801.

1 May 1780. SOLOMON HICKS e. 100 ac. Grassey Creek of Big Elkin below
his other entry. Entry No. 1802.

1 May 1780. SOLOMON HICKS e. 100 ac. first branch Big Elkin that puts
into creek above JAMES DAVIS. Entry No. 1803.

5 May 1780. ALEXANDER HOLTON e. 50 ac. N side Mulberry Creek..between
JOHN ROBINS & HICKERSONS..(ALEX. HOLTON marked out..GERVIS
SMITH written in). Entry No. 1804.

5 May 1780. ALEXANDER HOLTON e. 50 ac. N side Mulberry Creek..mouth
great branch..(ALEX. HOLTON marked out..GERVIS SMITH written
in). Entry No. 1805.

No date. THOMAS TERRY e. 200 ac. on Washington Road known by name Rich
Hills..including the spring. Entry No. 1806.

No date. THOMAS TERRY e. 200 ac. on Washington Road in the County line..
including the spring. Entry No. 1807.

No date. THOMAS TERRY e. 200 ac. on Washington Road including..(the
bottom of this page is torn completely away). Entry No. 1808.

No date. THOMAS TERRY e. 200 ac. on the Washington Road..joining WILLIAM
MCCLAINS line on the (torn) side next to Washington County.
Entry No. 1809.

6 April 1780. THOMAS ELLET e. 100 ac. joining his E line..including
mouth of falling branch of Warrior Creek. Entry No.
1810.

2 May 1780. JOHN YEARGAIN e. 150 ac. E WM. LENOIRS land that lyes both
sides Fishers Creek. Entry No. 1811.

No date. JOHN OREAR e. 150 ac. waters Little River on big branch above
Bletchers Creek..(JOHN OREAR, CLISBY COBB & JONATHAN HAINS
marked out..WILLIAM LENOIR written in). Entry No. 1812.

13 May 1780. HENRY PARKS e. 300 ac. branch Little Elkin at GABRIEL
LOVING corner..(HENRY PARKS marked out..GABRIEL LOVING,
SENR. written in). Entry No. 1813.

15 May 1780. WILLIAM LEWIS e. 150 ac. on ridge between Caleys Creek &
the hill creek near EDWARD HARRISES upper line..(WM.
LEWIS marked out..JOHN COMBS written in). Entry No. 1814.

15 May 1780. JAMES LOVE e. 150 ac. on Bear branch at N corner of
WILLIAM LEWIS line..up both sides Bear Branch. Entry No.
1815.

16 May 1780. JAMES LOVE e. 200 ac. Ridge that divides head Caleys Creek
..some of waters Hunting Creek..(JAMES LOVE marked out..
MATTHEW PHIPES (FIPPS) written in). Entry No. 1816.

16 May 1780. CHARLES CRENSHAW e. 50 ac. joining his entry in WILLIAM
LENOIRS line..WHITES bottom line..(CHARLES CRENSHAW marked
out..JOSEPH HERNDON written in). Entry No. 1817.

24 May 1780. CHARLES CRENSHAW e. 200 ac. on Brushey Mountain..waters of
Hunting Creek..joining his other entry. Entry No. 1818.

No date. JOHN BROWN e. 200 ac. branch N fork Lewis Fork..joining entrys
made by ISAAC PERLIER on land he now lives on. Entry No. 1819.

No date. JOHN BROWN e. 200 ac. branch N fork Lewis Fork..joining an entry made by ISAAC PERLIER on Bells branch..including the Cove.
Entry No. 1820.

18 May 1780. PETER HENDRICKS e. 100 ac. ridge at lone Gap..on branch
Stoney Lewis Fork. Entry No. 1821.

18 May 1780. MOSES WATERS e. 150 ac. waters Elk Creek..including
NORMANS (?). Entry No. 1822.

16 May 1780. MOSES WATERS e. 50 ac. Laurel branch Stoney fork above the
falls. Entry No. 1823.

16 May 1780. MOSES WATERS e. 50 ac. on Buck Branch of Stoney fork.
Entry No. 1824.

16 May 1780. BENJAMIN CUTHBATH e. 100 ac. being Fullentons Creek..waters
New River..at upper part said creek. Entry No. 1825.

24 May 1780. JOSEPH HERNDON e. 100 ac. head MOSES TOLIVERS Branch..
joining an entry the said HERNDON made on said branch.
Entry No. 1826.

24 May 1780. FRANCIS ELLEDGE e. 100 ac...joining THOMAS ELLIOTTS on
Warrior Creek..including mouth some branches. Entry No.
1827.

May 1780. JACOB ELLEDGE e. 150 ac. on Warriors Creek..joining his former
entry..extending up creek he lives on and with FRANCIS ELLED-
GES line toward Brushey Mountain..(JACOB ELLEDGE marked out..SABRET
CHOTE written in). Entry No. 1828.

May 1780. BENJAMIN OAKLEY e. 50 ac. joining his former entry..BOONS
field branch in his former line up towards MR. JAMES ISBELLS
..(BENJAMIN OAKLEY marked out..JOHN KELLAR written in). Entry No. 1829.

May 1780. BENJAMIN OAKLEY e. 50 ac. joining his former survey W side..
(BENJ. OAKLEY marked out..HUGH MONTGOMERY written in). Entry
No. 1830.

5 May 1780. GEORGE GORDON e. 200 ac. on Redies River where upper line
of Mulberry Field tract crosses the River. Entry No. 1831.

20 May 1780. CHARLES GORDON e. 300 ac. N side Yadkin River at MAJOR
JOSEPH HERNDONS upper line where it joins said river.
Entry No. 1832.

25 May 1780. CHARLES GORDON e. 100 ac. E & W line Mulberry Fields
tract. Entry No. 1833.

30 May 1780. WILLIAM MCCUBBINS e. 320 ac. some waters Hunting Creek..
below path from HENRY ROADS to DANIEL FULLERS..including
meadow branch..(WM. MCCUBBINS marked out..JOHN TURNBILL written in).
Entry No. 1834.

30 May 1780. JOHN PILES e. 50 ac. on Cainbrake branch..waters Redies
River..above JOHN SHEPHERDS. Entry No. 1835.

No date. DEVEROUX BALLARD e. 80 ac. waters said BALLARDS Mill Creek at
his other line of 150 ac...(DEVEROUX BALLARD marked out..
transfared to JAMES FLETCHER written in). Entry No. 1836.

NOTE: Beginning with entry #1837 and continueing to the end of the old
entry Book, the edges of the pages are completely worn and torn
away..will abstract what is left that is readable.

No date. DEVEROUX BALLARD e. 80 ac. joining EDWARD ..torn.. that he
made on ridge path that goes by mill he formerly owned to
WILLIAM LENOIRS..above ANDREWS field..(DEVEROUX BALLARD marked out..
JAMES FLETCHER written in). Entry No. 1837.

No date. DEVEROUX BALLARD e. 100 ac. joining CHARLES GIN ..torn.. that
side next to JACOB PATES..near ..torn.. goes from where
NATHANIEL BARNET formerly lived to MR. CRANES..(DEVEROUX BALLARD marked
out..JAMES FLETCHER written in). Entry No. 1838.

No date. DEVEROUX BALLARD e. 100 ac. on middle fork Hunting Creek..near
head above entry EDWARD FINCH made called Chesnut Level..in-
cluding the rich land..(DEVEROUX BALLARD marked out..JAMES FLETCHER
written in). Entry No. 1839.

No date. AARON KING e. 50 ac. N side Yadkin at JAMES DURLINS (DEERLIN)
N side..up branch that JOEL DURLIN..on both sides..(AARON
KING marked out..ROBERT EPPERSON written in). Entry No. 1840.

No date. AARON KING e. 50 ac. Yadkin River..N side JAMES DURLINS..up
Pounding Mill Branch..(AARON KING marked out..ROBERT EPPERSON
written in). Entry No. 1841.

29 May 1780. WILLIAM ROBERTS e. 100 ac. waters Lewis Fork. Entry No.
1842.

Torn. SAMUEL WILLIAM ROBERTS e. 100 ac. branch ISAAC PARLIER now lives
on joining entry said PARLIER lives on. Entry No. 1843.

Torn. SAMUEL SIMPSON e. 50 ac. on HENRY B-----HAMS upper line. Entry
No. 1844.

June (torn). FRANCIS REYNOLDS e. 350 ac. N side Yadkin River on upper
line tract he now lives on. Entry No. 1845.

Torn. ARCHIBALD MAHONE e. 100 ac. branch Elk Creek just above BUNCHES
       Camp. Entry No. 1846.

June 1780. ROBERT KIRKPATRICK e. 100 ac. left hand fork Reedy branch..
       below JOEL DIERS entry at THOMAS Cabbin joining said DIERS
entry..(ROBERT KIRKPATRICK marked out..THOMAS FERGUSON written in).
Entry No. 1847.

June 1780. ROBERT KIRKPATRICK e. 100 ac. Reedy Branch above JAMES DIERS
       entry..(ROBERT KIRKPATRICK marked out..NEHEMIAH FERGUSON
written in). Entry No. 1848.

June 1780. ROBERT KIRKPATRICK e. 100 ac. small branch runs into Yadkin
       River between where JAMES BARKLEY now lives..SIMON Mills..
path that leads off Reedy branch to the Indian Grave Gap. Entry No.
1849.

4 June 1780. STEPHEN TRIBBLE e. tw-- (torn) on (possible branch) of
       Warriors Creek of the Yadkin River. Entry No. 1850.

6 June 1780. STEPHEN TRIBBLE e. 100 ac. on Little Warrior Creek at
       JAMES DIERS upper ..torn... Entry No. 1851.

6 June 1780. RUSSEL JONES e. 50 ac. above his spring house. Entry No.
       1852.

June 1780. JOHN DIER, JUNR. e. 150 ac. Branch..into Yadkin River above
       where STEPHEN ..torn.. now lives joining lower side. Entry
No. 1853.

6 June 1780. GEORGE GORDON e. 300 ac. the Sawmill Creek. Entry No.
       1854.

6 June 1780. JOHN BROWN e. 200 ac. N side Yadkin..joining on N side
       tract formerly surveyed for him being land where ROBERT
RUS--(torn) now lives. Entry No. 1855.

6 June 1780. ISAAC ELLEDGE e. 100 ac. joining land he transferred to
       HAWKINGS DONATHAN..both sides creek towards mountain..
including Mill Shoal. Entry No. 1856.

Torn. MOSES WRIGHT e. 50 ac. Cutons (?) Creek..some waters Fishes River.
       Entry No. 1857.

9 June 1780. THOMAS CALLAWAY e. 50 ac. waters Obeds Creek at Cranberry
       path..(THOMAS CALLAWAY marked out..THOMAS GIBSON written
in). Entry No. 1858.

Torn. BURWELL BREWER e. 100 ac. adjoining his other survey..waters
       Beaver Creek..branch New River..(BURWELL BREWER marked out..CLOSS
TOMSON, JUNR. written in). Entry No. 1859.

Torn. DANIEL WHEATLEY e. 100 ac. Elk Ridge in his N line. Entry No.
       1860.

Torn. ELISHA DYER e. 200 ac. both sides Yadkin River adjoining WILLIAM
       BREWER & ROBERT SAUNDERS. Entry No. 1861.

1780. BARNARD FRANLKING e. 400 ac. on little Reedy fork Mitchels River
       ..on the JESSE FRANKLINS line. Entry No. 1862.

Torn. JESSE FRANKLIN e. 400 ac. little Reedy fork of Mitchels River.
       Entry No. 1863.

10 June 1780. JOHN GAMBILL e. 100 ac. (blurred) at or near HOLDBROOKS
       line. Entry No. 1864.

10 May 1780. BENJAMIN MORGAN e. 100 ac. between ..torn.. & dividing
       ridge waters on Little River. Entry No. 1865.

26 May 1780.   BENJAMIN MORGAN e. 100 ac. ..torn.. of Noheaded branch..a
               branch of Pine Swamp Creek. Entry No. 1866.

10 June 1780. MARTIN GAMBILL e. 200 ac. on Roaring River at his upper
               line. Entry No. 1867.

10 June 1780. BENJAMIN BRANHAM e. 25 ac. ..torn.. mouth great branch.
               Entry No. 1868.

9 June 1780.   JESSE TOLIVER e. 50 ac. at mouth ..torn.. second long
               branch. Entry No. 1869.

No date. JESSE FRANKLIN e. 100 ac. S side Mitchels River..(JESSE FRANK-
          LIN, JONATHAN CANTERYBERY marked out..DAVID RIGGS written in).
Entry No. 1870.

1 July 1780. WINEFORD ALEXANDER e. 80 ac. on Aleks Creek near Turkey
              Pen. Entry No. 1871.

Torn. BENJAMIN FLETCHER e. 150 ac. at WM. FLETCHERS open line or W
       corner..both sides Grassey branch..(BENJ. FLETCHER & JOHN PROPHETT
marked out..JAMES FLETCHER written in). Entry No. 1872.

Torn. JOB COLE e. 100 ac. between Fiddler JOHN ROBERTS & old JOHN RO-
       BERTS. Entry No. 1873.

Torn. WILLIAM ROBERTS e. 100 ac. fork Fishdam Creek above THOMAS LAXTONS
       improvement. Entry No. 1874.

Torn. RANDOLPH ALEXANDER e. 100 ac. Stewards Creek. Entry No. 1875.

Torn. THOMAS GILBERT e. 100 ac. on Deep Gap Creek at his other line.
       Entry No. 1876.

Torn. TOHMAS GILBERT e. 100 ac. some waters Pine Swamp at his line of
       land he bought of BENJAMIN CUTHBERD..down ridge on both sides of
path. Entry No. 1877.

Torn. CHARLES GILBERT e. 100 ac. longest fork Pine Swamp Creek..at its
       head..(CHARLES GILBERT marked out..CHARLES GORDON, JR. written
in). Entry No. 1878.

Torn. THOMAS HOPPER e. 50 ac. at his upper line above his house..
       (THOMAS HOPPER marked out..JAMES HAYS written in). Entry No.
1879.

Entry No. 1800 skipped.

No date. MATTHEW SPARKS, SENR. e. 200 ac. head of Oldfield Creek.
          Entry No. 1881.

No date. GEORGE GORDON e. 100 ac. in WILLIAM ..torn.. at waggon road..
          head Hoppers branch. Entry No. 1882.

18 Aug. 1780. RICHARD GWIN e. 640 ac. little Elkin & Yadkin waters..
               joining entry made by GABRIEL LOVEING & JOHN PARKS, JUNR.
& MEMUCAN HUNT, WILLIAM CARRELL & SIMON CARTER..(entry withdrawn). Entry
No. 1883.

18 Aug. 1780. BENJAMIN HERNDON e. ..torn.. hundred ac. on Buffalow..
               waters N fork New River..above Camp called Priests Camp..
(BENJ. HERNDON marked out..LAURENCE YANEL (YARNELL) written in). Entry
No. 1884.

24 Aug. 1780. JOB COLE e. 50 ac. below EDWARD HARRIS line..the Branch.
               Entry No. 1885.

26 Aug. 1780. JOHN SELLERS e. 200 ac. on Duncans Branch..on said DUNCANS
               line..(JOHN SELLERS marked out..LANDRINE EGGERS written in).
Entry No. 1886.

No date. Beginning at my corner on TURNBILLS line..S thence W..thence N
to my line to include fifty acres of land on the waters of
Bryer Creek from your most Humble Servt. ROBERT CHANDLER. Entry No.
1887.

1780. STEPHEN CARPERDER e. 250 ac. S side Yadkin River..on condt. line
between JAMES BARKLEY & NEHEMIAH FERGUSON..to said CARPENDERS
line. Entry No. 1888.

6 Sept. 1780. ALEXANDER HOLTEN e. 100 ac. S fork New River..near a
small island..(ALEXANDER HOLTEN marked out..JOHN BROWN
written in). Entry No. 1889.

9 Sept. 1780. ROWLAND JENKINGS e. 100 ac. New River at Rockey Shoal..
(ROWLAND JENKINGS marked out..SAMUEL WILCOXEN written in).
Entry No. 1890.

Sept. 1780. Not readable.. e. 150 ac. Little fork Hunting Creek..known
as Rockey Creek or JOHN CRANES Creek..(1st enterer marked
out..transfaired to JAMES SMOOTE written in). Entry No. 1891.

1 Nov. 1780. BENJAMIN GREER his vacation of a tract of land on one fork
Moravian Creek called CALEB LOWS fork..for one hundred
acres joining to CALEB LOW, JUNR & JOSHUA MITCHELS. Entry No. 1892.

Torn. WILLIAM LANDSDON e. 60 ac. on Joseph Fork of Buffalow at lower
fall. Entry No. 1893.

6 Nov. 1780. BENJAMIN ELLEDGE e. 150 ac. on Moravian Creek..joining an
entry made by WILLIAM MCGILL that he sold to JOHN PARSONS..
extending up both sides creek towards mountains. Entry No. 1894.

6 Dec. 1780. MOSES DENMAN e. 50 ac. ..torn.. of Yadkin River..joining
JOHN DENMANS that was entered by JOHN THRASHER & REUBIN
RO--- ..torn... Entry No. 1895.

5 Dec. 1780. blurred, crossed out, not readable.. e. 100 ac. at Mill
Seat on Holton Creek..(ISAAC WEVER written in). Entry No.
1896.

No date. WILLIAM MCCLAINE e. 150 ac. on head branch empties in N fork
New River. Entry No. 1897.

No date. WILLIAM MCCLAIN e. 100 ac. waters New River..N side Three Top
Mtn. Entry No. 1898.

No date. JOHN SELLERS e. 100 ac. below ARNOLDS improvement on Elk Creek
..(JOHN SELLERS marked out..ISAAC PARLIER written in). Entry
No. 1899.

No date. JOHN SELLERS e. 200 ac. head Elk Creek at LEVY JACKSONS line..
(JOHN SELLERS marked out..RICHARD BROWN written in). Entry No.
1900.

No date. JOHN SELLERS e. 100 ac. branch Elk Creek at his improvement..
(JOHN SELLERS marked out..ISAAC PARLIER written in). Entry No.
1901.

Torn. STEPHEN TILLEY e. 50 ac. on some waters of New River on his S line
..(STEPHEN TILLEY marked out..JOHN FORGUSON written in). Entry
No. 1902.

Dec. 1780. CHARLES GORDON e. 100 ac. N side Reddies River above small
clearing made by Old MR. THOMAS HOPPER..including the clearing and mouth of branch called Hoppers Branch. Entry No. 1903.

20 Dec. 1780. MICAJAH LEWIS e. 100 ac. on Moravian Creek..including
improvement where WILLIAM LANSNOW (LANSDOWN?) lives..
(MICAJAH LEWIS marked out..WILLIAM LAWS written in). Entry No. 1904.

Torn. JOSHUA GREER e. 50 ac. Moravian Creek..beginning upper line..
opposite side said Creek from his house. Entry No. 1905.

Torn. JESSEE RAY e. 200 ac. S Beaver..some waters New River at FRANCIS
VANNOYS line..including vacant land between said VANNOYS line..
WM. STURDIES line..(JESSEE RAY marked out..ELIZABETH RITTER written in).
Entry No. 1906.

Torn. WILLIAM COLVARD e. 300 ac. Muddy branch empties into Beaver Creek
..S including BAKERS Camp..(WM. COLVARD marked out..DEVALT POUTS
(FOUTS) written in). Entry No. 1907.

Torn. LEWIS CARLTON e. 150 ac. waters Beaver Creek..known by name Bryar
Knob..below the spring. Entry No. 1908.

No date. PETER JONES e. 100 ac. Little fork Cub Creek..(PETER JONES
marked out..WM. LOW written in). Entry No. 1909.

24 Jan. 1781. WILLIAM TOLBY e. 100 ac. E fork Roaring River at or near
JAMES BUNYARDS line..(WM. TOLBY marked out..WILLIAM TOLBY
written in again). Entry No. 1910.

No date. JAMES LOVE e. 10 ac. on Hunting Creek at his lower corner..S
side. Entry No. 1911.

No date. JAMES STAMPER e. 250 ac. N side Little River..including all
the good land near Buck Knob. Entry No. 1912.

No date. GABRIEL SMITHER e. 50 ac. on some waters S fork Stoney Fork..
at his other line he bought of MR. ROSS..(GABRIEL SMITHER
marked out..THOS. CALTON written in). Entry No. 1913.

No date. LARKING (LARKIN) CLEVELAND e. ..torn.. hundred ac. N fork
Lewis Fork ..torn.. upper line. Entry No. 1914.

6 March 1781. THOMAS WHITE e. 50 ac...a branch of Yadkin above THOMAS
SLONES..joining lands of THOMAS SLONE. Entry No. 1915.

6 March 1781. GEORGE LEWIS e. 50 ac. on Roaring River at his other
lower line..including the vacant land to WM. GAMBILLS
line. Entry No. 1916.

10 March 1781. JOHN SUTTEN e. 100 ac. on Sawmill Creek..near GEORGE
GORDONS lower line. Entry No. 1917.

No date. WILLIAM LANDSDON e. 50 ac. Tices (?) fork on his own line.
Entry No. 1918.

March 1781. WILLIAM HANEY e. 50 ac. E fork Roaring River..at or near
WILLIAM MEDLINS line. Entry No. 1919.

No date. JOHN OREAR e. 250 ac. middle fork Little River near OSBONS
path in fork of Creek..(PETER OREAR marked out..DANIEL HOPESS
(?) written in). Entry No. 1920.

No date. JOHN OREAR e. 150 ac. on Little River..N side two miles below
his house against a large Cranberry Patch..(JOHN OREAR, CLISBY
COBB & JONATHAN HAINES marked out..WILLIAM LENOIR written in). Entry
No. 1921.

NOTE: The writing has completely disappeared from this entry. Entry
No. 1922.

No date. JOHN HOPPER e. 100 ac. Naked Creek of New River..including all
the Black Walnut Cove..(JOHN HOPPER marked out..ROWLAND JUDD
written in). Entry No. 1923.

No date. WILLIAM CHAPMAN e. 50 ac. on Bob ..torn.. branch of Naked
Creek of New River. Entry No. 1924.

No date. SAMUEL SIMPSON e. 15 ac. on Wheatleys Creek..on his other line
..including the ..torn.. land between SLONES line and his own.
Entry No. 1925.

11 May 1781. JAMES BROWN, JUNR. e. 250 ac. N side Redy ..torn.. River..
mouth first branch below meadows. Entry No. 1926.

No date. WILLIS CHILDERS e. 300 ac. Ridge ..torn.. where said CHILDERS
lives. Entry No. 1927.

No date. FREDERICK BRAZEL e. 100 ac. on JOHN SHEPHERDS line up both
sides Cane branch. Entry No. 1928.

No date. FREDERICK BRAZWELL e. 50 ac. at a pine so as to incude the
Redys River Meeting House. Entry No. 1929.

5 June 1781. FREDRICK BRAZWELL e. 50 ac. waters Reddys River between
lines of JOHN SHEPHERD & JOHN ROBINS, JUNR...including
the good land betwæn them lines. Entry No. 1930.

No date. SPRUCE MACAY e. 200 ac. middle fork Rockey Creek..mouth first
branch. Entry No. 1931.

No date. SPRUCE MACAY e. 150 ac. on Rockey Creek at lower end Chinopen
thicket. Entry No. 1932.

8 June 1781. ABRAHAM DEMOSS e. 250 ac. branch Hunting Creek near head..
including some branches of Cub Creek. Entry No. 1933.

No date. JOHN SELLERS e. 200 ac. on Boons Branch of Elk Creek. Entry
No. 1934.

1781. WILLIAM STURDIE location for a ..torn.. acres between head Roaring
River..S ..torn.. little River on Top of the Main ..torn.. mountain. Entry No. 1935.

1781. WILLIAM STURDIE e. 100 ac. uppermost fork N fork Cranberry..a
branch of New River..(WM. STURDIE marked out..BENJAMIN MORGAN
written in). Entry No. 1936.

1781. BENJAMIN MORGAN & WILLIAM STURDIE Location for 100 ac. known by
name ..torn.. Top of the Peach Bottom Mountain..N fork Cranberry..
including said Gap..(WILLIAM STURDIE marked out). Entry No. 1937.

26 June 1781. BENJAMIN MORGAN e. 100 ac. Dividing Ridge..Pine Swamp &
Glady Creek between M---..torn.. GAMBILLS entry and main
Mountain near Pine Swamp..(BENJ. MORGAN marked out..WILLIAM STURDIE
written in). Entry No. 1938.

Torn. CHARLES MORGAN e. 100 ac. between Bauld Knob and top of main
Mountain on waters little River..near the Notch. Entry No. 1939.

Torn. WILLIAM STURDIE & ISAAC MORGAN Location for 100 ac. under E end
Bauld Knob..S fork Little River..above Corn Camp. Entry No. 1940.

Torn. WINNEFORD ALEXANDER e. 200 ac. on Roaring River called Long
Bottom..in CHARLES MORGANS line..S side River. Entry No. 1941.

Torn. WINNEFORD ALEXANDER e. 200 ac. on Roaring River in her former
survey. Entry No. 1942.

Torn. EDMOND DENNEY e. 80 ac. waters Roaring River..joining upper end
his other line..(EDMOND DENNEY marked out..transfard by WM.
TOLEFOR marked out..HEZEKIAH BARKER written in). Entry No. 1943.

Torn. JAMES FLETCHER e. 300 ac. waters New River on Potater Creek..half
a mile near the Virginia line on Potater Creek. Entry No. 1944.

Fletcher contd.
 James contd.
  1873,1838,1839,1872,
  1944
 James, Jr. 1436
 Reuben 502,1546
 William, Sr. 473
 William 281,583,626,674,
  1072,1118,1235,1247,
  1736,1775,1778,1789,
  1791
Floyd, William 874,875,
 876,932,976
Forbush (Forbus), James
 539
 John 285,1353,1558,1562
Ford, Peter 552
Foster, George 98,529,595
 Mark 714
Fox, James 721,1331,1697
Francis, Matthew 147,356,
 501,928,931,1006,
 1350,1381
Franklin, Barnard 312,1257,
 1276,1862
 James 850
 Jesse 1277,1758,1862,
  1863,1870
Frazier, William 255,668,
 1575,1576
Freeman, James 631,795,
 1656
Frobock, Thomas 366
Fugit, John 203,204
 Randolph 243,585
Fuller, Daniel 1801,1834
 Mordacai 635

Gambill, Henry 399
 John 660,1732,1864
 Martin 117,484,702,837,
  866,867,1080,1081,
  1682,1683,1867
 William 118,119,120,
  398,1916
 William, Jr. 121
Garrison, Isaac 200,845,
 846,975,1652
 James 1132,1590
 John 1288
 Zachariah 538
Ge----- (?), Charles 1838
German, Charles 892
Gibson, David 823
 George 709,967
 Humphrey 56
 Thomas 1858
Gilbert, Charles 1878
 Gideon 1353
 Thomas 1239,1600,1876,
  1877
Gilley, Francis 704
 Peter 704
Gilreath, Alexander 337,
 1190,1241,1300,1500,
 1501,1502,1795
 John 1724
 William 349,473,672,
  1305,1605,1656,1734

Glover, Benjamin 1121
Goins (Joines), Thomas
 406,494,497,1219,
 1220,1221,1286,1287,
 1595,1596,1597,1598
Goode, Peter 446,513,591,
 1002,1199,1325,1372,
 1526
Goodin, Thomas 838,839,
 840,841
Gordon, Alexander 12,250,
 258,260,452,453,648,
 1207,1267,1593
 Charles (Colo.) 28,46,
  149,178,343,374,573,
  693,727,728,941,1236,
  1508,1636,1767,1832,
  1833,1882,1903
 Charles, Jr. 424,1603,
  1878
 George 58,387,403,1091,
  1195,1341,1831,1854,
  1917
 Mary 54,1537,1656
 Thomas 505
Gouge, Joseph 224,225,
 479,1681
Grant, David 1679
 John 446
Graves, Joseph 225
Gray, Enerous 529
 James 179,691,1371
 John 1039,1292
 Samuel 179
 William 691,1367,1371
Grayham (Graham), Edward
 974,985
Grayson, Benjamin 530,1038
Green, John 89,164
Greenlee, James 228
Greenstreet, Peter 38,140,
 141
Greer, Aquiller 48,61,103,
 470
 Benjamin 25,217,629,1892
 Jesse 1180
 John 171,385,442,506,629,
  1120,1363
 John, Sr. 61,62
 John, Jr. 638
 Joshua 48,103,1905
Grimes, George 260
Guess (Guest), William 69,
 75,994,995,1015,1182
Gullet, Daniel 557,732,
 1175,1177,1178
 Jesse 734,1301
Gusson (?), John 848
Gwin (Gwyn), Peter 1009
 Richard 1651,1883

Hagaman, Joseph 1027
Hagood (Haigwood), Bird
 1580
 James 254,950,1116,1483,
  1484
 Parten 950,1684
Haines (Haynes), Jonathan
 827,835,837,864,1454,
 1812,1921

Hais (Hayes), Henry 881,
  1246,1718
  James 606,1879
  Reuben 1293
  Robert 885,1175
Hall, Jesse 814
  John 824,919,1776
  John, Sr. 464,1776
  John, Jr. 1777
  Samuel 339,507
Hambea (Hamby), 771,809
Hambrick, Benjamin 901
  Joseph 1627
  Patrick 506
  Robert 566
  Thomas 87,171,416,417,
    418,885,1628,1724
Hammon, Ambrose 38,852,858,
  859
  John 327,855,856
  Robert 301,717,723,860
  Thomas 1154
Hampton, Jacob 62,385
  James 249,338,1180
  Joel 1357
  Thomas 533,1188
Hand, Henry 60,1565,1566,
  1709
  John 1741
  Robert 1709
Haney, William 1919
Hankins, John Jobe 1175
  Richard 392,489,607,1328
  Robert 489,607,1285,1328
Harbin, William 113
Harden, Bradshaw 1736
  Henry 703
  William 518,803
Hardgrave, Francis 25,62,
  164,380,688
Hardiman, Uriah 472,777,
  1099
Hargis, William 116,777,
  861,1154
Harmon, John 734,1007
Harris, Dabney 1160
  Edward 500,1333,1835
  Stephen 828,829,918,
    1110,1567
Harrison, William 1485
Hart, James 1495
  Nathaniel 649 (?)
Harvel, David 409,410,
  1527,1528
  James 588,659,947
  Isham 276,277,278,882,
    1639
  William 697,737
Harvey, William 604
Haskins, John 267,915,916
  Jonathan 218
  Joshua 599,1029
Heady, Edward 311
Hedden, Elisha 451,1597,
  1738
  Elijah 494
  Jacob 309,1361
Henderson, Charles 1168
  James 354,1169,1368,
    1369,1582,1740

Henderson contd.
  Thomas 348,393,569,1170,
    1739,1740
  Thomas, Jr. 1760
Hendricks (Hendrix),
  Benjamin 388
  Garrett 388,1179,1261,
    1262,1263
  Joshua 388
  Peter 1824
Henson, John 747,1080
  Old Mr. 1088
  Paul 331,1184
  William 1316,1482,1712
Herndon, Benjamin 12,28,
  49,177,287,288,292,
  299,394,445,446,515,
  541,542,553,651,736,
  737,738,739,740,749,
  852,921,922,923,924,
  925,926,930,1008,1009,
  1010,1022,1052,1206,
  1215,1267,1324,1422,
  1423,1424,1425,1452,
  1453,1518,1519,1527,
  1528,1536,1697,1738,
  1884
Hagins (Higgins), John 589
  William 71,664,665
Hickerson (no given name)
  1804
  Charles 14,978,1247,1555
  David 978
Hicks (Hix), Solomon 1470,
  1762,1802,1803
Highsmith, Thomas 1164,1250
Hill, Francis 429,1376,1377
  James 400
  William 406,488,1108
Hinds (Hines), Samuel 780
  Simion 570
Hodges, Thomas 683
Hogs, Frd. 539
Holdbrook (Holbrook), John
  202,801
  Randolph 499,1219,1220,
    1346
Holdman (Holman), Daniel
  239,1621,1622,1623
  Joseph 41,572
  Thomas 268,633,1742
Holder, William 1217,1571
Holland, Vincent 1186
  William 815,1359
Hollaway (Holloway), Stephen
  856
Hollonsworth, Vinson 821
Holt, Joseph 1098
  William 334
Holton, Alexander 347,
  1165,1804,1805,1889
Honsley (Honley), Rowland
  138,608,958
Hooper, John 1923
  Thomas 341,1091,1500,
    1879,1903
Hopess (?), Daniel 1920
Hopkins, Joseph 1057
Horn (?), Richard 725

Mains, Martin 1135
Marshall, Jonas 663,678
Martin, Alexander 1181
  Isaac 1324,1325,1326
  James 80,81,847,848,892
  John 1330
  Joiles 508
Mash, Aaron 250,258,260,
  728,1042,1247
Massey, Elias 1605
  Joseph 729
Mason, Archibald 577
  John 676
  Mr. 1119
  Liah (?) 947
  Philip 679,1315,1380
Mathis, William 1453
Maxwell, William 1785
May, Abraham 1682
  Benjamin 302,1278
  Thomas 303,304,1477
Medkiff (Medcalf), Jacob
  901,1363
Medlin, William 1919
  William Owen 448
Miller, John 652
  Leonard 978
  William 647,959,1027,
  1093
Milligan, James 787
Minton, Meredith 24,618,
  1671,1710
Mir (Myers), Jacob 929
Mitchell, David 1156
  James 174,688
  Joshua 1892
  Nicholas 776,1315
  Randolph 478,1199,1204
  William 10,512,534,544,
  662,769,1060,1543
Mize, John 1557
Money, Joseph 289
Montgomery, Hugh 23,165,
  166,167,168,169,170,
  176,522,574,644,888,
  890,920,908,990,1064,
  1426,1733,1830
More (Moore), Elisha 1389
  John 265
Morgan, Benjamin 88,109,
  1865,1866,1936,1937,
  1938
  Charles 52,53,1939,1941
  Isaac 1940
  John 182,1317
  Joshua 171,555,1502,
  1627,17--
  William 290,512,609
Morris, George 2,9,160,
  634,658,907,937,938,
  939,942,1124,1158,
  1163,1670,1707
  George, Jr. 1434
  John 1571
  Squire 1434
Morrison, Alexander 1117,
  1174
  Samuel 311
  William 1117
Moss, Jophs 618,1381

Moss contd.
  Joseph 963
Mulkey, James 706,743,
  1744,1745,1746,1748
  Joseph 940
Mullens, Henry 910,1297
Munuy, Thomas 882
Murphey, John 1173

Nall, Robert 1432,1438,
  1467,1764,1765
  William 38,146,702,864,
  865,1076,1077,1078,
  1079,1106,1119,1281,
  1282,1284,1458,1586,
  1668,1704,1764
Neaves, Joshua 31
Netherly, Robert 365,645,
  1013
  Thomas 905
Newberry, Thomas 590,1340,
  1341
  Thomas, Jr. 1631
Nicholds (Nichols), Jacob
  16,137,1643
  Joshua 476,1119
Nicholson (Nickerlson),
  Samuel 10,327,512,881
Niece, Humphrey 1516
Norman, Edman 22
  Isaac 41,1488
  James 1641,1642
Norris, Ephraim 1693,1694
  John 1047,1693
Nutterville (Nuterfield),
  Volentine 123,629,1120,
  1305

Oakeley, Benjamin 201,1829,
  1830
Obair (Obarr), Robert 890,
  1021,1229
Oliver, John 1466
  Vanam 1201
Orastus, William 1688
Orear, John 52,1228,1454,
  1495,1456,1812,1920,
  1921
  Peter 1920
Osburn, Enoch 3,367,903,
  1654,1685,1726,1727,
  1785
Owen, Barnet 614,1296,1677,
  1678
  David 1721,1723
  James 388
  John 654,655
  Richard 1441
  Thomas 622,656,657,685,
  1104
  William 431
  William, Sr. 612,617,
  1721,1722
  William, Jr. 653,1041

Parker, Benjamin 1603
  Edward 384,535
  John 379,1103,1110,1761
  William 354
Parks, Aaron 639
  George 480
  Henry 122,1813
  Jacob 1141
  John 42,184,765,1320,
    1473,1620
  John, Sr. 43,94,300
  John, Jr. 107,108,1883
  Reuben 85,183,1474
  Thomas 12,63,92,107,183,
    453,495,610,807
  Thomas, Jr. 113,923
Parmely, Ephraim 778
  Giles 220,264,449,867,
    935,1025,1221
Parsons, John 1753,1894
Pate, Isaac 1129
  Jacob 854,1602,1838
Patrick, Paul 727,728,935,
    936,1050
Patton, James 405
Payn (Payne), George 521,
    1579
  John 50,420,691,750
  Thomas 710,711,712,713,
    714,766,767,768,772,
    1286,1287,1443,1595,
    1598,1651,1711
  Thomas, Sr. 907,1259
  Thomas, Jr. 1259,1273,
    1285,1288,1650
  Wm. 1651
Pearson, Peter 651,1306,
    1360,1475
Pennington, Abel 3,222,
    1184,1185,1186
  Benajah 371,698,1086,
    1088,1494
  Benajah, Jr. 698
  Benjamin 707,1021
  Edward 1151,1394
  Elijah 1087
  Micajah 368,370,899,
    1080,1086,1157,1352,
    1433,1491,1658,1661
  Micajah, Jr. 1152
  William 1087,1433,1695
Perkins, Ben 1560
  Joseph 55,1097
  Thomas 1245
  Timothy 55,70,1123
Perlier (Parlier), Isaac
    235,236,446,560,646,
    898,1819,1820,1843,
    1899,1901
Petty, William 579
Philips (Phillips), Gab-
    riel 1538
Phipes (Fipps), Matthew
    1816
Phouts (Fouts), Devalt
    1907
Piles (Pyles), John 1835
Pinkston, Edward 351,851,
    1224
  Zachariah 851

Pitman (Pittman), John
    173,1388
Poe, John 485,923
Pointer, George 257
Poor, Alexander 1048,1302,
    1303
Porter, Boyd 55
  Joseph 39,111,114
  Thomas 1234
Pound, Samuel 1285
Powers, Moses 100
Preston, Isaac 789,793,
    1159,1364,1365
  John 76
Price, Humphrey 774
Prophet (Proffit), John
    47,90,172,262,422,
    1131,1637,1750,1872
  William 557

Quary see McQuary

Ragland, William 445,1206
Ramey, James 38,95,585
Rash, Daniel 10,511
Ray, Benjamin 1774
  Jesse 1906
  Samuel 187
  William 2,5,658,1074,
    1194
Read (Reed), Henry 272,
    419,611,669,1448,
    1513
  Joseph 342
  Stephen 696,833
Reaves (Reeves), George
    517,613,638,966,
    1363,1657
  Isaac 285
  James 1541
Rees, Travis 523,1753
Reynolds, (erased) 769
  Charles 771,1584
  Elisha 322,1023,1547,
    1549,1607,1633,1634
  Francis 86,153,1023,
    1108,1109,1162,1238,
    1552,1553,1845
  James 86,261,584,823,
    1554
  Jenkins 503,1002
  William 314,315,724
Rice (no given name) 960
Richardson, John 1192
  Daniel 373,706,900,
    1442,1456,1748
Ridge, William 477
Riggs, Bethuel 1137,1190,
    1197
  David 1870
  Zeadock 1751
Ritter, Cattren 1609
  Elizabeth 1906
Roads (Rhodes), Henry 1834
Roberts, Bennett 718,1390
  Edward 1370
  Elizabeth 1422
  Jacob 1689

Roberts contd.
James 208
John 671,1149,1214,1235,
  1422,1789
John, Fiddler 1873
John, Old 1873
Lewis 50
Rosannah 1588
Thomas 1141
Widow 408
William 362,550,932,1689,
  1842,1843,1874
Robertson (Roberson), John
  155,744,1234
Robins, John 45,286,1420,
  1772,1804
John, Sr. 96,99,101,159,
  650
John, Jr. 818,1930
Reubin 750
Thomas 33,101,514,916,
  1142,1143,1144
Tirey 762
Robinson, John 587,847,
  1446,1447
William 1111
Rose, Benjamin 1771
Emanuel 223,313,1687
John 272,201,559,598
John, Jr. 735,764,765,
  1189
Ross, Laurence 19,82,958,
  1037,1225
Rowland, Charles 1135
Reuben 955
Russau (Rousseau), Hilliar
  45,46,244,1774
Rysdon, William 282,739

Sails (Sale), Cornelius
  345,513,739,1166,1310,
  1330,1698,1699
Leonard 1548,1550
Thomas 736
William 1166,1698
Sanders, Abraham 1083,1224
Francis 284
Robert 571,809,813,814,
  1861
Sandridge, Berry 1004
Saler (Saylor), John 1243
Sawyer, William 1030
Scott, Benjamin 636
John 636
William 460,575,942,1481
Scritchfield (Crutchfield),
  Arthur 188,394,406,488
Nathaniel 299,520,1799
Samuel 392,394,520,607,
  832,1596
Scritchworth, Joseph 1200
Scurley (?), John 1130
Scurlock (Shurlock), Joshua
  154,443,885,1559,1570
Sebastian, Benjamin 689,
  690
Sellers, John 646,1886,
  1899,1900,1901,1934
Sewell, Abraham 1175

Sewell contd.
Dosson 557,732,1176
Joseph 1178
Shan (?), Christefor 1059
Sharpe, William 869
Shaver, George 1235
Shepherd, James 27,516,619
John 64,65,875,876,1835,
  1930
John, Jr. 875
Robert 35,65,614,1769
Sherry, William 126,127,
  280,305
Shuffield (Shorefield),
  George 1420
Shufield, James 407,637
Shumate, John 1545
Shute, Henry 1437
Sigler, Jacob 1456,1586
Philip 1413
Simpson (Simson), John
  83,86,162,256,257,328,
  762
Samuel 819,1057,1148,
  1298,1772,1773,1844,
  1925
Sisk, John 1315
Thomas 830,965,1316
Timothey 807,1617
Sizemor (no given name) 827
Slone (Sloan), John 955
Thomas 7,1915
William 213,215,844,845
Smalley, Abner (Esq.) 541,
  542,553,787,826,1382
Smith, Alexander 1768
Benjamin 477,724
David 376
Edward 1327
Gervis 407,635,637,1241,
  1804,1805
Hugh 355,402,577,1079,
  1284,1445,1700
James 1257
John 1091
Jonathan 377,701,704,
  1660,1661
Moses 1150
Randolph 397,1181
Richard 331,450,911
Thomas 1185
William 174,343,443,444,
  1036,1356,1370,1405,
  1542,1731
Smither, Gabriel 1913
John 756,1752
Smithey, Garnet 444
Smoote (Smoot), James 1891
Sneed, Jonathan 57
Snoddy, William 21,227,
  228,553,576,788,789,
  790,792,992
South, Joseph 632,1587
Souther, John 252,1082
Lacarus 381
Michel 295,1082
Stephen 234,386,590,
  1082,1629
Sparks, James 1295
John 1396

Williams, Charles 1773
  Elijah 996
  James 308,317,318,377
  Owin 356,931,1061,1091
  Samuel, Jr. 56
  Thomas 826
Willis, Robert 523
Wisdom, John 361,537
  Joseph 359,360
  Thomas 360,1270
Witherspoon, David 563,
    1041,1582
  James 564,683
  John 67,564
  Mr. 578
  Thomas 562,1049,1050,
    1051
Wood, Edmond 663
  Elias 788
  Reuben 1429
Woodruff, Gideon 1750
  John Allen 780,1687
  Moses 288,1154,1164
Woolbanks, Richard 504,
    845,975,1107
Wright, Benjamin 686,1157
  Daniel 32,91,969
  John 726
  Joseph 945
  Micajah 513,592
  Moses 1857
  Samuel 34,179,307,404,
    736
  William 49,179,980,1155

Yarnell, Daniel 81,346,
    1382
  Laurence 1884
Yates, John 356,362,931,
    976,977
  Joshua 698
Yeargain, Andrew 84,1487,
    1720,1783
  Benjamin 1728,1729,1780,
    1781,1782,1789,1790,
    1791
  John 1811
Younce, John 1284
Young, Rachel 1648
Younger, Joseph 604

www.ingramcontent.com/pod-product-compliance
Lightning Source LLC
Chambersburg PA
CBHW021834020426
42334CB00014B/616